AN INTRODUCTION TO PENOLOGY

AN INTRODUCTION TO PENOLOGY

Sue Strickland-Lord

SOCIETY Publishing

www.societypublishing.com

An Introduction to Penology

Sue Strickland-Lord

Society Publishing
4164 Lakeshore Road
Burlington, ON L7L 1A4
Canada
www.societypublishing.com
Email: orders@arclereducation.com

ISBN: 978-1-77956-397-2 (Hardcover)

ABOUT THE AUTHOR

Sue Strickland-Lord is a college lecturer in Social Sciences, lecturing for over twenty years in several UK colleges. She specialises in Criminology and has a 1st Class degree in Criminology from the University of Winchester and a MSc in Criminal Justice, with merit from the University of Portsmouth. Sue achieved particularly high grades in her dissertations with pass percentages at 85% and she has been able to pass on those skills to many of her students who have excelled in their educational achievement. Sue works hard to introduce students to the world of Criminology and inspires students to research the subject thoroughly and understand it fully to support their own academic writing. Many of her students have gone on to gain their educational aspirations and go on to work in areas such as criminal justice, policing, law and prison services. Her own career as also included working with vulnerable victims and writing educational programmes within prison reform.

TABLE OF CONTENTS

LIST OF FIGURES

ABSTRACT

This handbook explores the historical evolution, theoretical foundations, and contemporary practices of penology. It traces the history of punishment from ancient retribution and deterrence practices in Mesopotamia, Greece, and Rome to the more humanitarian approaches of the Enlightenment period. Modern penal systems were shaped by key figures such as Cesare Beccaria and Jeremy Bentham, who advocated for proportional punishment and crime prevention. The handbook also discusses the development of the penitentiary system in the 19th century, emphasizing rehabilitation and the penal-welfare model, which addressed the social and psychological factors contributing to criminal behavior.

In the 20th century, penology incorporated elements of restorative justice, emphasizing reconciliation and reparation over punishment. Modern penology now alternates between retributive, rehabilitative, and restorative approaches. The role of religion in shaping penological practices, the rise of the prison-industrial complex, and the future of penology, particularly with the incorporation of technology, are all discussed. This book also highlights the ongoing debate over punitive versus rehabilitative approaches to balancing justice, public safety, and human rights. Additionally, the book briefly covers the juvenile justice system, emphasizing imperative concepts such as the system's primary focus on the rehabilitation of young offenders over retribution, and the juvenile court process.

PREFACE

This handbook provides an expansive exploration of penology, delving into both historical developments and current issues. The first chapter examines the history of punishment, tracing its evolution from retributive practices in ancient Mesopotamia and Greece to modern rehabilitative methods influenced by Enlightenment ideals. The narrative follows the gradual humanization of penal policies and the rise of institutions such as the penitentiary, emphasizing the growing importance of social factors in shaping punishment strategies.

In Chapter 2, the discussion transitions to fundamental theories of crime and punishment. The classical school, based on rational choice theory, views crime as a deliberate decision for which punishment serves as a deterrent. In contrast, the positivist school focuses on the impact of biological, psychological, and environmental factors, emphasizing rehabilitation over punishment. These opposing theories provide a foundation for understanding the various approaches to crime prevention that shape modern criminal justice systems.

The correctional system, discussed in Chapter 3, has multiple goals, including retribution, deterrence, incapacitation, and rehabilitation. These objectives reflect the larger debate in penology about balancing punitive and reformative strategies. Contemporary issues such as overcrowding and recidivism call into question the system's efficacy, urging reforms that prioritize more humane and effective offender management. In Chapter 4, punishment and rehabilitation are presented as complementary rather than opposing ideas. Historically, punishment was based on retribution and deterrence, but the rehabilitative model now seeks to address the underlying causes of criminal behavior, such as substance abuse and socioeconomic disadvantage. The integration of both models is proposed as a way to reduce recidivism and improve public safety.

The narrative about prison life in Chapter 5 emphasizes the profound impact incarceration has on individuals. The term "pains of imprisonment" refers to the psychological and social toll that inmates face, such as the loss of autonomy and strained social roles. The inmate subculture, complete with its own norms and hierarchies, is explored as a survival strategy in the harsh prison environment. The text also highlights the long-term effects of institutionalization, which make reintegration into society difficult after a lengthy prison sentence. Job training, mental health services, and family reunification programs have been shown to reduce recidivism and promote successful reintegration, consistent with modern penology's rehabilitative goals.

Chapter 6 introduces juvenile justice as a specialized branch of penology, emphasizing rehabilitation over punishment. This chapter highlights the distinct developmental needs of young offenders and argues that diversion programs and restorative justice practices are more effective than punitive approaches in addressing juvenile delinquency. In Chapter 7, probation and parole are discussed as alternatives to incarceration, with a focus on their role in promoting rehabilitation while maintaining community safety. When implemented effectively, these measures provide more humane responses to crime than incarceration and are more likely to result in lower recidivism rates.

The discussion on capital punishment in Chapter 8 delves into the ethical, legal, and practical issues surrounding it. While rooted in retributive justice, capital punishment is under increasing scrutiny for its questionable deterrent effect, racial biases, and moral implications, particularly in a global context that favors abolition.

Finally, the handbook concludes with emerging issues in penology, such as integrating technology into correctional systems, privatizing prisons, and the ongoing challenges of overcrowding, racial disparities, and solitary confinement. These issues reflect broader societal changes, pointing to a future in which restorative justice and rehabilitation take precedence over punitive measures, with the goal of creating a more just and effective criminal justice system.

Chapter **1**

THE HISTORY OF PENOLOGY

Contents

Penology, the study of the processes used by societies to manage crime and administer punishment, has an evolving and complicated history. Early penological practices, originating in Mesopotamia, Greece, and Rome, were frequently harsh and punitive, focusing on retribution and deterrence through physical punishment and public humiliation. The Enlightenment period of the 18th century marked a significant shift toward more humanitarian approaches, influenced by thinkers such as Cesare Beccaria, who advocated for proportionate punishment and crime prevention over retribution (Scott, 2008).

The penitentiary emerged as a central institution in penology during the 19th century, with a focus on offender reform and rehabilitation. This period also saw the rise of the "penal welfarism" model, which shifted the emphasis to understanding the social and psychological factors that contribute to criminal behavior (Faqir, 2015). Penology evolved further in the late twentieth and early 21st centuries with the introduction of restorative justice practices that emphasized reconciliation and reparation rather than punishment. Contemporary penology now balances various approaches, including retributive, rehabilitative, and restorative paradigms, reflecting broader societal values and debates on justice, human rights, and the efficacy of different penal strategies (Scott, 2008).

1.1. ORIGINS OF PUNISHMENT

The origins of punishment are deeply ingrained in human history, reflecting various cultural, social, and philosophical perspectives on justice, morality, and social order. The concept of punishment has evolved significantly over time, influenced by existing sociopolitical conditions, religious beliefs, and shifting notions of human rights and justice. In penology, the study of punishment and its effects, scholars examine the historical evolution of punitive practices to understand the underlying motives and consequences of different approaches to dealing with deviant behavior (Scott, 2008) (Figure 1.1).

In ancient societies, punishment was frequently characterized by a retributive nature, with the primary goal of exacting vengeance or retaliating against offenders for their transgressions. Early legal codes, such as the Code of Hammurabi in Mesopotamia around 1754 BCE, exemplify this retributive approach, imposing harsh punishments for a wide range of offenses, often based on the principle of lex talionis, or "an eye for an eye." The emphasis was on proportionality, which ensured that the punishment was appropriate for the severity of the offense. This early form of punishment served multiple functions, including deterring potential offenders, maintaining social order, and reinforcing the power of the ruling authority (Scott, 2008).

Figure 1.1. *Origins of capital punishment.*

Source: Crime Museum, LLC (2024).

In ancient Greece and Rome, punishment was also used to maintain civic order and authority. However, these societies implemented more complex and varied forms of punishment, such as fines, exile, and death, which were tailored to the nature of the offense and the offender's social status. Public punishment and spectacles, such as gladiatorial games and executions, were effective deterrents and reinforced the social hierarchy by publicly demonstrating the consequences of breaking the law. These practices were used not only for retribution, but also to assert state power and control over the population. In this context, punishment was intrinsically linked to the political structure, with its administration reflecting larger societal values and norms (Garland, 2018).

The advent of Christianity and its spread throughout Europe beginning in the 4th century CE marked a significant shift in punishment philosophy. Christian doctrines introduced the concepts of sin and divine retribution, which influenced medieval European penology by emphasizing penance and moral correction over retribution alone. During this time, the church became a dominant force in legal matters, frequently prescribing penitential practices as forms of punishment to encourage spiritual reflection and redemption (Faqir 2015). This spiritualization of punishment was reflected in practices such as public penance, pilgrimages, and various forms of corporal punishment designed to reconcile the sinner with the community and God.

By the 18th century, the Enlightenment had brought about significant changes in how punishment was perceived and implemented. Cesare Beccaria and Jeremy Bentham, two Enlightenment thinkers, criticized the arbitrary and often brutal nature of modern penal practices, calling for a more rational and humane approach to punishment. Beccaria's seminal work, On Crimes and Punishments (1764), argued against the death penalty and torture, proposing that punishment should be quick, certain, and proportionate to the crime in order to be effective. Bentham, on the other hand, introduced the utilitarian perspective, emphasizing that punishment should maximize overall happiness by preventing crime and reforming offenders (Garland, 2018). These ideas laid the foundation for the modern penal system, which began to shift towards a more rehabilitative model, focusing on the reform and reintegration of offenders rather than solely on retribution.

These Enlightenment principles were institutionalized during the 19th century with the establishment of penitentiaries and correctional facilities. The penitentiary model, particularly in the United States and Britain, was based on the notion that offenders could be rehabilitated through isolation, labor, and religious instruction. The goal was to create a controlled environment in which offenders could reflect on their actions and become morally transformed. However, this model was not without criticism; many contemporaries emphasized the negative psychological effects of prolonged isolation, as well as the often-brutal conditions within these institutions (Faqir, 2015). Despite these criticisms, the penitentiary has become an integral part of modern penal systems, reflecting the ongoing conflict between retributive and rehabilitative approaches in penology.

Throughout the 20th century, penology evolved, incorporating insights from psychology, sociology, and criminology. The "penal-welfare" model, which emerged in the mid-20th century, focused on the social and psychological factors that contribute to criminal behavior, advocating for rehabilitation and treatment rather than punishment. This approach reflected a growing understanding of the complexities of human behavior and the need for a more personalized approach to punishment. However, by the late 20th century, this rehabilitative focus was being challenged by a resurgence of retributive justice, fueled by rising crime rates and public demand for harsher punishments. This shift, known as the "punitive turn," has resulted in the expansion of the prison-industrial complex and a renewed emphasis on deterrence and incapacitation (Garland, 2018; Scott, 2008).

Contemporary penology grapples with a variety of competing philosophies and practices, reflecting broader societal debates about the purpose and efficacy of punishment. While punishment's origins were based on retribution and deterrence, modern penal systems have increasingly attempted to balance these traditional goals with a focus on rehabilitation, restorative justice, and human rights. As a result, the history of punishment demonstrates the evolving nature of human societies and their ongoing quest to define justice and maintain social order (Faqir, 2015; Scott, 2008).

1.2. EVOLUTION OF CORRECTIONAL SYSTEMS

Early correctional systems in ancient societies were primarily based on retributive justice, with the goal of exacting vengeance and deterring future crimes. This approach was evident in early legal codes such as Mesopotamia's Code of Hammurabi, which prescribed harsh penalties, including mutilation and death, based on the principle of lex talionis, or "an eye for an eye" (Scott, 2008). Correctional facilities, as we know them today, did not exist in these early systems; instead, punitive measures were immediate and often public, serving to punish the offender while also deterring others.

In Greece and Rome, the classical period brought more sophisticated approaches to punishment, such as fines, exile, and various types of corporal punishment. Prisons were used primarily to hold people awaiting trial or execution, rather than for long-term incarceration. In these societies, punishment was inextricably linked to maintaining social order and state power. Public spectacles of punishment, such as gladiatorial games or executions, served to reinforce societal norms and the ruling elite's power. These practices reflected a correctional philosophy that emphasized deterrence and the demonstration of state power over rehabilitation (Garland, 2018).

During the medieval period, the Christian church had an impact on correctional systems, introducing the concept of penance and moral correction as important components of punishment. The church advocated for penitential practices that sought to reform the soul rather than simply punishing the body. As a result, punishment frequently took the form of public penance, pilgrimage, or other acts of repentance. During this time, the use of confinement became more prominent, but primarily in the form of monastic orders or ecclesiastical courts, where the focus was on spiritual reflection and redemption rather than secular retribution (Scott, 2008).

The Enlightenment period saw a significant shift in penology and the establishment of modern correctional systems. Enlightenment thinkers like Cesare Beccaria and Jeremy Bentham criticized the arbitrary and brutal nature of modern punitive practices, advocating for more rational, proportionate, and humane approaches to punishment. Beccaria's On Crimes and Punishments (1764) advocated for the abolition of the death penalty and torture, claiming that the certainty and speed of punishment, rather than its severity, were more effective in deterring crime. Bentham's utilitarian philosophy emphasized that punishment should do the most good by deterring crime and rehabilitating offenders. These ideas paved the way for the modern penitentiary system, which aimed to reform criminals through isolation, labor, and moral instruction (Lipsey and Cullen, 2007).

In the 19th century, the penitentiary was established as a central institution in the correction system. The penitentiary model, as developed in the United States and Britain, was based on the idea that criminals could be rehabilitated through structured routines, hard work, and religious instruction. The Pennsylvania system, for example, emphasized solitary confinement and reflection as forms of moral reform, whereas the Auburn system combined labor and solitary confinement at night (Faqir, 2015). Despite these reforms, conditions in prisons were often harsh, and the intended rehabilitative effects were frequently hampered by overcrowding, insufficient resources, and punitive administration.

In the early 20th century, the "penal-welfare" model gained popularity, particularly in Western Europe and North America, reflecting a growing belief in the possibility of reforming offenders through individualized treatment. Correctional systems began to incorporate rehabilitative programs, such as education, vocational training, and therapeutic interventions, in response to emerging fields of psychology and sociology. This approach saw crime as a social pathology that could be treated, rather than a moral failing that should be punished. The establishment of probation, parole, and juvenile justice systems during this period also reflected the shift toward rehabilitation and the desire to reintegrate offenders into society (Faqir, 2015; Lipsey and Cullen, 2007).

However, the late 20th century saw a resurgence of punitive approaches in correctional systems, also known as the "punitive turn." Rising crime rates, political shifts toward conservatism, and public demand for harsher penalties resulted in a focus on deterrence and incapacitation over rehabilitation. During this time, prison populations grew significantly, the prison-industrial complex expanded, and harsher sentencing laws, such as "three-strikes" legislation in the United States, were implemented. The emphasis on punitive measures frequently came at the expense of rehabilitative programs, as resources were increasingly allocated to expanding incarceration capacity and enforcing harsher penal policies (Faqir, 2015; Garland, 2018).

In recent years, there has been a renewed interest in restorative justice and alternative correctional approaches, reflecting a growing awareness of the limitations and social costs of mass incarceration. Restorative justice emphasizes repairing the harm caused by crime through reconciliation and dialogue among offenders, victims, and the community, with the goal of restoring relationships rather than simply punishing. This approach is consistent with broader movements toward decarceration, particularly in response to concerns about racial disparities in the criminal justice system, prisoners' human rights, and the social and economic costs of high incarceration rates (Scott, 2008).

Correctional systems have evolved through a dynamic interplay of punitive and rehabilitative philosophies, reflecting broader societal values, political ideologies, and evolving understandings of crime and justice. While the history of corrections has seen significant shifts in emphasis—from retribution and deterrence to rehabilitation and restoration—modern correctional systems continue to grapple with balancing these competing aims in their efforts to promote public safety, justice, and social reintegration (Garland, 2018).

1.3. INFLUENTIAL FIGURES IN PENOLOGY

Several influential figures have made significant contributions to the field of penology. These individuals introduced theories, reforms, and practices that had a significant impact on the evolution of penal systems as well as our understanding of crime and justice. Their work covers centuries and reflects shifts in societal values, philosophical thought, and approaches to criminal justice.

Cesare Beccaria, an 18th-century Italian philosopher and jurist, was one of the founding and most influential figures in penology. In his seminal work, On Crimes and Punishments (1764), Beccaria argued against the use of torture and capital punishment, instead advocating for punishments proportionate to the crime. His rationalist approach emphasized crime prevention over retribution, arguing that the certainty of punishment was more effective than its severity in discouraging criminal behavior. Beccaria's ideas established the classical school of criminology and introduced the concept of legal reform, which influenced penal codes throughout Europe and the United States. His work is considered a cornerstone of modern penology, encouraging the principles of justice, fairness, and human rights in the treatment of offenders (Scott, 2008).

Jeremy Bentham, a contemporary of Beccaria, contributed significantly to the field of penology by developing utilitarian philosophy. Bentham's work was based on the principle of "the greatest happiness for the greatest number," which suggested that laws and punishments should aim to maximize societal well-being. He is best known for designing the Panopticon, a circular prison with a central observation tower that allowed a single guard to monitor all inmates without them knowing they were being watched. This architectural design was intended to induce a state of consciousness and permanent visibility in the prisoners, thus encouraging self-regulation and obedience (Faqir, 2015). While the Panopticon was never fully realized as Bentham envisioned, its underlying principles have influenced modern surveillance and disciplinary practices in prisons and beyond, reflecting the utilitarian emphasis on efficiency and control in penal systems.

John Howard, an 18th-century English philanthropist and social reformer, is another important figure in the history of penology. Howard's extensive inspections of prisons across England and Europe revealed appalling conditions for prisoners, such as overcrowding, a lack of sanitation, and corruption among jailers. His seminal work, The State of the Prisons in England and Wales (1777), advocated for comprehensive reforms such as the separation of prisoners by gender and offense, improved living conditions, and the establishment of a salaried prison staff to reduce corruption. Howard's efforts resulted in the development of the penitentiary model, which emphasized moral reform and rehabilitation for offenders through hard work, discipline, and religious instruction. His advocacy for humane treatment and institutional reform laid the groundwork for modern correctional practices and established him as a pivotal figure in penal reform (Scott, 2008).

Alexander Maconochie, a 19th-century British naval officer and penal reformer, expanded on the rehabilitative approach to punishment. While serving as governor of the Norfolk Island penal colony, Maconochie created the "mark system," a revolutionary method in which prisoners could earn points for good behavior, hard work, and educational attainment. These marks could be used to reduce sentences and gain early release, encouraging inmates to work on themselves and accept responsibility for their actions. Maconochie's ideas challenged the dominant punitive ethos of the time, emphasizing rehabilitation and reintegration over retribution and deterrence. Although his reforms faced opposition and were eventually discontinued, his concepts influenced subsequent developments in parole and probation systems, emphasizing the importance of rehabilitation in correctional philosophy (Garland, 2018).

The work of Louis Brandeis, a United States Supreme Court Justice and social reformer who advocated for the humane treatment of prisoners and the use of social science in legal decision-making, had a significant impact on penology during the 20th century. Brandeis championed the "Brandeis Brief," a legal argument that used empirical data and expert testimony to inform judicial decisions, emphasizing the importance of a more scientific and evidence-based approach to criminal justice (Lipsey and Cullen, 2007). His efforts contributed to the integration of psychological and sociological perspectives into penology, promoting a better understanding of the causes of criminal behavior and the creation of rehabilitative programs tailored to individual needs.

Michel Foucault, a twentieth-century French philosopher and social theorist, made significant contributions to penology with his critical analysis of power, discipline, and punishment. In his seminal work Discipline and Punish: The Birth of the Prison (1975), Foucault traced the historical development of penal practices from public executions to the modern prison system, arguing that punishment has shifted from a focus on the body to a focus on the spirit. He proposed the concept of a "disciplinary society," in which institutions such as prisons, schools, and hospitals use surveillance and normalization techniques to regulate behavior and maintain social control. Foucault's analysis questioned traditional notions of power and punishment, emphasizing the pervasive and insidious role of disciplinary practices in shaping individual and collective behavior. His work has had a profound impact on contemporary penology, encouraging critical reflection on the ethical and political dimensions of punishment and the role of prisons in society (Lipsey and Cullen, 2007; Scott, 2008).

These influential figures in penology have had a significant impact on the evolution of punishment and correctional practices, reflecting a variety of philosophical perspectives and social reform initiatives. Their contributions have helped to transform penal systems from purely punitive institutions to complex structures that strike a balance between retribution, deterrence, rehabilitation, and social control (Faqir, 2015). As penology evolves, the ideas and insights of these seminal thinkers remain relevant, informing ongoing discussions about justice, human rights, and the future of corrections.

1.4. IMPACT OF HISTORICAL EVENTS ON PENOLOGY

The Enlightenment of the 18th century was one of the first major events to have a significant impact on penology. This intellectual movement emphasized reason, individual rights, and the pursuit of knowledge while fundamentally challenging existing punitive practices. Cesare Beccaria and Jeremy Bentham, both Enlightenment thinkers, criticized the arbitrary and often brutal nature of punishment at the time. Beccaria's On Crimes and Punishments (1764) advocated for a rational approach to punishment, calling for the abolition of torture and capital punishment in favor of proportionate penalties aimed at deterring crime rather than exacting retribution. Bentham's utilitarian philosophy emphasized that the goal of punishment should be to maximize societal well-being, which influenced the development of penal reform and the emergence of the penitentiary system (Scott, 2008). These Enlightenment ideas laid the foundation for modern penology by promoting the principles of justice, fairness, and the prevention of crime.

The Industrial Revolution of the late 18th and early 19th centuries had a significant impact on penology. Rapid urbanization, population growth, and the rise of factory work resulted in increased social dislocation and crime. Traditional punitive methods, such as public executions and corporal punishment, became less effective and were deemed incompatible with new humanitarian values. In response, the penitentiary system evolved, emphasizing moral reform and rehabilitation of offenders through labor, discipline, and religious education.

This period saw the development of the "separate system," exemplified by the Eastern State Penitentiary in Pennsylvania, which emphasized solitary confinement to encourage reflection and repentance, and the "silent system," as seen in the Auburn Prison in New York, where inmates worked silently to instill discipline (Faqir, 2015). These systems reflected the belief that structured environments and moral education could reform offenders, which was consistent with society's overall emphasis on order, productivity, and control.

The abolition of slavery in the 19th century, followed by the Reconstruction era in the United States, had an impact on penology, particularly in the American South. The abolition of slavery resulted in the establishment of the convict lease system, in which African American prisoners, many of whom were arrested on dubious charges, were leased to private enterprises to work in conditions similar to slavery. This system served as a social and economic control mechanism, maintaining racial hierarchies and exploiting convict labor for profit. The convict lease system emphasized the intersection of race, economics, and penal practices, showing how punishment could be used to maintain social order and reinforce existing power structures (Garland, 2018).

The rise of the Progressive Era in the late 19th and early 20th centuries brought additional changes to penology, as reformers sought to address the social issues associated with industrialization and urbanization. Progressive reformers, influenced by emerging social sciences, advocated for a more scientific approach to criminal justice that prioritized rehabilitation, social reintegration, and individualized treatment. This era saw the development of probation and parole systems, the establishment of juvenile courts, and the implementation of indeterminate sentencing, all with the goal of tailoring interventions to offenders' specific needs and promoting rehabilitation (Faqir, 2015). These reforms reflected a shift away from purely punitive approaches and toward a more therapeutic model, which was consistent with the larger Progressive agenda of social improvement and reform.

The late 20th century saw a punitive shift in criminology, known as the "punitive turn," fueled by rising crime rates, political conservatism, and public demand for harsher penalties. This period was distinguished by the growth of the prison-industrial complex, harsher sentencing laws such as mandatory minimums and "three strikes" legislation, and a greater emphasis on deterrence and incapacitation (Garland, 2001). The drug war and subsequent mass incarceration disproportionately affected marginalized communities, particularly African Americans and Latinos, emphasizing racial and economic disparities in the criminal justice system (Garland, 2018). This shift toward punitive policies reflected broader sociopolitical concerns about crime, social order, and the perceived failure of rehabilitative programs.

In recent years, there has been a growing recognition of the limitations and social costs of mass incarceration, resulting in renewed interest in alternatives such as restorative justice. Restorative justice focuses on repairing crime-related harm through reconciliation and dialogue among offenders, victims, and the community, with the goal of restoring relationships rather than simply punishing. This approach reflects a broader societal shift toward decarceration and social justice, challenging traditional penal practices and advocating for more humane and effective crime-reduction strategies.

1.5. COMPARISON OF ANCIENT AND MODERN PENOLOGY

A comparison of ancient and modern penology demonstrates significant differences in goal, methodology, legal structures, societal role, and institutional frameworks, all of which are based on different philosophical approaches to crime and punishment.

Punishment was frequently used in ancient communities to retaliate and prevent others. Justice was strongly related to vengeance, with sanctions intended to cause pain or suffering to the perpetrator as a kind of societal retribution. This approach was based on a worldview that considered crime as an affront not only to the victim but also to the community and gods. The Code of Hammurabi, one of the oldest known legal laws, exemplifies retributive justice with its well-known precept of "an eye for an eye" (Johnston, 2021). Similarly, in ancient Greece and Rome, punishment was frequently severe and public in order to dissuade others via fear. The methods used ranged from corporal punishment, such as flogging and amputation, to lethal punishment, which was frequently carried out via crucifixion, stoning, or burning (Gagarin, 2011).

On the other hand, contemporary penology has mostly moved in the direction of a more restorative and rehabilitative approach, especially within the framework of Western legal systems. Beyond simple retaliation, the goal of punishment now encompasses the offender's rehabilitation, society's protection, and the healing of victims and communities. A profound philosophical shift was brought about by the Enlightenment, which placed a strong emphasis on the rights and dignity of the person. In his ground-breaking work On Crimes and Punishments (1764), scholars such as Cesare Beccaria advocated against capital punishment and other severe penalties, favoring proportionality in punishment and the use of rational-legal institutions to deter crime (Beccaria, 1986). According to this contemporary viewpoint, crime is a social problem that necessitates addressing underlying causes like poverty, education, and mental health, rather than just being a moral failure or an act of rebellion against the government or divine order (Garland, 2001). The techniques used in modern penology reflect this shift in goal. Instead of relying primarily on physical punishment, current systems prioritize incarceration, probation, and rehabilitation programs. The use of prisons as the principal method of punishment is a comparatively recent trend, with the first penitentiaries opening in the late 18th century. These institutions were intended to reform prisoners via labor, education, and moral instruction, rather than simply punish them (Foucault, 1977). Over time, the emphasis has shifted to rehabilitation, with numerous programs aimed at lowering recidivism and assisting criminals in reintegration into society. However, the usefulness and ethical implications of such strategies are still being debated within the field of criminology and criminal justice (Cullen and Gilbert, 2013).

The legislative structure controlling penology has also experienced substantial changes. Ancient legal laws, such as the aforementioned Code of Hammurabi, were frequently prescriptive and rigid, leaving little leeway for judicial interpretation. Rulers, priests, or local authorities administered justice, and punishments were usually rapid and severe. Ancient Rome's legal systems included certain elements of due process, but justice remained highly affected by social rank and political power (Gagarin, 2011). In contrast, modern legal systems place a stronger focus on individual rights, due process, and the rule of law. Modern penology operates inside a complex legal framework that includes extensive criminal codes, appeal procedures, and a variety of procedural safeguards intended to promote fairness and proportionality in the administration of justice. The emergence of international human rights law in the 20th century influenced modern penology by raising standards for prisoner care and the prohibition of harsh forms of punishment such as torture and the death penalty (Van Zyl Smit and Snacken, 2009).

The role of society in penology has also changed. In ancient times, punishment was frequently a communal affair, with public executions and other types of punishment functioning as spectacles to enforce social standards and dissuade misbehavior. The community was directly involved in the implementation of justice, whether through participation in trials, as in ancient Greece, or through communal sanctions such as ostracism or banishment. In modern civilizations, the community's function has changed. While public opinion and societal attitudes continue to have an impact on penological procedures, professional organizations such as the police, courts, and penitentiary facilities today bear the majority of the responsibility for justice administration. Modern penology, on the other hand, increasingly recognizes the importance of community involvement in the rehabilitation process, as evidenced by the rise of restorative justice practices that engage offenders, victims, and community members in a collaborative process of healing and restitution (Zehr, 2002).

Ancient penology lacked specialized institutions. Punishments were frequently administered instantly and openly, and there were few designated facilities for holding or rehabilitating offenders. The evolution of prisons as we know them is a comparatively recent occurrence. Early jails, such as the famed dungeons of medieval Europe, were frequently used to store captives awaiting trial or punishment rather than for long-term confinement (Foucault, 1977). The emergence of the penitentiary in the 18th and 19th centuries signaled a substantial change toward institutionalized punishment, with the purpose of reforming offenders through solitary confinement, labor, and religious instruction. Today's penal institutions encompass a wide range of facilities, from community-based correctional centers to maximum-security prisons, all designed to achieve certain purposes within the larger framework of criminal justice (Garland, 2001).

Philosophically, the foundation of penology has evolved from a retributive to a more comprehensive, multifaceted perspective. Ancient penology was frequently driven by religion or moral precepts, and the fundamental goal was to restore balance by punishing the offender proportionally to their crime (Johnston, 2021). Modern penology, influenced by Enlightenment ideas and later discoveries in social sciences, views punishment through a utilitarian lens, with the objective of maximizing society's well-being through crime prevention, offender rehabilitation, and public safety. This transition parallels broader cultural principles, as modern penology is more informed by human rights, social justice, and the possibility of redemption (Cullen and Gilbert, 2013).

A comparison of ancient and modern penology demonstrates a significant shift in the goal, tactics, legal frameworks, societal roles, and philosophical foundations of punishment. While ancient penology was essentially retributive, based on a worldview that prioritized vengeance and deterrence, modern penology takes a more nuanced approach to crime and punishment, emphasizing rehabilitation, social protection, and the restoration of both victims and offenders. This history mirrors broader shifts in societal norms, legal systems, and philosophical approaches, emphasizing the complex and dynamic nature of penology as a discipline.

1.6. ROLE OF RELIGION IN PENOLOGICAL PRACTICES

Religion has historically played an important and complex role in developing penological practices, influencing the evolution of legal systems, the moral and ethical foundations that underpin laws, and the ways used to rehabilitate offenders.

The junction of religion and penology represents the larger interaction between religious teachings and societal standards, in which religious ideas frequently serve as the foundation for concepts of justice, punishment, and compassion. This link has evolved throughout time, from religiously infused legal laws in ancient civilizations to the integration of religious activities into current correctional systems. However, the incorporation of religion into penology is not without controversy, as it raises concerns about imposing specific beliefs on diverse populations and the efficacy of religious-based rehabilitation.

Religion has historically influenced penological procedures, as seen by ancient civilization's legal laws. For example, the Code of Hammurabi, one of the oldest known legal laws, was inextricably linked to the religious beliefs of the time. The law, credited to Babylonian monarch Hammurabi, was thought to be divinely inspired and designed to protect justice as prescribed by the gods. This heavenly sanction gave the laws hallowed legitimacy, justifying the harsh and retributive punishments imposed for numerous transgressions. Similarly, the Mosaic Law, as represented by the 10 Commandments, embodies ancient Judaism's moral and ethical principles. These commandments, which are said to have been given by God to Moses, served as a basic legal and moral guide for the Israelites, shaping their society's norms and legal processes. In both cases, the intersection of religion and law fostered the notion that justice was a manifestation of divine will rather than a human invention. This relationship between religion and law created a framework in which punishment was viewed not simply as a response to crime, but also as a way of restoring moral order as defined by religious belief (Johnston, 2021).

Religion has also offered a moral and ethical framework that has influenced society's attitudes toward justice, mercy, and rehabilitation. In many theological traditions, justice is regarded as a fundamental moral principle, frequently accompanied by ideas of mercy and forgiveness. For example, Christianity emphasizes the value of forgiveness and redemption, which has inspired the development of more rehabilitative methods of punishment. Religious figures' moral teachings, such as Jesus Christ's emphasis on compassion and forgiveness, have penetrated society's views toward offenders, fostering the belief that people should be given the chance to change their ways and redeem themselves. This religiously driven attitude has helped to build penological methods that promote rehabilitation over retribution. The way nations have historically viewed the death penalty is another example of how religious morality has had an impact. Religious justifications for and against the death penalty have been invoked several times, demonstrating the intricate relationship between religious doctrine and cultural norms (Garland, 2001). Religion continues to play an important role in modern penology, particularly in terms of rehabilitation and reform.

Many correctional systems contain religious programs aimed at rehabilitating prisoners, believing that spiritual advice might help them achieve moral and psychological change. Counseling, religious services, and community service activities are common components of these programs, which are intended to assist inmates acquire a sense of moral responsibility and encourage personal transformation. These programs are based on the idea that religion can create a sense of purpose and meaning, which is necessary for the rehabilitation process. For example, prison ministries and faith-based projects frequently focus on assisting offenders in developing a relationship with a higher power, which can lead to good changes in behavior and attitude According to some research, involvement in religious programs helps reduce recidivism rates because offenders who participate in these programs are often better equipped to reintegrate into society after release. However, the usefulness of faith-based rehabilitation programs is still being debated, with detractors doubting their applicability to varied inmate groups with varying religious views or nonbelief.

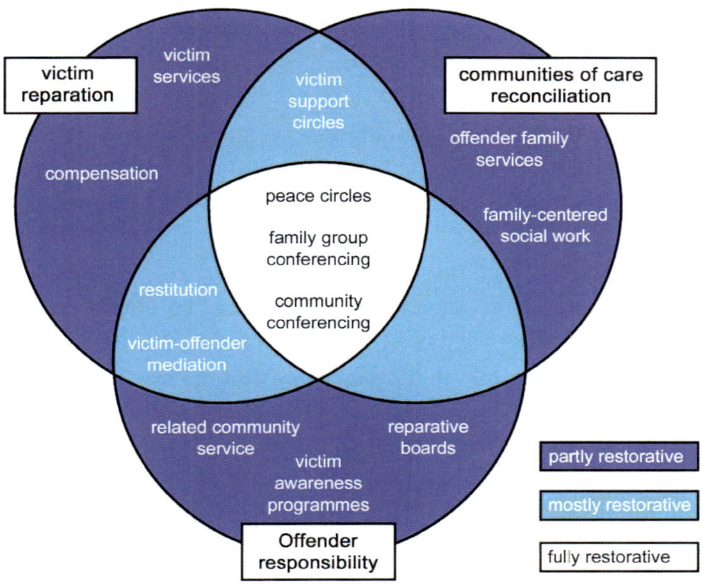

Figure 1.2. *Practice of restorative justice.*

Source: Weitekamp & Parmentier (2014).

Restorative justice is another example of how religion has influenced penological procedures. Restorative justice, which is based on the moral precepts of numerous faith traditions, stresses mending the harm caused by criminal activity rather than punishing individuals. This technique entails reconciling criminals with their victims and the larger community by fostering conversation, forgiveness, and reparation (Figure 1.2).

Restorative justice has long been an important aspect of conflict resolution in many indigenous societies, which frequently have a significant religious or spiritual basis. These approaches are gradually being implemented into modern legal systems, especially in cases involving juvenile offenders or minor crimes. Religious ideas, such as the Christian emphasis on reconciliation and forgiveness or the Buddhist focus on compassion and restoration, have supplied the ethical basis for these restorative practices. Restorative justice stands in stark contrast to the retributive concepts that dominate much of modern penology, providing an alternative approach that aims to heal rather than punish. However, incorporating restorative justice into modern judicial systems offers obstacles, notably in reconciling victims' interests and rights with the purpose of offender rehabilitation (Zehr, 2002).

Prison chaplaincy is another notable example of religion's influence on current penological procedures. Chaplains are employed by many correctional facilities to give convicts spiritual support, including religious services, counseling, and advice. Chaplains in jail reflect the view that spiritual treatment is an important part of the rehabilitation process. Chaplains frequently assist inmates in dealing with the emotional and psychological hardships of jail, offering solace and hope. They also serve an important role in helping offenders prepare for reintegration into society by providing moral and spiritual direction that can aid in the development of positive social and behavioral skills. The chaplaincy program can be especially effective for convicts who are experiencing guilt, humiliation, or hopelessness since it gives them a framework for understanding and dealing with their situation. However, chaplains' roles in prisons are not without criticism. Critics argue that the presence of religious figures in correctional facilities can lead to the imposition of specific religious beliefs on inmates, especially when participation in religious programs is viewed as required for favorable treatment or parole decisions (Beckford and Gilliat, 1998).

Despite its advantages, the incorporation of religion into penological activities is not without problems and criticism. One of the key concerns is that religious programs and chaplaincy services may impinge on inmates' religious freedom, particularly those who do not practice the dominant religion within the institution. This issue is especially important in multicultural settings, as inmates may come from many religious backgrounds or identify as non-religious. The imposition of specific religious ideas or practices can lead to ethical and legal issues, especially when inmates feel pressured into participating in religious activities in order to acquire favor or access certain privileges. Furthermore, there is a continuous dispute over the efficacy of religious-based recovery programs. While some studies suggest that these programs are beneficial, their effectiveness may be dependent on the inmate's personal views and level of religious commitment. This calls into question the applicability of religion programs and their ability to satisfy the requirements of a varied inmate community (Clear and Sumter, 2002).

1.7. FUTURE TRENDS IN PENOLOGY

The future of penology is set to change dramatically as nations contend with developing ideas of justice, increased use of technology, and a growing emphasis on human rights. These changes reflect broader developments in societal norms as well as advancements in domains such as technology, psychology, and criminal justice. As we look ahead, it seems obvious that penology will continue to be affected by intricate interactions between these forces, resulting in a more sophisticated and multifaceted view of crime and punishment.

One of the most significant future trends in penology is the incorporation of technology into many parts of the criminal justice system. Technological improvements are projected to have a significant impact on offender management, rehabilitation, and monitoring. For example, the usage of electronic monitoring devices, such as ankle bracelets, is expected to advance, allowing for real-time tracking of criminals and minimizing the need for physical detention. These technologies can also be used to enforce parole restrictions, lowering recidivism rates by providing a non-intrusive but effective form of supervision. Furthermore, artificial intelligence (AI) and big data analytics are projected to transform risk assessment tools, allowing for more precise predictions of recidivism and personalizing rehabilitation programs to individual requirements. AI-powered systems could help identify the most effective solutions for specific offenders, boosting rehabilitation outcomes and lowering recidivism rates (Hannah-Moffat, 2013).

A further interesting development is a growing emphasis on restorative justice as an alternative to traditional punitive measures. Restorative justice, which focuses on mending the harm caused by criminal activity via reconciliation between offenders, victims, and the community, is gaining popularity as a more humanitarian and successful strategy to combat crime. This strategy is especially significant in cases involving nonviolent offenses or where the victim and perpetrator are from the same community. Restorative justice programs have shown promise in lowering recidivism and increasing victim satisfaction by addressing the root causes of criminal conduct and instilling a feeling of accountability and empathy in offenders. Restorative justice is anticipated to grow in importance within penological procedures as views toward punishment continue to change, possibly even taking the place of some more conventional types of punishment (Zehr, 2002).

The future of penology is also anticipated to be influenced by the growing significance placed on human rights and treating offenders in an ethical manner. There is a growing global consensus that punishment should be proportionate and should respect the person's dignity, which is shown in the trend toward the abolition of the death penalty and the reduction of severe sentencing procedures. International human rights groups, including the United Nations, have played a pivotal role in advancing changes that prioritize rehabilitation over retribution in correctional systems across the globe. Therefore, rather than concentrating solely on punitive measures, future penological practices are expected to place a greater emphasis on the rehabilitation and reintegration of criminals into society. Rehabilitative measures appear to be more beneficial in the long run in reducing recidivism and increasing public safety, according to a growing body of evidence that supports this change (Van Zyl Smit and Snacken, 2009).

Furthermore, the growing acknowledgment of the social determinants of criminal conduct will very certainly have an impact on the future of criminology. Poverty, education, mental health, and substance misuse are increasingly recognized as major drivers of criminal activity. This awareness is propelling a trend toward more comprehensive approaches to crime prevention and offender rehabilitation, which target the root causes rather than simply punishing the symptoms of larger social problems. Programs that combine mental health treatment, educational opportunities, and substance addiction counseling are predicted to gain popularity as part of a comprehensive effort to reduce crime and increase social well-being. This trend reflects a broader movement toward recognizing crime as a complicated social issue that requires various solutions (Garland, 2001).

The future of penology is likely to witness a further shift away from simply punitive techniques and toward more rehabilitative, restorative, and technologically advanced practices. These trends reflect broader societal changes, such as a greater emphasis on human rights, the incorporation of technology, and a better knowledge of the social determinants of criminal conduct. As these trends continue to grow, they are likely to result in a more humane, effective, and just prison system that benefits both offenders and society at large.

Chapter 2

THEORIES OF CRIME AND PUNISHMENT

Contents

The study of crime and punishment has been fundamentally influenced by two major schools of thought in penology: classical and positivist. The classical school, which was heavily influenced by the works of Cesare Beccaria and Jeremy Bentham, promotes a rational, calculative approach to criminal behavior. It asserts that individuals have free will and engage in criminal behavior based on a cost-benefit analysis, weighing potential pleasure against the risk of punishment. This school emphasizes deterrence, arguing that predictable and proportionate punishments are effective deterrents to crime (Faqir, 2015).

In contrast, the positivist school, which emerged in the late 19th century, shifted the emphasis from the crime to the criminal. It contends that criminal behavior is influenced by biological, psychological, and social factors beyond a person's control. This viewpoint emphasizes rehabilitation and scientific research into offenders, advocating for tailored interventions rather than uniform punishments (Marsh et al., 2004). Contemporary penological discourse continues to debate the merits and limitations of these theories, acknowledging that a nuanced understanding of crime necessitates integrating insights from both deterministic and rationalist frameworks (Scott, 2008). These foundational theories continue to shape contemporary criminal justice policies and practices.

2.1. CLASSICAL SCHOOL OF CRIMINOLOGY

The classical school of criminology emerged in the late 18th century, representing a significant shift in the understanding and administration of criminal justice. The classical school, founded on the Enlightenment ideals of reason, liberty, and equality, sought to establish a systematic and rational approach to crime and punishment. This school of thought is primarily associated with two foundational figures: Cesare Beccaria and Jeremy Bentham. Their theories have profoundly influenced modern penological practices and criminal law (Scott, 2008).

Cesare Beccaria, an Italian philosopher, is considered the father of classical criminology. In his seminal work, On Crimes and Punishments (1764), Beccaria argued against the arbitrary and brutal practices of his time's criminal justice system. He emphasized the importance of a legal framework that is just, predictable, and rational. Beccaria proposed that when deciding to commit a crime, individuals are rational actors with free will who weigh the costs and benefits. This viewpoint holds that people commit crimes because the perceived benefits outweigh the costs. Thus, Beccaria proposed that punishment should be designed to discourage criminal behavior by outweighing the potential benefits of the crime. He introduced the concept of proportionality, advocating that the severity of punishment should correspond to the seriousness of the crime, thereby creating a rational scale of justice (Faqir, 2015; Scott, 2008). Beccaria's theories also emphasized the importance of punishment being certain and swift. He contended that for deterrence to be effective, individuals must perceive a high likelihood of punishment following a crime, and that punishment must be administered quickly in order to reinforce the link between the criminal act and its consequences. This idea was revolutionary in the context of 18th-century Europe, where punishments were often arbitrary, excessively harsh, and delayed, fostering a retributive rather than deterrent system (Williams, 2012).

Jeremy Bentham, a British philosopher and social reformer, expanded on the principles established by Beccaria. Bentham's utilitarian philosophy, based on the principle of "the greatest happiness for the greatest number," when applied to criminal justice, advocates for reducing pain and increasing pleasure throughout society. In An Introduction to the Principles of Morals and Legislation (1789), Bentham contended that all human actions, including criminal acts, are motivated by the desire for pleasure and the avoidance of pain. To effectively deter crime, punishments must be calibrated to be unpleasant enough to dissuade potential offenders while not being unjust or disproportionate (Vito and Maahs, 2015).

Bentham pioneered the concept of "panopticism" in prison design, in which inmates would be constantly observed, not necessarily by actual guards but under the impression of continuous surveillance. This concept of deterrence by visibility emphasized his belief in rational choice theory and the notion that potential offenders are deterred not only by the act of punishment but also by the possibility of being caught and punished (Levinson, 2002).

The classical school's emphasis on rationality, free will, and deterrence marked a shift from earlier views of crime as a manifestation of supernatural forces or innate depravity. The classical school laid the groundwork for the development of modern legal systems founded on the principles of fairness, equality, and proportionate punishment by advocating for a more humane and systematic approach to criminal justice (Faqir, 2015).

However, the classical school has not been without criticism. Scholars argue that it assumes a level of rationality and foresight that may fail to account for the complexities of human behavior or the numerous factors that contribute to criminal activity. The strict application of its principles can also lead to disparities in justice because it does not consider the social, psychological, or economic conditions that may influence an individual's decision-making processes (Williams, 2012).

Despite these criticisms, the classical school's contributions to criminology remain significant. Its foundational theories shaped the development of laws and policies emphasizing crime prevention through deterrence, as well as the structure of judicial systems around the world. The principles of certainty, swiftness, and proportionality in punishment continue to resonate in contemporary penological discourse, highlighting the enduring legacy of the classical school of criminology in the pursuit of a rational and just criminal justice system (Marsh et al., 2004).

2.2. POSITIVIST SCHOOL OF CRIMINOLOGY

The positivist school of criminology marks a significant paradigm shift from the classical school, which emphasized rationality and free will in understanding criminal behavior. The positivist school, which emerged in the late 19th and early 20th centuries, emphasized empirical science and advocated for a more scientific and deterministic approach to crime research. Rather than viewing crime as the result of individual choice or rational calculation, positivist criminologists sought to identify the external and internal factors that influence human behavior, such as biological, psychological, and social determinants. This school of thought introduced a nuanced understanding of criminal behavior, highlighting the need for tailored interventions and rehabilitative efforts over punitive measures (Scott, 2008).

Cesare Lombroso, an Italian criminologist known as the "father of modern criminology," had a profound influence on the positivist school of thought. In his seminal work, L'uomo delinquente (The Criminal Man, 1876), Lombroso argued that criminal behavior was not the result of rational choice, but rather an expression of innate characteristics and biological determinism. Based on Charles Darwin's theory of evolution, Lombroso proposed that criminals were atavistic throwbacks—biologically inferior beings who were less evolved than non-criminals. He claimed that physical anomalies like skull shape, facial asymmetry, and other anatomical defects were signs of a "born criminal." This biological determinism marked a stark departure from the classical emphasis on free will and rationality, suggesting instead that criminality was an inherent trait rather than a conscious choice (Faqir, 2015).

Enrico Ferri and Raffaele Garofalo, Lombroso's contemporaries, expanded on his work through advancing the positivist perspective. Ferri, a lawyer and sociologist, developed the concept of "social defense," which asserted that society must protect itself from individuals who are perceived to be inherently dangerous or biologically predisposed to crime. He believes that the criminal justice system should prioritize crime prevention through a scientific understanding of its causes rather than focusing solely on punishment. Ferri advocated for a multifaceted approach to crime prevention that considers psychological, environmental, and social factors when analyzing criminal behavior. This comprehensive approach reflected a growing recognition that crime is a complex phenomenon influenced by an array of factors other than biological determinism (Marsh et al., 2004).

Raffaele Garofalo, another key figure in the positivist school, introduced the concept of "natural crime," which he defined as actions that violate the fundamental sentiments of pity and probity—empathy and honesty—that are essential to society's survival. Garofalo contended that criminal behavior was not only a violation of legal codes but also a violation of natural law, which supported social cohesion and order. Garofalo extended positivist analysis beyond biological explanations by focusing on the moral and social dimensions of crime, emphasizing the importance of understanding the societal context in which crime occurs (Faqir, 2015; Williams, 2012).

While Lombroso, Ferri, and Garofalo established the positivist school with their emphasis on biology and sociology, the scope of positivist criminology expanded dramatically in the early 20th century with the introduction of psychological theories of crime. Scholars such as Sigmund Freud and Ivan Pavlov proposed the idea that criminal behavior could be understood in terms of psychological abnormalities or learned behaviors. According to Freud's psychoanalytic theory, criminal behavior can be the result of unconscious conflicts, unresolved childhood traumas, or deviant superego development. Pavlov's work on conditioned responses helped us understand how criminal behaviors could be learned and reinforced over time (Levinson, 2002).

The positivist school also made a significant contribution to the development of modern criminal justice policies and practices, particularly in terms of rehabilitation and offender treatment. Positivist criminologists paved the way for penal system reforms that sought to address offenders' social, psychological, and biological needs by shifting the focus away from punishment and toward understanding the root causes of criminal behavior. This rehabilitative approach has been instrumental in the development of numerous correctional programs, including psychological counseling, vocational training, and educational initiatives designed to reduce recidivism and promote reintegration into society (Scott, 2008).

Despite its groundbreaking contributions, the positivist school has been heavily criticized over the years. Critics argue that its deterministic approach to human behavior undermines individual agency and accountability by reducing complex social phenomena to simple causal explanations. The emphasis on biological determinism, particularly in Lombroso's work, has been widely criticized for its reductionist and frequently pseudo-scientific claims, which have been used to justify discriminatory practices and policies. Furthermore, the emphasis on identifying and treating "abnormal" individuals has raised ethical concerns about the potential for abuse and stigmatization, as well as the danger of pathologizing deviant behavior without considering broader social and economic contexts (Faqir, 2015).

Furthermore, the positivist school's emphasis on empirical methods and scientific analysis has sparked debates about the objectivity and reliability of its findings. While the scientific study of crime has undoubtedly advanced criminological knowledge, some scholars argue that the positivist approach overlooks the subjective and interpretive aspects of human behavior. The positivist emphasis on quantifiable data and measurable outcomes can occasionally obscure the sociopolitical dimensions of crime, including issues of power, inequality, and social justice (Williams, 2012).

Nonetheless, the positivist school of criminology remains an important part of the criminological landscape, providing valuable insights into the complexities of criminal behavior. Its emphasis on empirical research, scientific inquiry, and the examination of biological, psychological, and social factors has had a significant impact on current understandings of crime and criminality. By emphasizing the importance of addressing the root causes of criminal behavior, the positivist school has helped to develop more humane and effective criminal justice policies that prioritize prevention, rehabilitation, and social reintegration over retribution (Levinson, 2002).

2.3. RATIONAL CHOICE THEORY

Rational choice theory is a popular framework in criminology and penology that emphasizes the importance of individual decision-making in the context of crime and punishment. This theory is based on the classical school of criminology, which was heavily influenced by Enlightenment thinkers such as Cesare Beccaria and Jeremy Bentham, who argued that rational cost-benefit calculations govern human behavior, including criminal activity. According to rational choice theory, when making the decision to commit a crime, individuals engage in a cognitive process that weighs the potential rewards of the criminal act against the likely risks and consequences of being apprehended and punished. This theoretical perspective has significantly influenced contemporary criminal justice policies and practices, particularly in the realm of deterrence and the design of legal sanctions (Scott, 2008).

The rational choice theory of crime emerged in the late 20th century as a reaction to earlier criminological theories that emphasized deterministic explanations of criminal behavior, such as those proposed by the positivist school. Whereas positivist criminology concentrated on the biological, psychological, and sociological causes of crime, rational choice theory returned to the traditional concepts of free will and individual autonomy. It asserts that crime is the result of a deliberate decision by individuals who believe that the benefits of engaging in illegal activities outweigh the risks of detection and punishment. This viewpoint is consistent with Jeremy Bentham's utilitarian philosophy, which claimed that humans are motivated by the pursuit of pleasure and the avoidance of pain, and that criminal behavior can be understood as an attempt to maximize personal utility (Akers, 2011; Scott, 2008).

Bounded rationality is a central concept in rational choice theory. While the theory assumes that people are rational actors, it also recognizes that their decision-making processes are influenced by information limitations, cognitive biases, and situational contexts. As a result, offenders may not have complete or accurate information about the potential consequences of their actions, nor do they always conduct a fully rational cost-benefit analysis. Instead, decisions to commit crimes are frequently influenced by perceived opportunities, which are shaped by the individual's environment, social networks, and previous interactions with the criminal justice system. This concept of bounded rationality provides a more nuanced understanding of criminal behavior by acknowledging that rational choices are made within specific constraints and contexts (Matsueda et al., 2006) (Figure 2.1).

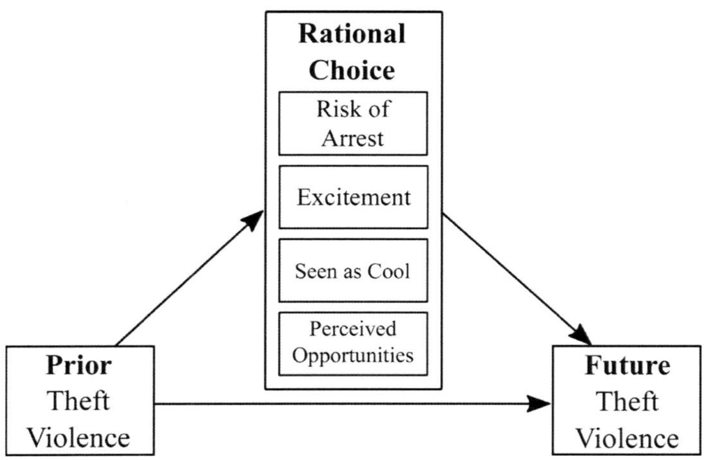

Figure 2.1. *Model of the rational choice theory.*

Source: Lanfear (2021).

Gary Becker, an economist, is a key proponent of rational choice theory, having applied economic principles to the study of crime in his seminal work

"Crime and Punishment: An Economic Approach" (1968). Becker contended that criminal behavior could be analyzed using the same economic models used to study market behavior. He proposed that individuals make a rational assessment of the expected utility of committing a crime, taking into account the likelihood of being caught and punished, the severity of the punishment, and the potential financial and social benefits of the crime. Becker's economic approach to crime has played an important role in shaping the development of deterrence theory, which holds that the certainty, swiftness, and severity of punishment are critical factors in deterring criminal behavior (Matsueda et al., 2006).

Ronald V. Clarke and Derek B. Cornish made a significant contribution to rational choice theory by expanding the theoretical framework to include the concept of situational crime prevention. Clarke and Cornish argued in their edited volume, "The Reasoning Criminal: Rational Choice Perspectives on Offending" (1986), that criminal decision-making is influenced not only by individual motivations and preferences, but also by situational factors that create opportunities for crime. They introduced the concept of "situational choice," which implies that the decision to commit a crime is influenced by the availability of suitable targets, the presence of capable guardians, and the perceived risks of detection. This perspective has led to the development of practical strategies for reducing crime through environmental design, such as increasing surveillance, improving lighting, and enhancing access control in public spaces (Levinson, 2002).

The rational choice theory has also influenced modern deterrence theories, which emphasize the role of legal sanctions in preventing criminal behavior. Deterrence theory, which is rooted in the classical school and refined by rational choice principles, holds that the threat of punishment can deter people from engaging in criminal behavior if the perceived costs of offending outweigh the benefits. Deterrence is divided into two types: general deterrence, which seeks to discourage the general public from committing crimes by demonstrating the consequences of criminal behavior, and specific deterrence, which seeks to prevent recidivism by imposing sanctions on individual offenders. According to rational choice theory, the effectiveness of deterrence depends on the perceived certainty, swiftness, and severity of punishment. Research suggests that the certainty of being caught is a more significant deterrent than the severity of the penalty (Akers, 2011; Williams, 2012).

Despite its contributions to criminological theory and practice, rational choice theory has received some criticism. One major criticism is that the theory is based on an overly simplistic and rationalistic model of human behavior, which ignores the complex psychological, social, and cultural factors that influence decision-making. Critics argue that the theory assumes a level of rationality and foresight that may not accurately reflect the realities of criminal behavior, especially when people act impulsively or under the influence of drugs. Furthermore, rational choice theory has been criticized for its focus on individual decision-making, which may overlook the broader structural and systemic issues that contribute to crime, such as poverty, inequality, and social disorganization (Scott, 2008).

Furthermore, empirical research on the effectiveness of deterrence has produced conflicting results, with some studies indicating that increasing the certainty of punishment can reduce crime rates, while others suggest that changing the severity of punishment has little to no effect on criminal behavior. This variability in findings has led to debates about the applicability and limitations of rational choice theory in explaining and preventing crime, especially in diverse social and cultural contexts (Matsueda et al., 2006).

Nonetheless, rational choice theory remains a fundamental framework in criminology and penology, providing valuable insights into the decision-making processes that drive criminal behavior. By emphasizing the importance of individual choice and rational calculation, the theory has helped to shape more targeted and evidence-based crime prevention strategies, such as situational crime prevention, deterrence policies, and behavioral interventions. The rational choice perspective has also encouraged a more dynamic and adaptive approach to criminal justice, acknowledging that effective crime control requires an understanding of the complex interplay between individual behavior, situational contexts, and broader social structures (Levinson, 2002).

2.4. SOCIAL LEARNING THEORY

Social learning theory emerged as a response to the limitations of both classical and positivist schools of criminology, combining psychological principles with sociological insights to emphasize that criminal behavior is learned through social contexts rather than being solely the result of individual choice or innate predispositions. This theory has significantly influenced modern understandings of crime, particularly in its exploration of the mechanisms by which behaviors are reinforced, modeled, and perpetuated within social environments (Akers, 2011) (Figure 2.2).

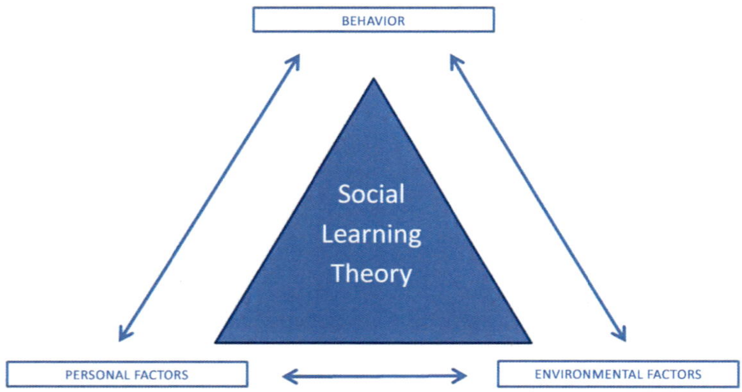

Figure 2.2. *Social learning theory.*

Source: Bond (2017).

Edwin H. Sutherland, who introduced the concept of differential association in his book Principles of Criminology (1939), is a seminal figure in the evolution of social learning theory. Sutherland proposed that criminal behavior is learned through interactions with others in a communication process, and that this learning includes both the techniques for committing crimes as well as the specific motives, drives, rationalizations, and attitudes that lead to criminal behavior. Sutherland argues that an individual becomes delinquent when there are more definitions favorable to the violation of law than definitions unfavorable to the violation of law. This theory challenged previous deterministic views by emphasizing the social context of crime and suggesting that criminal behavior is a result of socialization into a community that holds deviant values (Solakoglu and Yuksek, 2020).

The differential association theory paved the way for future developments in social learning theory, particularly Albert Bandura's contributions. Bandura, a well-known psychologist, developed Sutherland's ideas into his theory of observational learning, which he outlined in his book Social Learning Theory (1977). Bandura argued that people learn behaviors, values, and attitudes by observing others, particularly those who are regarded as role models. This process, known as modeling, occurs when people mimic the behaviors of others they see, especially when those behaviors appear to be rewarded or unpunished. In this way, criminal behavior can be learned indirectly, without direct reinforcement, by observing criminal acts being performed by others in one's social environment (Scott, 2008).

Bandura's social learning theory includes the concept of reinforcement, which refers to the process by which behaviors are strengthened or weakened based on their consequences. Bandura distinguished between direct reinforcement, which strengthens behaviors through direct rewards or punishments, and vicarious reinforcement, which teaches individuals by observing the consequences of others' actions. In the context of crime, vicarious reinforcement is important in the learning process because people are more likely to engage in criminal behavior if they see others being rewarded for similar actions or avoiding punishment. This perspective emphasizes the importance of both the immediate social environment and the larger cultural context in shaping attitudes toward crime and legality (Levinson, 2002; Pratt et al., 2010).

Ronald L. Akers, a criminologist, expanded on social learning theory by combining concepts from Sutherland's differential association theory and Bandura's social learning theory to create a comprehensive framework for understanding criminal behavior. Akers' version of social learning theory, described in his book Deviant Behavior: A Social Learning Approach (1973), emphasized the importance of four major components: differential association, differential reinforcement, imitation, and definitions. Differential association is the process of interacting with others who have deviant values or engage in criminal behavior, which influences one's own likelihood of offending. Differential reinforcement refers to the balance of rewards and punishments associated with behavior, which influences the continuation or cessation of criminal activity. Imitation involves the modeling of behavior observed in others, and definitions refer to the attitudes and meanings that individuals attach to behaviors, which can be favorable or unfavorable to law violation (Solakoglu and Yuksek, 2020; Williams, 2012).

Akers' social learning theory provides a detailed explanation of how criminal behavior is acquired and maintained. According to the theory, people are more likely to commit crimes when they associate with others who encourage deviant behavior, when that behavior is reinforced or rewarded, and when they adopt favorable definitions of criminal conduct. This perspective emphasizes the importance of social and environmental factors in shaping criminal behavior, suggesting that crime is deeply embedded in social processes and structures rather than being solely the result of individual pathology (Akers, 2011).

The social learning theory has important implications for penology and criminal justice policy. This theory proposes that interventions should focus not only on individuals but also on the social environments and networks in which they operate, emphasizing the social dimensions of crime. Social learning theory principles are consistent with programs that aim to reduce crime by changing social contexts, such as community-based initiatives, mentorship programs, and family interventions. For example, rehabilitation programs that seek to change offenders' associations and reinforce pro-social behaviors are founded on the idea that criminal behavior can be unlearned through exposure to positive role models and reinforcement of lawful conduct (Pratt et al., 2010; Scott, 2008).

Furthermore, social learning theory has influenced crime prevention strategies by addressing the broader cultural and societal factors that contribute to the normalization of deviance. This includes efforts to reduce the media's glamorization of crime, provide positive role models for youth, and create environments that encourage lawful behavior. The theory also supports the development of restorative justice practices that focus on repairing harm and reintegrating offenders into their communities, thus changing the social learning environments that may have contributed to criminal behavior in the first place (Vito and Maahs, 2015).

Despite its contributions, social learning theory has received some criticism. Some scholars argue that the theory lacks specificity in explaining how social learning processes differ across different types of crimes or cultural settings. There is also debate about the relative importance of social learning in influencing criminal behavior versus other factors such as biological predispositions or structural inequalities. Furthermore, while social learning theory emphasizes the role of reinforcement and modeling, it may not fully account for spontaneous or irrational acts of crime that do not fit neatly into a framework of learned behavior (Vito and Maahs, 2015; Williams, 2012).

Social learning theory remains an important perspective in criminology and penology, providing a solid framework for understanding the social processes that underpin criminal behavior. By emphasizing the importance of social interactions, observational learning, and reinforcement, the theory sheds light on how criminal behavior is acquired, maintained, and potentially unlearned. As a result, social learning theory continues to inform contemporary approaches to crime prevention, intervention, and rehabilitation, highlighting the importance of addressing the social dimensions of crime in efforts to create safer and more just communities (Solakoglu and Yuksek, 2020).

2.5. LABELLING THEORY

Labeling theory, a popular idea in criminology and penology, provides an appealing framework for comprehending the dynamics of crime and deviance. Labeling theory, developed in the mid-20th century by sociologists such as Howard Becker, Edwin Lemert, and Erving Goffman, contends that crime and deviance are the product of societal labels, rather than inherent in the act itself. This hypothesis proposes that when individuals are labeled as "deviants" or “criminals,” they may internalize these labels, leading to a self-fulfilling prophecy in which the labeled individuals continue to engage in deviant activity. Labeling theory has been an important topic of study in the realm of crime and punishment for over two decades. Researchers have explored its implications for the criminal justice system, including policy, social justice, and rehabilitation (Vito and Maahs, 2015).

Labeling theory questions traditional criminological viewpoints that see the individual as the major source of deviance. Instead, it focuses on the societal response to deviance and the mechanisms by which people are classified and treated as offenders. One of the major assumptions of labeling theory is that society’s reactions to particular acts can result in individual stigmatization, which promotes criminal behavior. According to Marsh et al. (2004) idea of primary and secondary deviance, first acts of deviance (primary deviance) are frequently modest and do not elicit a major societal response. However, when these acts are discovered and classified by society, individuals may develop a deviant identity (secondary deviance), which can lead to additional criminal activity and membership in deviant subcultures (Figure 2.3).

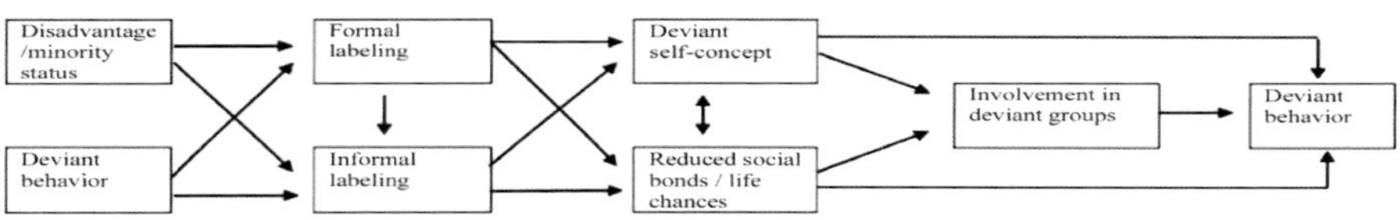

Figure 2.3. *Labeling theory.*

Source: Bernburg (2019).

The implications of labeling theory for penology are substantial, especially given the criminal justice system’s role in promoting or moderating deviant behavior. Scholars have suggested that the criminal justice system, via procedures such as arrest, prosecution, and jail, frequently plays an important part in identifying people as criminals. This approach can lead to a cycle of recidivism, as those who are classified and punished by the system may find it difficult to reintegrate into society, leading to additional deviance. Paternoster and Iovanni (2007) found that labeling can enhance criminal behavior, particularly among juveniles. The stigma associated with being called a criminal can result in social marginalization, limited access to legitimate opportunities, and increased association with deviant peers, all of which contribute to continued criminal activity. Furthermore, the impact of labeling is not evenly spread among demographic groups. According to research, labeling processes frequently connect with concerns of race, class, and gender, having a disproportionate influence on vulnerable communities. For example, research has shown that minority kids are more likely to be branded as delinquents and punished harsher than their white peers for the same acts. This tendency, known as the "racialization of crime," emphasizes the significance of labeling in sustaining socioeconomic inequities and institutional prejudices in the criminal justice system. These findings have far-reaching ramifications, implying that the criminal justice system's policies may exacerbate rather than alleviate social inequities, creating a vicious cycle of disadvantage for already marginalized populations (Marsh et al., 2004).

Labeling theory also has significant policy and practice consequences in the discipline of penology. One of the most important findings from labeling theory is the potential harm caused by formal interventions such as arrest and jail, especially for small transgressions. Scholars have argued for alternate approaches to crime and punishment that reduce offender stigma and prioritize rehabilitation over punishment. Restorative justice initiatives, for example, have been advocated as an alternative to traditional punitive methods, focusing on mending the harm caused by criminal action via conversation and reconciliation. These initiatives aim to minimize the stigma associated with criminal categorization while also providing offenders with possibilities for reintegration into society (Williams, 2012).

In recent years, there has been an increasing interest in applying labeling theory to current concerns in criminology, such as mass incarceration and reentry. The United States, in particular, has encountered major issues as a result of the mass incarceration of individuals, many of whom come from marginalized areas. Labeling theory offers a critical lens through which to assess the consequences of mass incarceration for individuals and communities. According to research, the labeling and stigmatization associated with incarceration can have long-term effects on people's social and economic prospects, making it harder for them to find work, housing, and social support following their release. These hurdles to reintegration might create a cycle of recidivism in which individuals are pushed back into criminal conduct owing to a lack of genuine possibilities (Levinson, 2002).

Furthermore, labeling theory can help explain the increase of the "collateral consequences" of criminal convictions, such as the loss of voting rights, restrictions on public assistance, and the denial of occupational licenses. These repercussions perpetuate the criminal label and further marginalize those who have previously paid their debts to society. Scholars have advocated for policies that lessen the long-term consequences of criminal labels, such as expunging criminal records and eliminating barriers to reintegration (Maruna, 2011).

These improvements are viewed as critical in breaking the cycle of recidivism and encouraging social reintegration.

Despite its long-standing significance, labeling theory has been criticized and limited. Some experts contend that the theory does not sufficiently explain why some people resist or reject deviant labels, whereas others absorb them. Furthermore, labeling theory has been criticized for emphasizing the social reaction to deviation rather than the reasons for deviant conduct itself. However, labeling theory supporters claim that its strength resides in its capacity to emphasize the social processes and power dynamics that lead to the formation of deviance and the persistence of social inequities (Scott, 2008).

Thus, labeling theory remains an important paradigm for understanding the complicated interaction between crime, punishment, and society. Its emphasis on societal reactions to deviance and the impact of labels on people's identities and behaviors has far-reaching consequences for the criminal justice system and larger social policy. As modern cultures contend with issues such as mass imprisonment, systemic inequality, and the difficulties of reintegration, labeling theory offers crucial insights into how social labels and stigmatization can perpetuate cycles of deviance and poverty. Future research and policy initiatives that use the insights of labeling theory have the potential to generate more just and effective ways to crime and punishment, eventually leading to a more equitable and compassionate criminal justice system.

2.6. CRITICAL CRIMINOLOGY

Critical criminology is an important subfield of criminology that provides a radical critique of established approaches to crime and punishment. Critical criminology, which originated in Marxist thinking and was influenced by many schools of critical theory, aims to explain crime and justice through the prism of social inequality, power relations, and oppressive structures. Unlike traditional criminological theories, which frequently focus on human behavior or disease as the underlying causes of crime, critical criminology investigates the socioeconomic and political settings that determine both criminal activity and reactions to it. This viewpoint is critical for understanding how laws, criminal justice agencies, and societal norms can perpetuate existing hierarchies and inequities.

A major element of critical criminology is its emphasis on socioeconomic inequality and its consequences for crime and justice. Critical criminologists contend that crime cannot be properly understood without taking into account the larger social environment in which it occurs, notably how class, race, gender, and economic status influence criminal behavior and societal reactions to it. For example, the overrepresentation of minority groups in jail is frequently claimed as proof of structural prejudices in the criminal justice system. According to Wacquant (2009), mass incarceration in the United States disproportionately impacts African Americans and Latinos, reflecting larger patterns of racial and economic inequality. Critical criminologists argue that these differences are not coincidental, but rather reflect a criminal justice system that works to sustain the status quo by marginalizing and regulating disadvantaged communities.

Another important part of critical criminology is the study of power dynamics. This method examines how the criminal justice system serves as a mechanism of social control, benefiting some groups at the expense of others. According to this viewpoint, the law is not a neutral arbiter of justice, but rather a vehicle by which dominant groups exercise power and retain their privileged position in society. Laws are frequently enacted and enforced in ways that safeguard the interests of the strong while criminalizing actions associated with the less powerful. For example, white-collar crimes, which are generally committed by those in positions of economic power, are frequently penalized less severely than street crimes, which are more likely to be committed by individuals from lower socioeconomic backgrounds. This selective enforcement and differential treatment highlights the role of the criminal justice system in perpetuating social hierarchies (Vito and Maahs, 2015).

Critical criminology also exposes the prejudices and oppression that exist within the criminal justice system, while advocating for the rights of underprivileged people. It refutes the concept that the law is impartial, arguing instead that legal processes frequently reflect and strengthen existing social inequities. Feminist criminologists, for example, have criticized the criminal justice system's failure to handle crimes against women, such as domestic abuse and sexual assault, claiming that these failures are indicative of greater social misogyny. Similarly, critical race theorists have investigated how racial prejudices pervade every level of the criminal justice system, from policing practices to sentencing decisions These criticisms emphasize the ways in which the criminal justice system can operate as a weapon of oppression rather than a vehicle for providing justice (Scott, 2008).

Critical criminology not only examines existing systems but also advocates alternative viewpoints on crime and punishment. It invites a reassessment of fundamental assumptions about criminal behavior, calling into question the effectiveness of punitive policies that focus primarily on punishment rather than addressing the underlying reasons for crime. For example, critical criminologists frequently support restorative justice approaches, which aim to repair the harm caused by criminal activity via conversation and reconciliation among offenders, victims, and the community. Restorative justice is an alternative to standard punitive measures that prioritizes accountability and healing over vengeance. This approach is consistent with the critical criminological view that justice should be about more than just punishing offenders; it should also include addressing the societal factors that contribute to crime and striving toward a more just and equitable society (Zehr, 2002).

Furthermore, critical criminology emphasizes the necessity of viewing crime as a social construct formed by the goals of powerful organizations. Those in positions of authority frequently determine what constitutes criminal behavior, defining certain activities as deviant or criminal while dismissing others. For example, political and economic forces have strongly influenced the criminalization of drug use, which frequently targets vulnerable people, but other damaging activities, such as corporate environmental pollution, may not be criminalized at all. This selective criminalization reflects greater power dynamics, where the definition and implementation of the law promote the interests of the powerful at the cost of the less powerful (Reiman and Leighton, 2016).

Critical criminology is not without criticism. Some scholars contend that its emphasis on systemic issues such as class and race risks overlooking the agency of criminals. Furthermore, critical criminology's emphasis on systemic analysis might lead to a negative assessment of the criminal justice system's reform prospects. However, proponents of critical criminology say that these criticisms overlook the theory's larger goal, which is to highlight the social settings and power dynamics that affect criminal behavior and the criminal justice response. Critical criminology focuses on these wider structures in order to identify inequities in the current system and advocate for more equitable and compassionate responses to crime and punishment.

2.7. APPLICATION OF CRIMINOLOGY THEORIES IN PENOLOGY

The use of criminological ideas in penology is an important part of understanding and addressing crime and punishment in the criminal justice system. Criminological theories provide the underlying foundations for developing penal legislation, designing correctional programs, and administering justice. Since the early 2000s, there has been a growing research focus on how various criminological theories influence penological practices, with a particular emphasis on the theories' effectiveness in reducing recidivism and encouraging rehabilitation. The convergence of these theories with penology has resulted in both traditional and creative approaches to crime and punishment, reflecting our changing understanding of criminal conduct and the social context in which it occurs.

One of the most influential criminological theories used in penology is the deterrence theory, which holds that the dread of punishment could deter people from engaging in criminal behavior. This idea has historically influenced punitive measures, such as mandatory sentencing laws and the imposition of the death penalty, with the assumption that harsh punishments will prevent both individual offenders and society as a whole from committing crimes. However, recent research has called into doubt the effectiveness of deterrence-based techniques, notably their ability to reduce recidivism. Studies have shown that while strong sanctions may temporarily incapacitate offenders, they do not always address the underlying causes of criminal behavior, leading to high rates of reoffending once individuals are freed (Nagin, 2013). As a result, there has been a trend toward investigating alternative approaches that prioritize rehabilitation and tackling the social causes of crime.

The social learning theory, which emphasizes the importance of environment and socialization in the development of criminal conduct, has had a considerable impact on penological procedures. This hypothesis contends that people learn criminal behaviors from their encounters with others, particularly those in their immediate social surroundings. In the field of penology, social learning theory has resulted in the development of rehabilitative programs aimed at altering offenders' social dynamics and cognitive habits. Cognitive-behavioral therapy (CBT) is an evidence-based strategy that has been widely applied in correctional facilities to assist offenders realize and change the cognitive patterns and behaviors that contribute to their criminal actions (Lipsey, Landenberger, and Wilson, 2007). According to research, CBT programs are helpful in reducing recidivism rates, especially when they are targeted to individual offenders' specific needs and risks.

Another critical theory used in penology is the strain hypothesis, which holds that societal pressures and the inability to pursue socially acceptable goals can lead to criminal activity. This idea has had a particularly strong influence on measures targeted at alleviating socioeconomic conditions that lead to crime. For example, correctional programs that provide offenders with education, vocational training, and job opportunities are based on the belief that lessening economic stress can reduce the chance of reoffending. Research has shown that offenders who participate in educational and vocational programs while incarcerated are more likely to obtain work upon release and less likely to return to criminal behavior (Davis et al., 2013). The use of strain theory in penology emphasizes the need to resolve structural inequities and societal forces that contribute to criminal conduct.

Moreover, the labeling theory, which investigates the impact of society's reactions and labels on individuals' self-identity and behavior, has influenced penological policies aimed at lowering the stigma against offenders. Labeling theory proposes that when people are classified as criminals, they may internalize this identity and continue to participate in criminal activity as a result. In response, some penological approaches have attempted to mitigate the harmful consequences of criminal labeling by emphasizing restorative justice techniques and community-based alternatives to incarceration. These techniques aim to reintegrate criminals into society while reducing recidivism by avoiding the stigmatizing impacts of traditional punishment tactics (Maruna, 2011).

As a result, the use of criminological theories in penology is critical for establishing successful crime prevention, punishment, and rehabilitation programs. The incorporation of ideas such as deterrence, social learning, strain, and labeling into correctional methods demonstrates an increasing awareness of the complex social dynamics that contribute to criminal behavior. By incorporating these theoretical frameworks into penological procedures, the criminal justice system can shift toward more holistic and effective crime-fighting methods, ultimately leading to improved outcomes for both offenders and society.

Chapter 3

THE CORRECTIONAL SYSTEM

Contents

The correctional system, a critical component of the larger criminal justice system, includes the structures and processes used to manage people who have been accused or convicted of criminal offenses. The correctional system, based on the field of penology, which studies the theory and practice of punishing and rehabilitating offenders, aims to achieve several core objectives: deterrence, incapacitation, retribution, and rehabilitation (Scott, 2008).

Deterrence attempts to prevent future criminal behavior by instilling fear of punishment in both the general public (general deterrence) and specific offenders (specific deterrence). Incapacitation removes offenders from society to reduce their capacity to commit future crimes, often through imprisonment. Retribution focuses on imposing a penalty proportionate to the offense, satisfying society's desire for justice. Rehabilitation, perhaps the most progressive goal, aims to reform offenders through educational programs, psychological treatment, and vocational training, eventually facilitating their reintegration into society as law-abiding citizens (Lipsey and Cullen, 2007).

Scholars frequently question the efficacy of the correctional system, questioning the balance between punitive measures and rehabilitative efforts. Furthermore, the systemic issues of overcrowding, recidivism, and the ethical treatment of inmates pose ongoing challenges that highlight the need for continuous reform and research within the field of penology (Levinson, 2002).

3.1. GOALS OF THE CORRECTIONAL SYSTEM

The correctional system's goals are multifaceted and based on the principles of penology. Penology provides a theoretical and empirical foundation for understanding how societies respond to crime and what goals these responses aim to achieve. The correctional system's objectives can broadly be classified into four primary goals: retribution, deterrence, incapacitation, and rehabilitation (Scott, 2008).

The most traditional goal of the correctional system is retribution, which reflects the belief that punishment should be proportionate to the offense. This concept is based on the notion of "just deserts," which holds that punishment is a moral response to crime that meets the societal demand for justice. According to the retributive model, offenders should receive their just punishment, not to deter future crime or to rehabilitate the offender, but as a response to the moral transgression itself. Retribution serves to validate societal norms and values, reinforcing the social contract that binds communities together. In this sense, the correctional system functions as a moral communication mechanism, signaling to society that certain behaviors are unacceptable and will result in corresponding penalties (Clear et al., 2013).

Deterrence, on the other hand, focuses on preventing future crime by imposing a punishment. Deterrence is classified into two types: general and specific deterrence. General deterrence aims to deter the general public from committing crimes by demonstrating the negative consequences of criminal behavior. The idea is that visible punishment of offenders will raise public awareness that crime does not pay, reducing the overall incidence of crime in society. Specific deterrence focuses on the individual offender, with the goal of discouraging them from committing future offenses through punishment. The effectiveness of deterrence as a correctional goal is subject to ongoing debate within penology, with some studies suggesting that certain forms of punishment may have limited deterrent effects or may even contribute to increased recidivism (Lowenkamp et al., 2006).

Incapacitation aims to protect society by removing dangerous people from the community. This goal is primarily achieved through imprisonment, in which offenders are physically restrained and thus prevented from committing future crimes. Incapacitation is a utilitarian approach that prioritizes public safety over the offender's rights or chances for rehabilitation. The efficacy of incapacitation as a correctional strategy is frequently measured by crime rate reductions, particularly for serious and violent offenses. Critics argue that relying on incapacitation can lead to over-incarceration and the erosion of civil liberties, raising ethical and practical concerns about the long-term viability of this approach (Lipsey and Cullen, 2007).

Rehabilitation is the most progressive and, perhaps, most contentious goal of the correctional system. Rehabilitation seeks to transform offenders into law-abiding citizens by addressing the underlying causes of criminal behavior, such as substance abuse, a lack of education, or inadequate job skills. The rehabilitative model emphasizes individuals' capacity for change and growth, advocating interventions that promote personal development and social reintegration. Educational courses, vocational training, psychological counseling, and substance abuse treatment are all possible components of rehabilitation programs. The success of rehabilitation efforts is frequently assessed through recidivism rates, with lower rates indicating more effective rehabilitation (Scott, 2008; Williams, 2012). However, rehabilitation requires substantial resources and a paradigm shift away from punitive measures, which can be challenging to achieve in practice given the prevailing public and political attitudes toward crime and punishment.

The correctional system's goals are determined by complex interactions between societal values, political pressures, and empirical evidence. While retribution, deterrence, incapacitation, and rehabilitation all have different motivations, they are not mutually exclusive and frequently overlap in practice.

A prison sentence, for example, could serve to incapacitate an offender and deter others while also providing opportunities for rehabilitation. The challenge for policymakers and practitioners is to balance these goals in order to effectively address crime while upholding principles of justice and human rights (Lowenkamp et al., 2006).

Contemporary penological scholarship continues to investigate the efficacy and ethical dimensions of these correctional goals, advocating for evidence-based practices that prioritize the humane and just treatment of offenders. There is growing recognition that an overly punitive correctional system can undermine its own goals by exacerbating social inequalities and failing to reduce recidivism rates. As a result, there is a push for more nuanced approaches that include restorative justice principles, which seek to repair the harm caused by crime through reconciliation and community involvement (Clear et al., 2013).

3.2. TYPES OF CORRECTIONAL FACILITIES

Correctional facilities are an essential component of the criminal justice system, designed to confine, manage, and rehabilitate individuals accused or convicted of crimes. According to penological insights, correctional facilities can be broadly classified into several types based on their roles, composition, and the nature of the inmates they house. These facilities include jails, prisons, juvenile detention facilities, and specialized institutions like halfway houses and community corrections centers. Each type serves distinct functions within the correctional framework, reflecting the various objectives of punishment, deterrence, incapacitation, and rehabilitation (Clear et al., 2013).

Jails are usually temporary facilities run by local governments, such as city or county governments. They primarily house people awaiting trial, sentencing, or transfer to other facilities, as well as those serving short sentences of less than one year. Jails serve as both pre-trial detention centers and facilities for minor offenders who do not require long-term incarceration. The jail population's composition is thus highly fluid, with inmates entering and exiting frequently, posing unique challenges for management, security, and service provision. Because of their short-term nature, jails often emphasize control and security over rehabilitation, with limited access to educational or therapeutic programs (Wortley, 2002).

Prisons, on the other hand, are long-term facilities designed to house people convicted of serious crimes and sentenced to significant periods of confinement, usually lasting more than a year. Prisons are typically run by state or federal governments and are classified into four security levels: minimum, medium, maximum, and super-maximum (supermax) security. Minimum-security prisons, also known as "federal prison camps," are the least restrictive environments, housing nonviolent offenders with a low risk of escape. These facilities focus on rehabilitation and provide a range of educational, vocational, and treatment programs to prepare inmates for reintegration into society (Staphan, 2008).

Medium-security prisons strike a balance between security and rehabilitation, allowing inmates more freedom of movement and access to programs than higher-security facilities. Maximum-security prisons, on the other hand, are designed to house the most dangerous offenders, and they include strict security measures such as controlled movement, surveillance, and isolation. Supermax prisons are the highest level of security, typically used to confine inmates who pose a significant threat to others or have a history of violent behavior within the prison system. These facilities are characterized by extreme isolation and limited contact with staff or other inmates, raising concerns about the psychological impact of long-term solitary confinement (Scott, 2008; Staphan, 2008).

Juvenile detention centers are specialized correctional facilities that house young offenders, typically under the age of 18, who have been charged or adjudicated for criminal activity. These facilities seek to strike a balance between public safety and youth development, focusing on rehabilitation and reintegration rather than punishment. Juvenile detention centers offer a variety of services, including education, counseling, and behavioral therapy, to address the underlying causes of delinquency. The penological approach to juvenile justice recognizes that young offenders are developmentally different from adults and may be more susceptible to rehabilitation if provided with appropriate interventions (Williams, 2012; Wortley, 2002).

In addition to traditional correctional facilities, there are specialized institutions such as halfway houses and community corrections centers that provide transitional environments for offenders nearing the end of their sentences or on probation or parole. Halfway houses are structured, supervised environments in which offenders can reintegrate into society while receiving assistance such as job training, substance abuse counseling, and life skills education. Community corrections centers serve a similar purpose, but they frequently place a greater emphasis on monitoring and controlling offenders' movements through electronic surveillance or regular check-ins with probation officers (Lipsey and Cullen, 2007).

The diversity of correctional facilities reflects the changing understanding of crime, punishment, and rehabilitation in penology. The traditional punitive model, which focuses on retribution and deterrence, has gradually evolved into a more rehabilitative and restorative approach, particularly for nonviolent and juvenile offenders. This shift is based on empirical research demonstrating that rehabilitative efforts can reduce recidivism and promote public safety more effectively than strictly punitive measures (Levinson, 2002).

However, the implementation of rehabilitation in correctional facilities is frequently uneven and influenced by a variety of factors, including political climates, public opinion, and resource availability. For example, while minimum and medium-security prisons may provide extensive rehabilitative programs, maximum-security and supermax facilities frequently prioritize security over treatment, limiting opportunities for inmate rehabilitation. Furthermore, overcrowding and understaffing in many correctional facilities can further impede the delivery of effective rehabilitation services, exacerbating existing systemic challenges (Scott, 2008).

Furthermore, broader social and economic contexts, such as systemic inequalities and racial disparities in incarceration rates, influence the role and composition of correctional facilities. Minority populations, particularly African Americans and Hispanics, are overrepresented in the U.S. prison system, reflecting larger patterns of social disadvantage and differential treatment within the criminal justice system. These disparities raise critical questions about the fairness and efficacy of correctional practices, emphasizing the need for reform efforts that address both the conditions within facilities and the larger structural factors contributing to crime and incarceration (Staphan, 2008; Wortley, 2002).

3.3. INMATE CLASSIFICATION

Inmate classification is an essential component of the correctional system, acting as a key mechanism for managing and organizing the prison population. Inmate classification, which is based on penological principles, entails assessing individuals to determine the most appropriate housing, security level, and rehabilitative interventions based on various risks and needs. Effective classification is essential for ensuring the safety and security of both inmates and staff, optimizing resource allocation, and increasing the overall effectiveness of the correctional system (Levinson, 2002) (Figure 3.1).

The classification process typically begins with an intake assessment, during which newly admitted inmates are comprehensively evaluated, including their criminal history, current charges, behavior, psychological status, and any special needs or vulnerabilities. This assessment determines the inmate's initial custody level, which dictates the level of supervision and security required. Custody levels typically range from minimum to maximum security, with each level reflecting varying levels of risk and corresponding restrictions on movement and privileges. Minimum-security inmates are frequently deemed low-risk and may be housed in less restrictive settings with greater access to rehabilitative programs and employment opportunities. Maximum-security inmates, considered high-risk, are subject to stricter controls, such as limited movement, increased surveillance, and reduced access to programs (Farr, 2000).

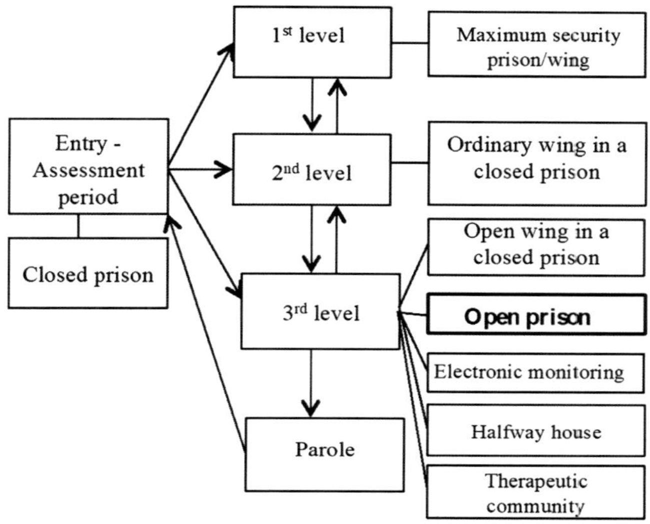

Figure 3.1. *Classification of prisoners in the Spanish prison system.*

Source: Martí (2021).

One of the primary goals of inmate classification is to separate individuals with different degrees of risk, thereby reducing the likelihood of violence and misconduct within correctional facilities. This separation is based on a number of important classifications, including security, risk, and needs classifications. The security classification of an inmate is based on the potential threat to the facility's, other inmates,' and staff's safety. It considers the nature and severity of the offense, prior history of violence, escape history, and gang affiliation. Risk classification evaluates an inmate's likelihood of engaging in disruptive or criminal behavior while incarcerated, taking into account past behaviors, institutional history, and psychological evaluations. Needs classification identifies specific needs that must be addressed to promote rehabilitation and reduce recidivism, including substance abuse, mental health, education, vocational training, and medical care (Arbach-Lucioni et al., 2012).

The importance of accurate and comprehensive classification cannot be overstated, as misclassification can have serious consequences for both individual inmates and the entire correctional facility. Over-classification, in which inmates are assigned to higher security levels than necessary, can result in increased costs, overcrowding, and limited access to rehabilitative programs. It can also exacerbate the negative psychological effects of incarceration, such as stress, anxiety, and depression, potentially increasing the likelihood of misconduct and recidivism. Under-classification, in contrast, where inmates are placed in lower security levels than warranted, can compromise the facility's safety and security by increasing the risk of violence, escape, and other forms of misconduct (Scott, 2008; Williams, 2012).

To improve the accuracy and effectiveness of inmate classification, correctional facilities are increasingly relying on evidence-based assessment tools and protocols. These tools are intended to provide a systematic and objective assessment of an inmate's risk and needs, utilizing validated measures that have been shown to predict outcomes such as institutional misconduct, recidivism, and successful reintegration into society. For example, the Level of Service Inventory-Revised (LSI-R) is a popular risk-needs assessment tool that takes into account a variety of factors such as criminal history, education and employment, family and marital status, substance abuse, and attitudes. By identifying areas of risk and need, the LSI-R helps to inform decisions about custody level, programming, and supervision (Arbach-Lucioni et al., 2012; Wortley, 2002).

In addition to these standardized assessment tools, inmate classification includes dynamic factors that can change over time, such as behavior, program participation, and progress toward addressing identified needs. This dynamic approach allows for the reclassification and adjustment of custody levels and interventions as an inmate's situation changes. For example, an inmate who exhibits good behavior and successfully completes a substance abuse treatment program may be reclassified to a lower security level and given additional privileges. In contrast, an inmate who engages in misconduct or fails to participate in required programs may be reclassified to a higher security level with more restrictive conditions (Farr, 2000; Williams, 2012).

Specialized classification is an important aspect of the inmate classification process, especially for populations with special needs or vulnerabilities. This includes inmates who are minors, women, the elderly, mentally ill, or have medical issues. Juvenile inmates, for example, require age-appropriate housing and programming that prioritizes education, rehabilitation, and development. Women inmates, who frequently have different paths to crime and different needs than men, may require gender-responsive classification that considers trauma history, parental status, and health care needs. Mentally ill inmates need specialized assessment and treatment plans to address their psychiatric conditions and reduce the risk of self-harm or harm to others (Levinson, 2002).

Inmate classification is also important for gang management in correctional facilities. Gangs, also known as Security Threat Groups (STGs), are a major concern in many correctional facilities, contributing to violence, drug trafficking, and other types of organized criminal activity. Inmate classification systems frequently include procedures for identifying gang affiliation and distinguishing known gang members from rival groups in order to reduce the possibility of conflict and maintain institutional order. This could include putting gang members in specialized housing units, limiting their movement and communication, and closely monitoring their activities (Scott, 2008).

Despite advancements in inmate classification, there are still challenges in ensuring consistent and fair application of classification procedures across facilities and jurisdictions. Variations in staff training, resources, and institutional culture, as well as biases based on race, ethnicity, and socioeconomic status, can all contribute to disparities in classification practices. Minority inmates are frequently disproportionately assigned to higher security levels, reflecting larger patterns of racial disparity within the criminal justice system (Arbach-Lucioni et al., 2012; Farr, 2000). Addressing these disparities will necessitate ongoing efforts to standardize classification practices, provide staff training on cultural competence and implicit bias, and implement oversight mechanisms to ensure accountability and transparency.

3.4. CORRECTIONAL STAFF ROLES AND RESPONSIBILITIES

Correctional staff are critical to the operation and management of correctional facilities, serving in a variety of roles that extend beyond enforcing rules and regulations. Their responsibilities are inextricably linked to the larger goals of the correctional system, which include ensuring safety and security, enforcing disciplinary measures, providing care and support, and facilitating rehabilitation. Insights from penology provide a comprehensive understanding of the complexities and challenges associated with the roles of correctional staff (Williams, 2012) (Figure 3.2).

Correctional staff are primarily in charge of maintaining the facility's security and order. This includes keeping track of inmate behavior, conducting routine searches to prevent contraband smuggling, and intervening in conflicts or disturbances. Maintaining order is critical for the safety of both inmates and staff, as well as the smooth operation of the facility. Correctional officers frequently need to strike a balance between strict rule enforcement and discretion. This balance is necessary to avoid escalation of tensions and foster a more stable environment within the prison (Griffin et al., 2010).

In addition to enforcing rules and security protocols, correctional officers play an important role in inmate rehabilitation. Penological research has influenced modern correctional philosophy, which emphasizes rehabilitation alongside punishment and deterrence. Correctional personnel, particularly those involved in educational and therapeutic programs, make direct contributions to rehabilitative efforts by offering instruction, counseling, and support. These positions necessitate a distinct set of skills from those traditionally associated with correctional work, emphasizing empathy, communication, and the ability to motivate and encourage positive behavioral change. For example, correctional educators and counselors work to equip inmates with the skills and knowledge required for reintegration into society, such as literacy, vocational training, and cognitive-behavioral therapy (Levinson, 2002).

Figure 3.2. *Sheriff's office recruiting female correction officers.*

Source: Strickland (2024).

In addition to these rehabilitative functions, correctional staff are in charge of inmates' daily care and welfare. This includes providing basic necessities like food, clothing, shelter, and medical care. Ensuring the humane treatment of inmates is a fundamental responsibility of correctional staff, and it is critical for upholding individuals' rights and dignity within the corrections system. Healthcare provision is especially important because inmates have higher rates of physical and mental health issues than the general population. Correctional staff, including medical professionals and mental health workers, are tasked with identifying and responding to these needs, which can range from routine medical care to more intensive mental health interventions (Scott, 2008).

Correctional staff are also responsible for managing specialized populations within the prison system. This includes inmates with mental illnesses, those with substance abuse problems, juveniles, elderly inmates, and people with disabilities. These populations frequently require individualized approaches to supervision and care that reflect their specific needs and vulnerabilities. Correctional staff who work with mentally ill inmates, for example, must be trained to recognize symptoms of mental health crises and respond appropriately, often in collaboration with healthcare providers (Wortley, 2002). Similarly, staff who work with juvenile offenders must use age-appropriate strategies that prioritize education, development, and rehabilitation over punitive measures.

Penological research emphasizes the significance of staff-inmate interactions and the impact they can have on the overall prison environment. Positive staff-inmate interactions can help to create a safer, more rehabilitative correctional environment by increasing trust, lowering tensions, and encouraging compliance with rules and expectations. In contrast, negative or adversarial relationships can exacerbate conflicts, increase misconduct, and undermine rehabilitative efforts. Correctional officers are therefore encouraged to engage in "dynamic security," which entails proactive engagement with inmates to understand their needs, behaviors, and potential risks. This approach differs from "static security," which focuses only on physical barriers and surveillance without fostering interpersonal relationships (Griffin et al., 2010).

Correctional staff's roles and responsibilities are not without challenges and risks. Correctional officers, in particular, work in a high-stress environment with the potential for violence, trauma exposure, and a high level of scrutiny and accountability. These conditions can lead to burnout, job dissatisfaction, and mental health issues among staff, reducing their effectiveness and the overall operation of the correctional facility. Addressing these challenges requires a comprehensive approach, including adequate training, support systems, and organizational policies that promote staff well-being and resilience (Vito and Maahs, 2015). Training and professional development are critical components of preparing correctional officers to effectively perform their various roles and responsibilities. Security procedures, conflict resolution, communication skills, crisis intervention, and cultural competence are among the topics covered in most training programs. Ongoing training is essential for keeping staff up to date on best practices and emerging issues in the corrections field. Furthermore, staff must be educated on the ethical dimensions of their work, including the importance of respecting inmates' rights and avoiding abuse or misconduct (Griffin et al., 2010).

3.5. TREATMENT PROGRAMS IN CORRECTIONAL FACILITIES

Treatment programs in correctional facilities have become a cornerstone of modern penology, representing a shift away from punitive measures and toward more rehabilitative strategies focused on addressing the underlying causes that contribute to criminal conduct. These programs are intended not just to help offenders better manage their time in jail, but also to prepare them for reintegration into society after they are released. These projects aim to reduce recidivism by addressing issues such as substance misuse, mental health illnesses, a lack of education, and poor life skills. Treatment programs, by focusing on offender rehabilitation, contribute to the criminal justice system's broader goals, such as public safety and social reintegration.

Substance abuse treatment is one of the most common treatment programs in correctional facilities. Given the strong link between substance misuse and criminal conduct, these programs are critical in combating one of the primary causes of crime. Alcoholics Anonymous (AA) and Narcotics Anonymous (NA) are two programs that are often used in prisons to help inmates overcome their addictions. These programs, which are frequently modeled on the 12-step model, promote peer support and personal accountability, both of which are critical components of recovery. In addition to peer-led support groups, some correctional facilities offer more complete substance misuse treatment programs, including detoxification, counseling, and relapse prevention methods. According to research, offenders who participate in substance addiction treatment are less likely to re-offend, especially if these programs are supplemented with aftercare support following release (Lipsey and Cullen, 2007) (Figure 3.3).

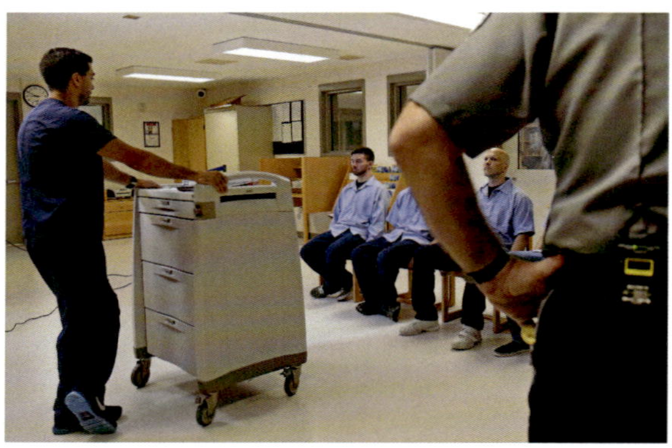

Figure 3.3. *Opioid detox in county jails.*

Source: Westervelt (2019).

Mental health therapies are an important component of correctional facility treatment programs. Inmates have a considerably greater prevalence of mental health issues than the general community, with many experiencing depression, anxiety, bipolar disorder, and schizophrenia (Fazel et al., 2016).

Addressing these mental health disorders is critical for both the inmates' well-being and the security of the correctional facility. Counseling, psychiatric care, and crisis intervention are typical mental health services provided in prisons. Some jails also have specialist wards for convicts with serious mental health concerns, where they can get more intense care. The provision of mental health services in correctional facilities has been demonstrated to reduce self-harm, aggression, and recidivism, emphasizing the significance of these programs in the rehabilitation process (Bakura, 2020).

Educational and vocational training programs are critical components of correctional facilities' rehabilitation initiatives. These programs attempt to provide inmates with the skills and information they need to find work and live productive lives once they are released. Education programs can include everything from basic reading and numeracy training to high school equivalency (GED) programs and even college courses. Vocational training, on the other hand, provides inmates with practical skills in trades such as carpentry, plumbing, and culinary arts, potentially increasing their employability in the job market. Studies have consistently demonstrated that participation in educational and vocational training programs greatly reduces recidivism rates because offenders who learn these skills are better prepared to find work and reintegrate into society (Latessa and Lovins, 2019).

Behavioral therapy, particularly cognitive-behavioral therapy (CBT), is a significant component of correctional treatment programs. CBT is founded on the idea that criminal behavior is learned and that by modifying maladaptive cognitive patterns, people can change their behavior. In penal facilities, CBT sessions assist convicts in building healthier coping mechanisms, enhancing decision-making abilities, and minimizing impulsive conduct. These programs frequently address issues including anger management, aggression, and substance misuse. Research has shown that CBT is helpful in reducing recidivism, especially when it is targeted to individual offenders' specific needs and risk factors. The success of CBT in correctional settings emphasizes the need to address the psychological and behavioral aspects of criminal behavior during the rehabilitation process (Latessa and Lovins, 2019).

Another important component of correctional treatment programs is reentry programs, which prepare offenders for life once they are released. These services help people find housing, get jobs, and access community resources. Reentry programs frequently include job placement services, aid in obtaining identity documents, and referrals to social services. The purpose of these programs is to facilitate the transition from incarceration to community life, hence lowering the chance of recidivism. Reentry programs are especially crucial given the multiple problems that recently released inmates experience, such as stigma, a lack of social support, and restricted economic possibilities. According to research, comprehensive reintegration programs that begin while incarcerated and continue after release are among the most effective techniques for reducing recidivism (Bakura, 2020).

The implementation of treatment programs in correctional facilities indicates a significant movement in penological thinking, from punishment to rehabilitation. These initiatives understand that addressing the underlying reasons for criminal behavior—such as addiction, mental illness, and a lack of education—is critical to reducing recidivism and enhancing public safety. Treatment programs assist the criminal justice system's greater goals by giving inmates the tools and support they need to alter their lives, including the reintegration of criminals into society as law-abiding individuals. While there are still obstacles to ensuring the accessibility and effectiveness of these programs, the evidence supports their importance in modern penology.

3.6. OVERCROWDING IN CORRECTIONAL FACILITIES

Overcrowding in correctional facilities is a key issue that presents considerable obstacles to the United States criminal justice system. This phenomenon, which is defined by the incarceration of people beyond the capacity of jails, has been exacerbated by a number of reasons, including legislative policies, the War on Drugs, and insufficient implementation of alternative sentencing options. Overcrowding has far-reaching implications, affecting not just convicts' well-being and correctional staff safety, but also the correctional system's overall efficacy in fulfilling its rehabilitative aims. Addressing this issue requires a comprehensive rethinking of sentencing policies, investment in rehabilitation programs, and the study of community-based alternatives, all of which are critical for developing a more just and effective criminal justice system (Figure 3.4).

The legislative environment in the United States has been a substantial contributor to jail overpopulation. Mandatory minimum sentencing legislation, established as part of the late 20th century's tough-on-crime strategy, has played a critical role in raising incarceration rates. These laws, which impose fixed penalties for certain crimes, frequently limit judicial discretion, resulting in unduly harsh sentencing, especially for nonviolent offenses. The three-strikes rules, which impose life terms on anybody guilty of three or more serious criminal offenses, have also contributed to the increase in prison populations.

Figure 3.4. *Overcrowded prison facility.*

Source: The Problem of Prison Overcrowding | Law Paper Example (2024).

While these rules were intended to deter repeat criminals, they frequently led to the detention of individuals for minor infractions, putting a burden on correctional facilities. The War on Drugs, which began in the 1980s, has also had a significant impact on the jail population. This strong campaign against drug-related charges resulted in the widespread incarceration of those engaged in nonviolent drug activities, disproportionately harming marginalized populations, notably people of color. Sentencing inequalities for drug offenses, which are frequently impacted by characteristics such as race and socioeconomic level, have compounded the problem, resulting in an overrepresentation of some groups in the prison system (Alexander, 2020).

Another major cause of correctional facility overpopulation is a lack of effective alternatives to incarceration. Although probation, parole, and other diversion programs are meant to give alternatives to jail, their restricted scope and insufficient resources have made them ineffective in addressing the root causes of criminal conduct. Probation and parole systems are frequently underfunded and overloaded, resulting in a lack of personalized care and support for people under supervision. As a result, the chance of recidivism increases since individuals are not given the tools and resources they need to properly reintegrate into society. The lack of effective alternatives emphasizes the importance of comprehensive reform that promotes rehabilitation over punishment and provides substantial support to those involved in the criminal justice system (Tonry, 2019).

Prison overpopulation has serious and far-reaching repercussions for both inmates and correctional staff. Inmates in overcrowded facilities frequently live in poor conditions, with restricted access to basic essentials including healthcare, nourishment, and sanitation. The demand for healthcare services in jails is especially worrying, as overcrowding can accelerate the spread of infectious diseases and impede the provision of effective care. Furthermore, overcrowding restricts access to rehabilitative programs like education and vocational training, which are critical for lowering recidivism and promoting successful reintegration into society. Overcrowding has a substantial influence on inmates' mental health, with higher rates of stress, anxiety, and depression reported in these circumstances. Overcrowding poses significant issues for correctional staff, including increased workloads, increased stress levels, and increased likelihood of violence and discontent within the facilities. Overcrowded prisons put both staff and inmates' safety at risk, as tensions can quickly develop due to a lack of space and resources (Lowenkamp et al., 2006).

The link between jail overpopulation and recidivism is especially alarming. Overcrowded prisons are frequently unable to provide the resources and services required to treat the underlying reasons for criminal conduct, such as substance misuse, mental health concerns, and a lack of education. As a result, offenders are more likely to re-offend after being released, continuing the incarceration cycle and contributing to the current overcrowding situation. The restricted availability of rehabilitation programs in overcrowded prisons exacerbates the problem, as inmates are unable to build the skills and support networks required for successful reintegration into society (Tonry, 2016).

Addressing the issue of prison overpopulation necessitates a multidimensional approach that includes sentencing reform, investment in rehabilitation programs, and the investigation of community-based alternatives to imprisonment. Sentencing reform, particularly the reduction or deletion of statutory minimum sentences, has the potential to drastically reduce the prison population by returning judicial discretion and enabling more customized, rehabilitative approaches to sentencing. Investment in rehabilitation programs within correctional facilities is also critical for addressing the underlying reasons for criminal behavior and lowering recidivism rates. Educational, vocational, and mental health programs have been found to be effective in preparing offenders for successful reintegration into society (Moore, 2017). Furthermore, community-based alternatives to incarceration, including probation, parole, and electronic monitoring, represent a viable way to reduce the prison population while maintaining public safety. These alternatives not only assist in reducing overcrowding but also allow individuals to stay linked to their families and communities, which is critical for successful recovery.

Comprehensive change is required to address the root causes of overcrowding, which include legislative policies, the War on Drugs, and a lack of alternatives to incarceration. Overcrowding has a variety of implications, ranging from poor inmate health to higher recidivism rates, emphasizing the need for a more compassionate and efficient criminal justice system. It is feasible to ease the load on correctional facilities by implementing sentence reform, investing in rehabilitation programs, and investigating community-based alternatives.

3.7. INNOVATIVE PRACTICES IN CORRECTIONAL FACILITIES

Penology has seen constant modification in practices and ideologies. In recent years, there has been a growing realization that traditional punishment tactics, which include long sentences, isolation, and few rehabilitation initiatives, frequently fail to reduce recidivism and enable successful reintegration into society. As a result, correctional facilities around the world are progressively implementing creative techniques to address the multifaceted needs of jailed people, with the ultimate goal of promoting rehabilitation and lowering the likelihood of recidivism. This investigation delves into numerous creative methods that have emerged within correctional facilities, assessing their success and significance within the larger context of penology.

One of the most striking changes in correctional practices is the transition to evidence-based rehabilitation programs. These programs are based on research that has identified distinct criminogenic requirements, such as substance addiction, a lack of education, and antisocial conduct, which, when addressed, can greatly lower the probability of recidivism. Cognitive-behavioral treatment (CBT), for example, has become an essential component of rehabilitation efforts in many penal facilities. CBT programs assist offenders in discovering and overcoming faulty thought patterns that lead to criminal behavior. Lipsey, Landenberger, and Wilson's (2007) meta-analysis indicated that CBT was related to a significant reduction in recidivism rates among participants, suggesting the usefulness of this technique in achieving behavioral change within the correctional setting. By targeting the underlying cognitive processes that contribute to criminal behavior, CBT represents an important innovation in the effort to rehabilitate offenders and reintegrate them into society.

In addition to cognitive-behavioral therapies, correctional facilities are increasingly adopting restorative justice approaches to repair the harm caused by criminal behavior. Restorative justice emphasizes mending the harm done to victims and communities over simply punishing the criminal. This strategy frequently includes guided meetings between offenders and their victims, during which both sides can vent their emotions and work toward a resolution. Restorative justice approaches have been shown in research to increase victim satisfaction, lessen the need for revenge, and reduce recidivism rates. Restorative justice, which fosters a sense of accountability and empathy, is a potent alternative to traditional punitive methods that align with the rehabilitative goals of modern penology (Latimer, Dowden, and Muise, 2005).

Another creative technique that has gained traction in recent years is the implementation of educational and vocational training programs in correctional facilities. The link between education and reduced recidivism is well-documented, with research continuously demonstrating that jailed individuals who participate in educational programs are much less likely to re-offend after release. Correctional education programs, which range from basic reading and high school equivalency classes to college-level coursework and vocational training, equip offenders with the skills and information needed to find work and live productive lives after they are released. In certain prisons, agreements with local community colleges and universities have permitted convicts to receive accredited degrees while jailed, further boosting their chances of successful reintegration. These educational opportunities benefit not only the individuals who participate but also help to make communities safer by lowering the general rate of recidivism (Lipsey and Cullen, 2007).

The use of technology in correctional settings is yet another key advancement in the discipline of penology. The implementation of digital tools such as online learning platforms, telemedicine, and virtual visitation systems has the potential to significantly improve service delivery within correctional facilities. Online learning platforms, for example, can give inmates access to a variety of educational resources, allowing them to learn at their own speed and gain essential skills. Telemedicine services allow offenders to obtain prompt medical care, including mental health therapy, without the need for expensive and logistically difficult transfers to outside healthcare facilities. Virtual visitation systems enable convicts to keep in contact with their families and support networks, which is critical for their emotional health and effective reintegration. According to research, keeping family relationships while incarcerated is linked to lower recidivism rates and better post-release outcomes. Correctional facilities can use technology to improve the accessibility and quality of their services, thereby aiding penology's rehabilitative aim (Latimer et al., 2005).

Furthermore, correctional facilities are increasingly recognizing the need to meet the special requirements of specific populations, such as women, minors, and those with mental illnesses. Traditional correctional techniques have frequently been created with a one-size-fits-all approach, neglecting to consider the unique requirements of different populations. However, new advances have attempted to adapt therapies to better serve these populations. For example, gender-responsive programs have been established to address the specific issues that jailed women experience, such as trauma histories, substance misuse, and caring duties. These programs frequently incorporate trauma-informed care, parenting training, and substance misuse treatment tailored to the needs of women (Clear et al., 2013). Similarly, juvenile justice systems have increasingly adopted rehabilitative programs that prioritize young offenders' developmental needs, such as education, family participation, and community-based alternatives to incarceration. Mental health courts and specialized mental health units within correctional facilities offer focused treatments for those suffering from mental illnesses, providing therapy and support rather than depending primarily on punitive measures. These individualized therapies reflect a more nuanced understanding of the different needs of the jailed population and mark a significant step forward in the discipline of penology.

Despite the positive consequences of these new techniques, problems persist in their implementation and sustainability. Evidence-based rehabilitation programs, for example, rely on the availability of skilled personnel, enough financing, and a supportive institutional culture. Similarly, the implementation of restorative justice procedures and instructional programs necessitates a shift in the mindsets of correctional officers and policymakers, who may be more acclimated to traditional punitive measures. Furthermore, the use of technology in correctional facilities presents issues of privacy, security, and the digital divide, as not all inmates have equal access to digital resources. Addressing these difficulties needs continuous research, investment, and collaboration among correctional facilities, legislators, and community organizations (Bakura, 2020).

By addressing incarcerated people's cognitive, educational, and emotional needs, these technologies have the potential to reduce recidivism, enhance successful reintegration, and ultimately contribute to safer communities. However, attaining the full potential of these techniques necessitates overcoming considerable obstacles, such as the need for proper resources, training, and cultural change within correctional facilities. As the science of penology evolves, it is critical that these creative approaches are supported and refined so that they may effectively satisfy the needs of the jailed population while also achieving the larger goals of justice and public safety.

Chapter 4

PUNISHMENT AND REHABILITATION

Contents

Punishment and rehabilitation are two key concepts in the field of penology, reflecting opposing views on how societies respond to criminal behavior. Punishment, which has traditionally been associated with retribution, deterrence, and incapacitation, aims to impose a penalty on the offender in response to their criminal actions. This approach emphasizes justice and the preservation of societal order, frequently putting the interests of victims and the community ahead of those of the offender. In contrast, rehabilitation focuses on the offender's reformation, with the goal of addressing underlying issues such as substance abuse, psychological disorders, or socioeconomic factors that contribute to criminal behavior. The rehabilitative model encourages interventions designed to help offenders reintegrate into society as law-abiding citizens (Scott, 2008).

Scholarly discourse on these approaches has evolved, revealing that punishment and rehabilitation are not mutually exclusive and can coexist within a comprehensive criminal justice strategy. According to research, a balanced approach that includes elements of both punitive and rehabilitative programs may be more effective in reducing recidivism and improving public safety (Levinson, 2002). As a result, the ongoing debate in penology focuses on the most ethically justifiable and practical ways to manage criminal behavior, taking into account broader societal values and evolving understandings of justice.

4.1. RETRIBUTION VS. REHABILITATION

Retribution and rehabilitation are two distinct approaches to addressing criminal behavior, each with its own philosophical underpinnings and practical objectives. Retribution, one of the oldest theories of punishment, is based on the concepts of moral balance and justice, with the primary goal of imposing a penalty proportionate to the offender's harm. This approach is based on the principle of just deserts, which states that offenders should face punishment proportionate to the gravity of their crime. Rehabilitation, on the other hand, aims to transform offenders into law-abiding citizens by addressing the root causes of their criminal behavior, such as social, psychological, and economic factors (Xie et al., 2023).

Retribution is often associated with a deontological view of justice, which emphasizes the moral obligation to punish wrongdoing. According to this viewpoint, punishment serves a symbolic function, affirming societal norms and reinforcing the moral order by visibly censuring deviant behavior. Retribution is not always intended to reduce future crime; rather, it is justified by the moral obligation to punish offenders with "just deserts" for their actions. The retributive model is closely related to the concept of proportionality, which states that the severity of punishment must correspond to the gravity of the offense. This principle is critical in preventing excessive or insufficient penalties, ensuring fairness and equity in the administration of justice (Bennett, 2010; Scott, 2008).

However, retribution is subject to significant criticism, particularly from scholars who argue that it frequently fails to achieve meaningful outcomes other than satisfying a desire for vengeance. Critics argue that retributive justice can perpetuate cycles of violence while doing little to address the underlying causes of criminal behavior. Furthermore, purely punitive measures have shown to have limited efficacy in reducing recidivism, with some studies indicating that harsh penalties may even exacerbate criminal tendencies by fostering resentment and social alienation among offenders (Vito and Maahs, 2015).

Rehabilitation, on the other hand, is based on the idea that criminal behavior is frequently a symptom of larger social and individual problems that can be addressed through targeted interventions. Rehabilitation seeks to reduce recidivism by modifying offenders' behavior through education, therapy, vocational training, and other supportive services. This approach is closely related to utilitarian principles, which prioritize the greatest good for the greatest number by emphasizing crime prevention and offenders' reintegration into society. The rehabilitative model asserts that most offenders can change if given the appropriate resources and support, aligning with the concept of penal welfarism, which sees crime control as a public health issue rather than a matter of punishment (Levinson, 2002; Xie et al., 2023).

Empirical research has shown that rehabilitation programs can significantly reduce reoffending rates, particularly when tailored to individual offenders' specific needs and risk factors. Cognitive-behavioral therapy, substance abuse treatment, and educational programs have all been shown to have a positive impact on criminal behavior reduction, especially when delivered consistently and in a structured manner. However, the rehabilitative model is not without its problems and criticisms. Some argue that rehabilitation can be paternalistic, limiting individual autonomy by imposing state-determined notions of "reform" on offenders (Lipsey and Cullen, 2007). There are also practical concerns about the accessibility and quality of rehabilitative services, particularly in underfunded or overcrowded correctional facilities.

The debate over retribution and rehabilitation is more than just theoretical; it has significant implications for the design and implementation of criminal justice policies. In practice, many modern criminal justice systems strive to strike a balance between these two approaches, incorporating punitive and rehabilitative elements to achieve a more comprehensive response to crime. This blended approach is evident in policies that combine incarceration with opportunities for education, treatment, and skill development, reflecting a recognition that effective crime prevention requires both accountability and support (Bennett, 2010).

The incorporation of retributive and rehabilitative principles reflects a broader societal shift toward a more nuanced understanding of justice, one that acknowledges the complexities of human behavior and the multifaceted nature of criminal activity. Modern penology has moved toward a more balanced and effective approach to managing criminal behavior by recognizing that punishment and rehabilitation can complement rather than contradict each other (Williams, 2012). This shift emphasizes the importance of evidence-based practices as well as ongoing research to improve our understanding of what works in terms of crime reduction and public safety.

4.2. EFFECTIVENESS OF PUNISHMENT IN DETERRENCE

The effectiveness of punishment as a deterrent has long been a major concern in the field of penology, sparking heated debate among scholars, policymakers, and practitioners. According to deterrence theory, the threat or application of punishment can prevent crime by discouraging potential offenders from engaging in unlawful behavior. This theory operates on two levels: general deterrence, which aims to discourage the broader public from committing crimes by demonstrating the consequences of criminal behavior, and specific deterrence, which seeks to prevent re-offending by imposing penalties on individuals who have already committed a crime (Bennett, 2010).

General deterrence is based on the assumption that potential offenders make rational decisions after weighing the costs and benefits of their actions. In theory, if the perceived severity, certainty, and speed of punishment are sufficiently high, people will refrain from committing crimes in order to avoid the associated penalties. However, empirical research into the effectiveness of general deterrence paints a mixed picture. According to research, the link between increased punishment severity and crime reduction is complex. While some research indicates that harsh penalties can have a deterrent effect, particularly for specific types of crimes such as economic offenses, the overall impact on crime rates is frequently minimal or inconsistent (Nagin, 2013) (Figure 4.1).

The low certainty of punishment is one of the primary reasons for general deterrence's limited effectiveness. The likelihood that offenders will be caught, prosecuted, and punished is an important factor in deterrence. When the chances of detection and punishment are slim, even harsh penalties may fail to deter crime effectively. Many jurisdictions have low clearance rates for crimes like burglary and assault, which undermines the deterrent effect of harsh punishments. This finding implies that increasing the certainty of punishment, rather than its severity, may be a more effective strategy for reducing crime (Fagan and Meares, 2008).

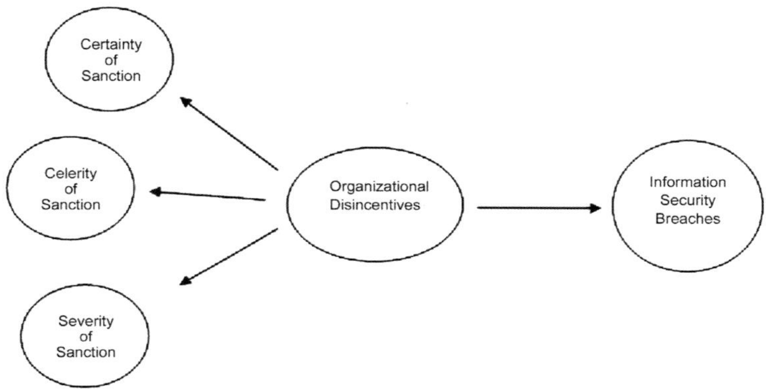

Figure 4.1. *General deterrence theory model.*

Source: Kuhn et al. (2014).

Specific deterrence aims to prevent recidivism by punishing those who have previously committed a crime. The assumption is that experiencing punishment firsthand will deter offenders from engaging in future criminal behavior due to the unpleasant consequences they have faced. However, the empirical evidence for specific deterrence is equally ambiguous. According to some studies, harsher punishments, such as longer prison sentences, do not significantly reduce recidivism and may even increase it in some cases (Wortley, 2002). Several factors contribute to this counterintuitive finding.

First, incarceration can have criminogenic effects, exacerbating rather than decreasing criminal behavior. Prisons frequently expose inmates to violent and antisocial environments, which can strengthen criminal identities and networks. The stigma associated with a criminal record, as well as the erosion of social and economic ties while incarcerated, can impede reintegration into society, increasing the likelihood of recidivism. Second, specific deterrence may be ineffective because many offenders do not perceive the punishment to be sufficiently aversive or are afraid of future application. Habitual offenders, for example, may consider incarceration a normal part of life rather than a significant deterrent (Bennett, 2010).

Beyond the individual and rational calculations of offenders, cultural and social factors also play a significant role in shaping the effectiveness of punishment as a deterrent. Research has shown that in societies or communities where legal institutions are perceived as legitimate and trustworthy, the deterrent effect of punishment is generally stronger. This perception fosters a moral alignment with the law, where individuals are more likely to comply with legal norms because they believe in the legitimacy of the legal system and the fairness of its processes. In contrast, in communities where there is widespread mistrust of the police and the criminal justice system, the deterrent effect of punishment is weaker. Here, individuals may view legal sanctions as arbitrary or unjust, which undermines their willingness to abide by the law (Garland, 2018).

Deterrence theory also faces challenges in accounting for the diverse motivations behind criminal behavior. Many crimes are not motivated by rational calculations, but rather by impulsive decisions, emotional states, or social and economic conditions. Crimes of passion, addiction-related offenses, and crimes committed while under the influence of drugs or alcohol, for example, frequently occur without prior planning or a rational assessment of the potential consequences (Fagan and Meares, 2008). In such cases, the threat of punishment is unlikely to be effective deterrent because the decision-making process is not based on a cost-benefit analysis.

Furthermore, the effectiveness of deterrence is frequently context-dependent, varying according to crime type, offender characteristics, and socio-legal settings. For example, white-collar criminals, who typically operate in environments where the likelihood of detection and punishment is low, may be more sensitive to the deterrent effect of increased surveillance and sanctions. Individuals involved in street-level drug offenses, who frequently face high levels of social and economic disadvantage and have limited legitimate opportunities, may be less responsive to the deterrent effects of punishment (Nagin, 2013).

In recent years, scholars have increasingly advocated for a more nuanced understanding of deterrence, one that incorporates insights from psychology, sociology, and criminology to account for the complexities of human behavior and the social contexts in which crimes occur. This approach emphasizes the importance of evidence-based practices, as well as the need to tailor deterrence strategies to the specific contexts and populations they seek to affect. Strategies that increase the certainty and speed of punishment, such as targeted policing and community-based interventions, have been shown to be more effective in reducing crime than those that simply increase the severity of punishment (Fagan and Meares, 2008; Nagin, 2013).

4.3. REHABILITATION PROGRAMS FOR OFFENDERS

Offender rehabilitation programs are in modern penal systems, reflecting a shift from punitive approaches and toward strategies that focus on reintegration and recidivism reduction. The primary goal of rehabilitation is to address the underlying causes of criminal behavior, thereby encouraging positive change in offenders and ultimately improving public safety. This approach is based on the belief that most individuals can reform when given appropriate support and resources, aligning with the principles of restorative justice and penal welfare (Bennett, 2010).

Cognitive-behavioral therapy is one of the most extensively researched rehabilitation programs. CBT is based on the premise that criminal behavior is learned and thus can be unlearned by restructuring cognitive processes. This therapeutic approach focuses on identifying and changing distorted thinking patterns that contribute to criminal behavior, such as impulsivity, poor problem-solving abilities, and pro-criminal attitudes. Numerous studies have shown that CBT is effective in reducing recidivism, especially when combined with other interventions tailored to the needs of high-risk offenders (Bernfeld et al., 2003). By addressing the cognitive deficits associated with criminal behavior, CBT aims to provide offenders with the skills they need to make better decisions and manage their behaviors effectively.

Substance abuse treatment programs are another critical component of offender rehabilitation, especially given the high prevalence of substance use disorders in criminal populations. These programs are intended to address the substance dependency that frequently underpins criminal behavior, giving offenders the tools they need to manage addiction and reduce their chances of reoffending. Research has shown that comprehensive substance abuse treatment, particularly when combined with other rehabilitative services, can significantly reduce drug use and criminal activity among participants. Treatment options range from inpatient detoxification and therapeutic communities to outpatient counseling and medication-assisted treatment, with varying levels of intensity and support based on the severity of the addiction and the individual's needs (Chamberlain, 2012).

Educational and vocational training programs are also critical components of successful rehabilitation strategies. These programs aim to improve offenders' employability by providing them with necessary skills and credentials, increasing their chances of finding stable employment after release. Employment is essential for successful reintegration because it provides financial stability, fosters social ties, and reduces the likelihood of recidivism.

Educational programs typically include basic literacy and numeracy instruction, high school equivalency courses, and post-secondary education opportunities, whereas vocational training teaches practical skills in trades such as carpentry, welding, and culinary arts. Empirical evidence suggests that participation in educational and vocational training programs is associated with significant reductions in recidivism rates, particularly when these programs are closely aligned with labor market demands (Williams, 2012).

In addition to these core rehabilitation programs, there are specialized interventions that cater to the specific needs of specific offender populations. For example, sex offender treatment programs aim to reduce the risk of reoffending by addressing deviant sexual arousal, cognitive distortions, and other criminogenic needs associated with sexual offending. These programs frequently use a combination of CBT, relapse prevention, and psychopharmacological treatments to reduce risk factors and promote long-term behavioral change. Similarly, programs for violent offenders emphasize anger management, emotional regulation, and conflict resolution skills, in order to reduce the likelihood of future violent behavior (Levinson, 2002).

Several factors, including program integrity, staff training, and offender engagement, have a significant impact on the effectiveness of rehabilitation programs. According to research, the quality of program implementation is a critical determinant of success; programs that are poorly implemented or do not adhere to established best practices are less likely to produce positive results. This emphasizes the importance of ensuring that rehabilitation programs are delivered by well-trained personnel who are capable of engaging offenders effectively and maintaining the therapeutic environment required for change. Furthermore, offender motivation and willingness to change are critical to the success of rehabilitation efforts. Programs that are tailored to the specific needs and risk levels of offenders, and that actively engage them in the rehabilitation process, tend to yield better outcomes (Bennett, 2010).

Despite the growing body of evidence supporting the effectiveness of offender rehabilitation programs, challenges remain in their implementation and evaluation. One significant issue is the disparity in access to and quality of rehabilitation services between correctional facilities. Overcrowded prisons, limited funding, and a shortage of qualified staff can all impede the delivery of effective rehabilitation programs, especially in underserved jurisdictions. Furthermore, the heterogeneity of offender populations necessitates a more nuanced rehabilitation approach that takes into account diverse backgrounds, needs, and risks. This emphasizes the importance of taking a personalized approach to rehabilitation, one that integrates a variety of services and supports to address the multiple dimensions of criminal behavior (Bernfeld et al., 2003).

4.4. CHALLENGES IN PROVIDING REHABILITATION SERVICES

Rehabilitation services have emerged as a cornerstone of modern penology, reflecting a growing recognition of the need to address the root causes of criminal behavior and facilitate offenders' reintegration into society. However, the implementation of effective rehabilitation programs faces numerous challenges that jeopardize their effectiveness and reach. These challenges are multifaceted, spanning institutional, structural, and individual levels, and are compounded by sociopolitical factors shaping the broader criminal justice landscape (Lowenkamp et al., 2006).

One of the primary challenges of providing rehabilitation services is determining resource allocation. Correctional facilities frequently face significant budgetary constraints, which can limit the availability and effectiveness of rehabilitative programs. Underfunded prisons may lack the infrastructure, trained personnel, and materials required to provide comprehensive rehabilitation services. Classrooms, teaching materials, and skilled instructors, for example, are all required for educational and vocational training programs, which necessitate financial investment. Similarly, substance abuse treatment and mental health services necessitate specialized personnel, such as counselors and psychologists, who may be in short supply due to budget cuts or hiring freezes. This resource scarcity can result in long waitlists reduced program intensity, and a limited range of services offered, thereby diminishing the potential impact of rehabilitation efforts on reducing recidivism (Bernfeld et al., 2003; Griffin et al., 2010).

Overcrowding in correctional facilities is another major impediment to the effective delivery of rehabilitation services. Many prisons, particularly in the United States, are severely overcrowded due to high incarceration rates caused by punitive policies and mandatory sentencing laws. Overcrowded conditions create an unfavorable environment for rehabilitation because they frequently result in increased tension, violence, and a lack of personal space, all of which can undermine the therapeutic atmosphere required for effective intervention. Furthermore, overcrowding puts a strain on available resources and staff, making it difficult to provide individualized attention and support to offenders. The sheer volume of inmates may overwhelm rehabilitation programs, resulting in diluted services that fail to meet the diverse needs of the incarcerated population (Bennett, 2010).

Staffing issues also present a significant challenge in the delivery of rehabilitation services. The effectiveness of rehabilitation programs is heavily reliant on the quality and consistency of their delivery, which is in turn dependent on well-trained and motivated personnel. However, correctional facilities frequently face high staff turnover, burnout, and a lack of professional development opportunities. Correctional officers may experience stress and job dissatisfaction as a result of the demanding nature of their work environment, which can include dealing with violent or uncooperative inmates, witnessing traumatic events, and working long hours. These conditions can cause high levels of burnout, resulting in frequent staff turnover and the loss of experienced personnel who are critical to the success of rehabilitation efforts. Furthermore, many correctional staff may not receive adequate training in rehabilitative techniques or the principles of therapeutic intervention, which can limit their ability to effectively engage with offenders and deliver evidence-based programs (Chamberlain, 2012; Wortley, 2002).

The diversity of the offender population adds to the challenge of providing effective rehabilitation services. Offenders come from various backgrounds and have a wide range of criminogenic needs, risks, and motivations. Some offenders may have mental health issues, substance use disorders, or developmental disabilities, whereas others may have experienced significant trauma or come from economically disadvantaged families. This diversity necessitates a highly individualized rehabilitation approach, with programs tailored to each offender's specific needs and circumstances. However, many correctional systems lack the capacity or flexibility to provide such individualized services, instead relying on standardized programs that may not be effective for all offenders. The one-size-fits-all approach can result in the provision of inappropriate or inadequate interventions that fail to address the root causes of criminal behavior, thereby limiting their effectiveness in reducing recidivism (Scott, 2008).

Another significant barrier to rehabilitation is the cultural and institutional resistance to change within correctional systems. The punitive ethos that has long dominated many criminal justice systems persists, resulting in an emphasis on security and control rather than rehabilitation and reform. This punitive mindset can be deeply ingrained in correctional staff, policymakers, and the general public, posing a barrier to the implementation of rehabilitative practices. Correctional officers and administrators may prioritize maintaining order and discipline over providing rehabilitative services, viewing the latter as secondary or even incompatible with the prison's primary goals. This cultural resistance can hinder the implementation of evidence-based practices and limit the effectiveness of rehabilitation programs, as staff may be unwilling to engage with or fully support rehabilitative initiatives (Vito and Maahs, 2015).

Sociopolitical factors also play an important role in shaping the challenges associated with providing rehabilitation services. Public and political support for rehabilitation can fluctuate dramatically, often influenced by prevailing social attitudes toward crime and punishment, media portrayals, and political discourse. In some cases, there may be a strong public demand for punitive measures, motivated by a desire for retribution or a belief that rehabilitation is ineffective or overly lenient. This can result in policies that prioritize punishment over rehabilitation, such as mandatory sentencing laws, "three strikes" rules, and other tough-on-crime measures that limit access to rehabilitative programs. Furthermore, political leaders may be hesitant to advocate for rehabilitation due to concerns about appearing soft on crime, particularly in electoral contexts where crime is a salient issue. This lack of political will can result in insufficient funding and support for rehabilitative initiatives, further constraining their implementation and effectiveness (Clear et al., 2013).

The stigmatization and marginalization of offenders, both within the prison system and in society as a whole, pose a significant challenge to providing rehabilitation services. Offenders frequently face discrimination and prejudice, which can limit their ability to access rehabilitation programs and successfully reintegrate into society after release. Certain groups of offenders in prison, such as those convicted of sexual offenses or those with mental health issues, may be barred from participating in rehabilitation programs because they are deemed dangerous or undesirable. Upon release, offenders frequently encounter barriers to reintegration, such as difficulties finding employment, housing, and social support, which can undermine rehabilitation gains and increase the risk of recidivism (Bernfeld et al., 2003). Addressing these challenges requires a concerted effort to reduce stigma and promote a more inclusive and supportive approach to offender rehabilitation.

4.5. RECIDIVISM RATES AND REHABILITATIONS

Recidivism, or the tendency of previously convicted individuals to re-offend, is a major concern in the area of penology, especially when considering the dual goals of punishment and rehabilitation within the criminal justice system. The continually high rates of recidivism observed around the world, particularly in the United States, have prompted serious concerns about the effectiveness of current penal systems and the balance between punishing measures and rehabilitative initiatives. This discussion delves into the complex relationship between recidivism rates and rehabilitation, comparing the effectiveness of punishment and rehabilitative strategies in reducing reoffending and emphasizing the importance of taking a balanced approach that incorporates both aspects in the pursuit of a more just and effective criminal justice system.

The concept of recidivism is an important metric for determining the effectiveness or failure of punitive treatments. High recidivism rates frequently imply that the correctional system has failed to address the root causes of criminal behavior. According to the Bureau of Justice Statistics in the United States, over two-thirds of freed inmates are rearrested within three years, and more than 75% are rearrested within five years. These data highlight the flaws of a system that depends mainly on punitive measures, such as imprisonment, without appropriately addressing offenders' rehabilitative needs. This predicament has spawned a heated debate in penology over the role of punishment vs rehabilitation, with many researchers arguing for a paradigm change toward a more rehabilitative strategy that tries to reduce recidivism by addressing the underlying causes of criminal conduct (Davies, 2013).

Punishment, traditionally typically considered a means of deterring crime by the enforcement of sanctions, has long been an integral part of criminal justice systems. Deterrence theories propose that the dread of punishment deters people from engaging in criminal conduct, but retributive justice requires that criminals be punished proportionally to the severity of their actions. However, high recidivism rates in many nations indicate that punishment alone may not be enough to prevent reoffending. This has resulted in an increased interest in rehabilitative strategies that focus on changing offenders and providing them with the skills and assistance they need to successfully reintegrate into society (LeBel et al., 2008).

Rehabilitation, as opposed to punishment, aims to treat the root reasons for criminal conduct, such as substance misuse, mental health disorders, a lack of education, and unemployment. Effective rehabilitation programs strive to prevent recidivism by giving prisoners the tools they need to live law-abiding lives once released. Numerous studies have shown that rehabilitation has a positive impact on lowering recidivism. For example, cognitive-behavioral therapy (CBT), which tackles the cognitive distortions and behavioral patterns that contribute to criminal conduct, is one of the most successful rehabilitative techniques, lowering recidivism by up to 25%. Similarly, educational and occupational training programs have been demonstrated to considerably reduce recidivism, with participants being 43% less likely to re-offend than those who do not. These findings underline the significance of rehabilitation in lowering recidivism and enhancing the long-term outcomes of former offenders (Davis, 2013).

Despite the documented benefits of rehabilitation, various barriers prevent its widespread application in the criminal justice system. One key impediment is a lack of financing and resources for rehabilitation programs. Rehabilitation necessitates significant investment in terms of skilled personnel, infrastructure, and continuing care for offenders both while incarcerated and after release. In many circumstances, the expenses of rehabilitation are viewed as exorbitant, resulting in an overreliance on punitive measures that are typically less expensive in the short term but less effective in the long run. Furthermore, there is frequently political and ideological opposition to rehabilitation, with certain officials and members of the public arguing for harsher fines and longer terms as a means of preserving public safety. This punitive approach, however, fails to address the root causes of recidivism and may end up doing more harm than good by sustaining a cycle of reoffending (Bernfeld et al., 2003).

Another barrier to effective rehabilitation is the stigma and discrimination that former convicts endure after their release. Even after people have finished rehabilitative programs and are ready to reintegrate into society, they frequently face substantial challenges, such as finding work, housing, and social acceptance. The social stigma associated with a criminal record might jeopardize the rehabilitation process and raise the likelihood of recidivism. According to research, those who are socially excluded or marginalized are more prone to engage in criminal conduct to cope with their circumstances. To be genuinely effective, rehabilitation must be combined with broader community measures to help former criminals' reintegration and lessen the stigma associated with criminal convictions (LeBel et al., 2015).

The balance between punishment and rehabilitation in the criminal justice system is complex, necessitating careful assessment of the goals and consequences of both approaches. While punishment is an important deterrent to crime and a kind of retributive justice, it is obvious that it cannot be used alone to address the issue of recidivism. Rehabilitation takes a more holistic approach, addressing the underlying reasons for criminal conduct and equipping offenders with the tools they need to successfully reenter society. To be effective, rehabilitation must be appropriately funded, supported by evidence-based approaches, and incorporated into a larger societal framework that encourages former offenders' reintegration (Lowenkamp et al., 2006).

As a result, the high rates of recidivism observed in many criminal justice systems show the limitations of a punitive response to crime and the need for a stronger emphasis on rehabilitation. Rehabilitation can help to reduce recidivism and improve public safety by addressing the root causes of criminal conduct and giving offenders the skills and assistance they need to live law-abiding lives. However, the effectiveness of rehabilitation is contingent on overcoming considerable hurdles such as funding restrictions, political opposition, and societal stigma. As such, policymakers and practitioners must collaborate to develop a criminal justice system that strikes a balance between punishment and rehabilitation, ensuring that offenders are not only held accountable for their actions but also given the opportunity to reform and reintegrate into society.

4.6. RESTORATIVE JUSTICE PRACTICES

Restorative justice is a paradigm change in the field of penology that challenges established approaches to punishment by emphasizing the necessity of healing the harm caused by illegal action.

In contrast to retributive justice, which emphasizes punishment as a form of deterrent and societal retribution, restorative justice tries to bring together offenders, victims, and society to address the effects of crime and encourage healing for all parties involved (Johnstone, 2011). This method is closely aligned with rehabilitative goals in penology, as it promotes offenders' reintegration into society while also addressing victim needs and lowering recidivism rates.

The concept of accountability is central to restorative justice, and it differs dramatically from the punitive accountability required by traditional justice systems. Restorative techniques require offenders to recognize the harm they have caused, accept responsibility for their acts, and actively participate in processes designed to make amends. This can include direct apologies, restitution, community service, or other reparative measures agreed upon by the parties concerned. Restorative justice fosters a sense of responsibility in offenders, which promotes behavioral change and personal growth, both of which are necessary components of successful rehabilitation (Johnstone, 2011).

Empirical studies have shown that restorative justice techniques reduce recidivism. Research shows that offenders who participate in restorative justice programs are less likely to re-offend than those who face traditional punitive measures. This decrease in recidivism is due to various elements inherent in restorative practices. For starters, restorative justice involves offenders in meaningful discourse about the consequences of their conduct, which frequently results in increased empathy and understanding of the harm done. This emotional engagement is crucial for changing offenders' cognitive habits and lowering the chance of future criminal activity. Furthermore, the inclusive character of restorative justice, which includes victims and community members, fosters a supportive environment that can help the offender reintegrate (Latimer et al., 2005).

Restorative justice also provides major advantages to victims, who are frequently marginalized in traditional legal systems. Traditional systems prioritize the criminal, relegating victims to the status of passive participants or observers. Restorative justice, on the other hand, prioritizes victims, providing them with a voice and the opportunity to express their needs and viewpoints. Victims can find this participating position powerful since it allows them to reclaim control and closure. Furthermore, restorative justice allows for a more customized type of justice because victims have direct influence over the reparative measures made by offenders, ensuring that these actions address their unique injustices (Davis, 2013).

Despite its merits, restorative justice in the correctional system confronts a number of problems. One key impediment is cultural and institutional opposition to reform within criminal justice systems, which are frequently strongly rooted in retributive ideas. Shifting to a restorative model necessitates a fundamental rethinking of justice, punishment, and rehabilitation, which may be regarded with suspicion by legal experts, lawmakers, and the general public. Furthermore, restorative justice may not be appropriate in many cases, particularly those involving extreme violence or when power imbalances between the criminal and victim are significant.

Critics also contend that restorative justice procedures, if not well managed, have the potential to re-traumatize victims or put undue pressure on them to forgive perpetrators. Another problem is also the variety of restorative justice procedures, which can vary dramatically depending on the setting and individuals involved. This heterogeneity can result in variations in outcomes, raising concerns about the fairness and equity of restorative justice. Standardizing processes while allowing for flexibility and responsiveness to specific instances is a difficult challenge that necessitates careful study and continual research (Latimer et al., 2005).

Given these limitations, incorporating restorative justice into traditional correctional systems necessitates a balanced approach. This strategy should include extensive training for facilitators, clear instructions to protect all parties' rights, and procedures for monitoring and evaluating outcomes. Furthermore, restorative justice should not be viewed as a replacement for all punitive measures, but rather as a complementing strategy that can coexist with traditional justice techniques. For example, combining restorative techniques with rehabilitative programs such as education, counseling, and substance addiction treatment can improve their effectiveness and provide a more comprehensive approach to crime (Bernfeld et al., 2003; Griffin et al., 2010).

The future of restorative justice in penology is dependent on further investigation of its ability to change how societies comprehend and respond to crime. As the science of penology evolves, it is becoming clear that addressing the core causes of criminal behavior and rebuilding the social fabric harmed by crime is critical to establishing safer communities. Restorative justice, with its emphasis on healing, accountability, and community involvement, is a potential step toward a more humane and functional justice system. Restorative justice reduces recidivism by moving the focus from punishment to rehabilitation and repair, while also fostering a more just and caring society.

4.7. FUTURE DIRECTIONS IN PUNISHMENT AND REHABILITATION

In contemporary penology, the conversation about punishment and rehabilitation has changed to future paths that emphasize transformative justice, technological integration, and a sophisticated understanding of recidivism. Historically, punitive systems have alternated between retributive justice, which emphasizes punishment equal to the offense, and rehabilitative approaches, which seek to reform convicts and reintegrate them into society. However, the future of these paradigms appears to be a more holistic approach that incorporates parts of both retribution and rehabilitation, as well as technological breakthroughs and shifting societal ideals.

One key trend in the future of punishment and rehabilitation is an increased emphasis on restorative justice approaches. Restorative justice, which focuses on healing the harm caused by criminal activity through mediated discourse between victims and offenders, aims to address the core causes of crime and promote reconciliation (Goel et al., 2021). This strategy departs from typical punitive methods, instead trying to foster empathy, accountability, and community involvement in the justice system. Restorative justice appears to be more effective than traditional punitive techniques in terms of reducing recidivism and increasing victim satisfaction. As a result, future penological tactics are expected to incorporate restorative ideas in a more systematic manner, notably in community-based programs and alternative sentencing structures.

Technological improvements are also expected to transform the landscape of punishment and rehabilitation. Electronic monitoring, predictive analytics, and virtual reality are examples of innovations that have the potential to transform correctional management and rehabilitation interventions. Electronic monitoring, for example, enables more nuanced and adaptable supervision of offenders, lowering the need for jail while maintaining oversight (Scott, 2008). Predictive analytics can help estimate recidivism risk and personalize interventions to individual requirements, potentially increasing the effectiveness of rehabilitation programs. Furthermore, virtual reality technologies provide immersive environments for skill development and therapeutic interventions, opening up previously untapped paths for rehabilitation (Latimer et al., 2005).

The expanding understanding of recidivism and the factors that contribute to criminal conduct informs future punishment and rehabilitation strategies. Socioeconomic determinants, mental health difficulties, and substance addiction are increasingly being highlighted in research as factors driving criminal conduct. Addressing these underlying issues through thorough, individualized treatment plans marks a change away from one-size-fits-all approaches and toward more personalized interventions. This viewpoint is consistent with the growing emphasis on therapeutic jurisprudence, which investigates how legal procedures and outcomes influence psychological well-being and seeks to improve the therapeutic potential of legal interventions (Johnstone, 2011).

Additionally, the incorporation of therapeutic jurisprudence into correctional practices emphasizes the importance of collaboration among legal professionals, mental health practitioners, and social service providers. This interdisciplinary approach not only treats offenders' psychological and social needs but also promotes successful reintegration into society. Future correctional systems are expected to embrace models that focus on holistic care and rehabilitative support, creating conditions that promote personal development and lower the likelihood of recidivism.

Another important factor for future punishment and rehabilitation policies is the push toward decarceration and a reassessment of incarceration's place in the criminal justice system. Growing awareness of the negative impacts of mass incarceration on persons and communities has fueled the demand for less dependence on jail and the exploration of alternative penalties. Diversion programs, community service, and restorative justice circles are examples of a larger social shift towards more egalitarian and humane approaches to criminal justice. These solutions strive to address criminal conduct while limiting the negative social and psychological consequences of jail, resulting in more long-term outcomes for both offenders and society (Vito and Maahs, 2015).

The potential for these future initiatives to improve the efficacy and justice of punishment and rehabilitation is dependent on continued research, policy innovation, and social commitment to addressing the intricacies of criminal conduct. Scholars and practitioners must continue to assess and refine the efficacy of developing techniques using empirical data and ethical considerations. The field of penology can evolve toward a more just and rehabilitative future by adopting a comprehensive strategy that incorporates restorative methods, technology breakthroughs, therapeutic jurisprudence, and decarceration initiatives.

Chapter 5

PRISON LIFE

Contents

Prison life, a widely studied topic in penology, encompasses the social, psychological, and structural dynamics that inmates face. Penology, the study of the processes and institutions involved in the punishment and rehabilitation of offenders, provides a nuanced understanding of the complexities of incarceration. Inmates are subject to a highly regulated environment characterized by deprivation of liberty, which fundamentally alters their social roles and identities (Liebling and Arnold, 2004) (Figure 5.1).

Figure 5.1. *An illustration of life in prison.*

Source: Prison Life for Inmates - What Is Prison Like - Zoukis Consulting (2023).

According to research, Gresham Sykes' concept of the "pains of imprisonment" encompasses the loss of autonomy, security, and access to heterosexual relationships, all of which contribute to psychological stress and identity transformation. Prison subculture, defined by its own set of norms and values, emerges as a response to institutional constraints, resulting in phenomena such as the "inmate code" and the formation of social hierarchies among prisoners (Scott, 2008).

Furthermore, the concept of "institutionalization" emphasizes the long-term effects of incarceration, in which inmates become accustomed to the prison environment and frequently struggle with reintegration into society after release. Academic studies also emphasize the role of correctional staff, whose interactions with inmates can either aggravate or mitigate the harshness of prison life, thereby influencing rehabilitation outcomes (Crewe, 2012).

5.1. INMATE SUBCULTURE

Inmate subculture is a central theme in penology, providing profound insights into the social dynamics and behavioral patterns that emerge within correctional facilities. This subculture, defined by a set of informal norms, values, and practices that differ from those of society, emerges in response to the prison's unique environment. Understanding the inmate subculture is critical for comprehending the complexities of prison life and the challenges of reform and rehabilitation within these institutions (Liebling and Arnold, 2004).

The "inmate code," a set of unwritten rules that govern prisoner behavior, is a fundamental concept in the study of inmate subculture. This code focuses on inmate loyalty, resistance to authority, and maintaining a stoic demeanor in the face of adversity. Violations of the inmate code can result in severe consequences, such as ostracism or violence from fellow inmates. In an environment where personal autonomy is severely restricted, the inmate code serves as both a survival mechanism and a way of asserting identity and agency (Crewe, 2012).

The inmate subculture has its roots in the deprivation model, which holds that the harsh conditions of incarceration—such as the loss of liberty, autonomy, and security—drive prisoners to form alternative social structures. In his seminal work "The Society of Captives," Gresham Sykes identified the "pains of imprisonment" as a catalyst for the development of a distinct inmate subculture. These deprivations cause inmates to form alliances, establish hierarchies, and develop a set of shared values that help them cope with the psychological and physical challenges of prison (Crewe, 2012; Scott, 2008).

The importation model also has a strong influence on inmate subculture, as it contends that the values, attitudes, and behaviors that prisoners bring with them from the outside world play an important role in shaping the prison environment. According to this viewpoint, pre-existing social identities, such as gang affiliations, racial or ethnic background, and socioeconomic status, are brought into the prison and contribute to the formation of subcultural groups among the inmates. These groups frequently serve as the foundation for the power dynamics and social stratification seen within prisons (Sirisutthidacha and Tititampruk, 2014).

The inmate subculture is not monolithic, but rather divided into subgroups, each with its own unique characteristics and norms. Gangs, for example, are a major component of inmate subculture, wielding significant power over prison life. Prison gangs frequently control illegal activities, such as drug trafficking, while also providing protection and social support to members. However, their presence also contributes to the perpetuation of violence and conflict within the prison. Rival gangs compete for dominance (Liebling and Arnold, 2004).

Another important aspect of inmate subculture is the concept of "prisonization," which refers to the process by which inmates internalize prison-specific norms and values. Over time, prisoners may become increasingly reliant on the prison's social structures, making it difficult for them to adjust to life outside of prison. This institutionalization process can have long-term effects, as inmates who have been deeply "prisonized" may struggle with reintegration into society, facing challenges such as impaired social relationships, decreased employability, and a heightened risk of recidivism (Sirisutthidacha and Tititampruk, 2014).

The interaction between correctional officers and inmates is also important in shaping inmate subculture. The authority and control exercised by prison staff can either reinforce or undermine the inmate code, depending on the nature of the interactions. Studies have shown that punitive and authoritarian approaches by correctional officers can exacerbate tensions and strengthen the solidarity of inmate subcultures, while more rehabilitative and humane approaches may reduce the harshness of prison life and promote positive behavioral changes among inmates (Crewe, 2012).

The diversity of the prison population, which includes people of various races, ethnicities, and cultures, complicates research into inmate subculture. This diversity has the potential to create subgroups within the inmate population, each with its own set of norms and values. Racial and ethnic tensions, in particular, can play a significant role in shaping the dynamics of inmate subculture. Prisoners frequently align themselves with others who share their background, both for protection and social support (Sirisutthidacha and Tititampruk, 2014).

5.2. PRISON GANGS AND VIOLENCE

Prison gangs and the violence around them provide valuable insights into the social structures, power dynamics, and behavioral patterns that emerge within correctional facilities. These gangs, which are frequently organized along racial, ethnic, or geographical lines, play a dominant role in shaping the inmate subculture and have a significant impact on the lives of prisoners. The violence that accompanies the activities of these gangs not only poses serious threats to the safety and security of prisons but also complicates efforts aimed at rehabilitation and reform (Liebling and Arnold, 2004) (Figure 5.2).

The formation and spread of prison gangs is inextricably linked to the broader social and environmental conditions of confinement. Gangs provide inmates with a sense of belonging, protection, and identity in an environment characterized by deprivation, isolation, and a lack of autonomy. Gresham Sykes and others proposed the deprivation model of prison life, which holds that the harsh realities of incarceration, such as the loss of freedom, security, and social connections, drive prisoners to seek alternative social structures. Prison gangs meet this need by offering members a support network that provides both psychological and physical safety. In exchange for this protection, inmates are expected to follow the gang's rules and participate in its activities which often include violent confrontations with rival groups and the maintenance of the gang's power within the prison hierarchy (Crewe, 2012).

Figure 5.2. *Prison gangs.*

Source: Misra (2024).

The significance of violence in prison gang operations cannot be overstated. Violence is used as both a tool of coercion and a means of establishing and maintaining dominance in the prison setting. Gangs use violence to enforce their rules, punish dissent, and protect their territories from competitors. The use of violence also helps to improve the gang's reputation and discourages challenges to its authority from both other inmates and correctional staff. This violent culture is deeply ingrained in the gang's identity and is often ritualized through initiation rites, retaliatory attacks, and the enforcement of a strict code of conduct among members (Zamble and Porporino, 2013).

Power dynamics within prison gangs are shaped by both internal hierarchy and external alliances. Within a gang, leadership is typically determined by a combination of seniority, reputation, and the ability to command the respect and loyalty of fellow members. Leaders are in charge of making strategic decisions, negotiating with rival gangs, and coordinating the gang's activities within and outside of prison. These leaders' influence extends beyond the prison walls, as many gangs maintain connections with street gangs and criminal organizations outside the prison. These external connections frequently facilitate the flow of contraband, such as drugs and weapons, into prison, further fueling the cycle of violence (Pyrooz et al., 2011).

The importation model of inmate behavior also offers a useful framework for understanding the role of prison gangs. This model suggests that the values, attitudes, and behaviors that inmates bring with them from the outside world have a significant impact on the prison environment. Many prison gang members were involved in gang activities prior to their incarceration, and they carry with them the same norms and loyalties that governed their street behavior. The prison environment, with its lack of formal social controls and high levels of violence and deprivation, exacerbates these tendencies, resulting in the formation of tightly-knit, highly organized groups that mirror the structures of street gangs (Zamble and Porporino, 2013).

Racial and ethnic divisions are especially prevalent in prison gangs, with many of the most powerful gangs organized along these lines. In the United States, prison gangs such as the Aryan Brotherhood, the Mexican Mafia, and the Black Guerrilla Family are all defined by their racial or ethnic origins. These divisions frequently result in violent conflicts between gangs as they compete for control of resources such as drugs, contraband, and protection rackets. The racialization of gang violence in prisons reflects broader societal tensions, as the prison environment magnifies and intensifies pre-existing racial and ethnic hostility (Liebling and Arnold, 2004).

Prison gangs and violence have far-reaching consequences for both the criminal justice system and society as a whole. The presence of gangs inside the prison complicates efforts to maintain order and discipline, as correctional officers must navigate complex power dynamics and the constant threat of violence. Gang influence also undermines rehabilitation efforts, as inmates who are deeply ingrained in gang culture are less likely to participate in educational or vocational programs and are more likely to re-offend upon release. Gang-related violence spreads from the streets to prisons and back again, creating a cycle of violence that perpetuates criminal behavior and destabilizes communities (Pyrooz et al., 2011).

Furthermore, the strategies used by correctional authorities to combat prison gangs may have unintended consequences. Solitary confinement, for example, is commonly used to isolate gang leaders and prevent them from communicating with other members. However, this practice has the potential to worsen inmates' psychological conditions and exacerbate the very issues it seeks to address. Similarly, transferring gang members to different facilities in an attempt to break up their networks can unintentionally spread gang influence to new prisons, creating more widespread problems (Sirisutthidacha and Tititampruk, 2014).

Penological research also emphasizes the difficulties of addressing the underlying causes of prison gang violence. While increased security and punitive measures may provide temporary relief, they do little to address the underlying social and economic factors that motivate people to join gangs in the first place. Effective intervention requires a comprehensive approach that includes not only improved security and intelligence within prisons, but also targeted rehabilitation programs that address issues such as substance abuse, mental health, and inmates' lack of educational and employment opportunities (Pyrooz et al., 2011).

5.3. PRISON STAFF-INMATE RELATIONSHIPS

The relationship between prison staff and inmates is a critical component of the carceral experience, with a significant impact on the overall operation of correctional institutions and the outcomes of incarceration. This relationship is complex, and shaped by power dynamics, institutional policies, and individual behaviors. Interactions between staff and inmates not only reflect the larger goals of punishment and rehabilitation but also play a critical role in shaping the daily lives of those within the prison system (Worley et al., 2021).

At the center of the staff-inmate relationship is the inherent power imbalance that defines the prison environment. Correctional officers and other prison staff have authority over inmates, controlling their movements, access to resources, and overall well-being. This power is required to maintain order and security within the institution, but it also creates an environment in which relationships can quickly become adversarial. Prison staff can use power to enforce rules and impose disciplinary measures, as well as to exert more subtle forms of influence, such as granting or withholding privileges. The manner in which this power is used has significant implications for the nature of the relationship between staff and inmates (Pyrooz et al., 2011).

Research in penology has highlighted the concept of the "dual role" that correctional officers frequently play, acting as both security enforcers and rehabilitation facilitators. This duality can result in conflicting demands and expectations, as officers must balance the need for control with the need to assist inmates' reform efforts. The conflict between these roles is a significant factor in shaping the staff-inmate relationship. Officers who prioritize security over rehabilitation may create an environment of hostility and mistrust, in which inmates see staff as oppressors rather than allies. In contrast, officers who successfully integrate their roles can create a more supportive environment that encourages positive behavioral changes among inmates (Worley et al., 2018).

The prison's organizational culture influences the quality of interactions between staff and inmates. Prison cultures that prioritize punishment and control tend to foster more authoritarian relationships, with staff relying heavily on formal authority and punitive measures to keep things in order. In such environments, the staff-inmate relationship is frequently antagonistic, with inmates resisting officers' control and officers viewing inmates as threats to be managed. This adversarial dynamic can lead to a cycle of conflict, where punitive actions by staff provoke defiance and misconduct by inmates, which in turn leads to additional punishment (Levinson, 2002).

In contrast, prisons with a rehabilitative culture tend to foster more positive relationships between staff and inmates. In these settings, staff are encouraged to interact with inmates in ways that promote respect, fairness, and personal growth. Officers in rehabilitative environments are more likely to influence inmate behavior through informal interactions and positive reinforcement rather than formal discipline. This approach can result in a more cooperative environment in which inmates are more willing to follow rules and participate in rehabilitative programs. The staff-inmate relationship in these contexts is frequently characterized by mutual respect and a shared commitment to the rehabilitation goals (Crewe, 2012).

Communication is also an important aspect of the staff-inmate relationship. Effective communication is critical for maintaining order, resolving conflicts, and encouraging rehabilitation within the prison. According to studies, when prison staff communicates openly and respectfully with inmates, tensions can be reduced and trust built. Poor communication, defined as hostility, indifference, or a lack of transparency, can exacerbate misunderstandings and lead to conflict. Communication is also important in the implementation of correctional programs, as inmates are more likely to engage with programs and adhere to institutional rules when they feel the staff is listening to their concerns and treating them fairly (Liebling and Arnold, 2004; Worley et al., 2018).

Individual staff members' attitudes and behaviors play an important role in shaping the staff-inmate relationship. Officers who approach their jobs with empathy, professionalism, and dedication to ethical behavior are more likely to form positive relationships with inmates. These officers are frequently able to defuse potentially volatile situations and encourage inmates to accept responsibility for their actions. On the other hand, officers who exhibit authoritarian or abusive behavior can contribute to an environment of fear and resentment, undermining the potential for rehabilitation and increasing the likelihood of misconduct and violence within the prison (Worley et al., 2021;

Zamble and Porporino, 2013). Another important factor in the staff-inmate relationship is the concept of "correctional officer burnout." Because of the high-stress nature of their work, correctional officers frequently experience burnout, which is characterized by emotional exhaustion, cynicism, and a sense of ineffectiveness. Burnout can have a negative impact on officers' interactions with inmates, resulting in more punitive and less supportive behavior. As a result, the quality of the staff-inmate relationship may deteriorate, making it difficult to achieve security and rehabilitation goals. Addressing burnout through organizational support, training, and resources is thus necessary for maintaining positive staff-inmate interactions (Williams, 2012).

The relationship between staff and inmates is influenced by societal attitudes toward punishment and rehabilitation. Societal attitudes toward crime and punishment influence correctional institutions' policies and practices, which in turn affect how staff and inmates interact. In societies that value retribution and deterrence, prison staff may be more likely to use punitive tactics in their interactions with inmates. In contrast, in societies that prioritize rehabilitation and reintegration, staff may be more supportive and focused on helping inmates prepare for life after incarceration (Pyrooz et al., 2011; Scott, 2008).

5.4. MENTAL HEALTH ISSUES IN PRISONS

Mental health issues in prisons pose a significant and complex challenge to the field of penology, reflecting the larger intersection of the criminal justice system and public health. The prevalence of mental health disorders in the incarcerated population is significantly higher than in the general population, highlighting the critical need for effective interventions, appropriate care, and policies that address the root causes of this disparity. The prison environment, characterized by deprivation, stress, and social isolation, frequently aggravates pre-existing mental health conditions and can contribute to the development of new psychological disorders (Fazel et al., 2016) (Figure 5.3).

Among the most notable aspects of prison mental health is the high prevalence of serious mental illnesses such as depression, anxiety, schizophrenia, bipolar disorder, and post-traumatic stress disorder (PTSD). According to studies, a significant proportion of inmates suffer from one or more of these conditions, often at rates several times higher than in the general population. This high prevalence is partially due to the fact that individuals with mental health issues are more likely to come into contact with the criminal justice system, whether due to behaviors related to their disorders, a lack of access to mental health care, or socioeconomic factors that increase their risk of incarceration (Haney, 2003).

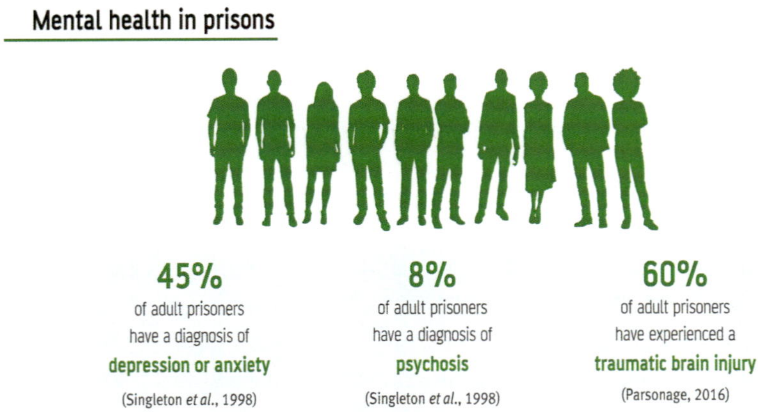

Figure 5.3. *Mental health issues in prisons.*

Source: Centre for Mental Health (2024).

The concept of "criminalization of mental illness" is critical for understanding why so many people with mental health disorders end up in prison. In many cases, the criminal justice system functions as a de facto mental health facility, especially in societies where community-based mental health services are insufficient or underfunded. This criminalization occurs when people with untreated or poorly managed mental illnesses engage in behavior that results in their arrest and incarceration. Once in prison, these people frequently face a lack of adequate mental health care, which complicates their conditions (Williams, 2012).

Prison environments, with their numerous stressors, can exacerbate pre-existing mental health issues. The deprivation model, as investigated in penological studies, demonstrates how a loss of freedom, autonomy, and social connections can cause significant psychological distress. Inmates face a variety of "pains of imprisonment," such as isolation, the constant threat of violence, and the stigma associated with incarceration, all of which can have a negative impact on their mental health. These stressors are especially harmful to individuals with pre-existing mental health conditions, who may find the prison environment overwhelming and destabilizing (Fazel et al., 2016; Haney, 2003).

The phenomenon of "prisonization," or the process by which inmates conform to the norms and values of prison life, can also have a negative impact on mental health. As inmates adjust to the harsh realities of incarceration, they may develop protective behaviors and attitudes in the prison setting but maladaptive outside of it. This adjustment can include emotional numbness, hypervigilance, and an increased proclivity for violence, all of which are associated with poor mental health outcomes. The longer a person is in prison, the more deeply ingrained these behaviors can become, making it more difficult to reintegrate into society and increasing the risk of recidivism (Haney, 2003; Pyrooz et al., 2011).

Solitary confinement, a common practice in correctional facilities, has received widespread criticism for its negative impact on mental health. Extended isolation and sensory deprivation in solitary confinement can cause a variety of psychological symptoms such as depression, anxiety, hallucinations, and paranoia. Individuals with pre-existing mental health conditions are especially vulnerable to the negative effects of solitary confinement, which can cause a rapid deterioration in psychological well-being. The use of solitary confinement as a disciplinary measure or for the management of inmates with severe mental health issues raises significant ethical and humanitarian concerns, because it frequently exacerbates the very conditions it is intended to manage (Fazel et al., 2016).

In addition to the direct impact of the prison environment on mental health, there is a serious lack of adequate mental health care within prisons. Many correctional facilities lack the necessary mental health services, resulting in inadequate treatment, delayed diagnoses, and insufficient support for inmates suffering from severe mental illnesses. The lack of qualified mental health professionals in prisons exacerbates the problem, as overburdened staff may be unable to provide the necessary level of care. Lack of care can worsen mental health conditions, increase vulnerability to self-harm and suicide, and increase the likelihood of behavioral problems that lead to disciplinary action or extended sentences (Fazel et al., 2016; Scott, 2008).

Another significant issue in prisons is the intersection of mental health and substance abuse. A large proportion of inmates with mental health disorders also have substance use disorders, a phenomenon known as "dual diagnosis." Substance abuse can both conceal and exacerbate underlying mental health conditions, resulting in a vicious cycle of dependency and deteriorating mental health. In the prison setting, access to drugs and alcohol may be restricted, resulting in withdrawal symptoms and worsening of mental health conditions. However, the availability of illicit substances within prisons can contribute to ongoing substance abuse, complicating efforts to address mental health issues (Williams, 2012).

Addressing mental health issues in prisons necessitates a multifaceted approach that includes both increased access to mental health care within correctional facilities and broader criminal justice reforms. Effective interventions must include comprehensive mental health assessments for all incoming inmates, appropriate and timely treatment, and ongoing support throughout the incarceration period. Furthermore, there is a need for specialized training for correctional staff to recognize and respond to mental health crises, as well as the implementation of alternative disciplinary approaches that do not rely on solitary confinement or other punitive measures that can harm mental health (Levinson, 2002).

Furthermore, addressing the broader social determinants of mental health, such as poverty, homelessness, and a lack of access to health care, is critical for reducing the criminalization of mental illness and breaking the cycle of incarceration for people with mental illnesses. This necessitates a shift from a punitive model of criminal justice to one that emphasizes rehabilitation, treatment, and support for people with mental illnesses (Haney, 2003).

5.5. PRISON RIOTS AND ESCAPES

Prison riots and escapes are major topics in penology, a branch of criminology that studies the theory and practice of prison administration and criminal rehabilitation. These occurrences are not simply symptomatic of individual behaviors, but they are also inextricably linked to systemic and structural issues within the criminal system. Analyzing prison riots and escapes from a penological perspective necessitates a thorough understanding of the underlying reasons, the sociopolitical context, and the ramifications for both the prisoners and society as a whole.

Prison riots are frequently indicative of larger problems inside the prison system. They are generally caused by poor conditions such as overcrowded cells, inadequate food, a lack of medical treatment, and a general disregard for prisoners' fundamental necessities (Useem & Morrison Piehl, 2008). These situations foster a sense of irritation and animosity, which can quickly escalate into violent conflicts. When convicts believe their issues are being disregarded or trivialized, collective fury can erupt as riots. The Attica Prison Riot of 1971, for example, was a direct reaction to the inhumane circumstances at the Attica Correctional Facility in New York. Prisoners' requests for better living conditions, political rights, and humane treatment were met with violent repression, resulting in numerous casualties and increased awareness of the prison system's dismal conditions (Hurowitz, 2021).

In addition to bad conditions, abuse and neglect can drive prison riots. Physical or psychological abuse by jail staff, combined with systematic negligence, frequently exacerbates an already stressful environment within prisons. Collective unrest is more likely in circumstances where prisoners face arbitrary punishment, excessive force, or psychological agony. Such abuse not only violates inmates' basic human rights but also undermines the legitimacy of prison officials, resulting in a breakdown in the order that the penal system seeks to preserve (Rubin, 2019).

Furthermore, jail riots are occasionally sparked by wider political or social demonstrations. Prisons, as microcosms of society, frequently mirror the larger social and political challenges of the day. When prisoners believe they are being used as symbols or pawns in larger societal disputes, rioting can be used as a form of resistance or protest (Useem and Piehl, 2008). This was evident during the California Prison Riots of the early 2000s when overcrowding and gang conflicts were not isolated issues within the prison, but rather symptomatic of broader social problems, such as racial tensions and the criminal justice system's failure to address the root causes of crime (Useem and Piehl, 2008).

The implications of prison riots are far-reaching. They frequently cause major damage to jail buildings, requiring months or even years to repair. The financial cost of these repairs is high, but the personal cost is far greater. Riots regularly result in injuries or deaths among prisoners and staff, heightening tensions between inmates and prison officials. In some circumstances, the aftermath of a riot can prompt policy changes targeted at addressing the underlying conditions that caused the disturbance. However, these improvements are frequently reactive rather than proactive, addressing just the symptoms rather than the underlying causes of jail system problems (Useem and Piehl, 2008).

Prison escapes, as opposed to riots, usually stem from the activities of a single person or small group motivated by desperation or careful planning. A profound sense of hopelessness among prisoners can be shown in escapes, which are driven by a desire to evade unjust sentences or harsh circumstances (Armstrong, 2001). Some believe that leaving a system they believe to be unfair is their last chance to regain some semblance of independence or autonomy. Notable escape stories, like Joaquín "El Chapo" Guzmán's jail break-outs from Mexico, highlight the extent some prisoners will go to in order to get their freedom back; these situations frequently require complex preparation, outside help, and the taking advantage of institutional flaws (Hurowitz, 2021).

Though successful escapes from modern prisons are becoming increasingly difficult due to advancements in security technology, such as electronic monitoring, surveillance systems, and fortified physical barriers, inmates have responded by utilizing complex strategies, like smuggling in tools or taking advantage of dishonest prison staff, to aid in their escape. Despite these difficulties, successful escapes continue to occur, raising serious questions about the efficacy of prison security measures and the possibility of corruption within the penal system (Armstrong, 2001).

The impact of prison escapes goes beyond the immediate consequences for the individuals involved. Successful escapes frequently result in heightened scrutiny of prison security measures, stronger protocols, harsher penalties for individuals involved, and even larger reforms to the penal system. However, these procedures are frequently used in a reactionary fashion, similar to how prison uprisings were handled. Rather than addressing the root causes of inmate escape, such as harsh sentences, poor living circumstances, or systematic injustice, these improvements tend to focus on strengthening security and preventing future escapes (Rubin, 2019).

Prison riots and escapes expose systemic issues within the criminal system. They are not isolated events but rather reflect deeper issues about inmate treatment, prison conditions, and the larger social and political framework in which these institutions operate. In many situations, these events serve as catalysts for change, leading reforms that seek to solve the urgent problems inside the system. However, unless a comprehensive effort is taken to address the core causes of these concerns, such as overcrowding, abuse, neglect, and the larger socioeconomic imbalances that lead to criminality, the cycle of unrest and escape is likely to persist (Useem and Piehl, 2008).

5.6. PRISON CONDITIONS AND HUMAN RIGHTS

Penology, which studies the moral and practical dimensions of incarceration, is centered on the analysis of prison circumstances and how they relate to human rights. Penology, the study of criminal punishment and prison administration, covers a wide variety of issues pertaining to the care of inmates and the running of prisons. In order to guarantee that the procedures used in correctional facilities are morally upright and helpful in the reintegration of prisoners into society, this discussion focuses on the concepts of humane treatment and the efficacy of rehabilitation within the penal system.

Prison facilities, typically beset by concerns such as overcrowding, inadequate healthcare, and limited access to rehabilitative services, pose substantial obstacles to the well-being and dignity of convicts. A common problem that lowers living standards and increases conflict among inmates is overcrowding. The occurrence of overcrowding intensifies pre-existing issues, including inadequate nutrition, poor sanitation, and a lack of medical attention, resulting in an atmosphere that is harmful to prisoners' physical and mental well-being. In addition to endangering the inmates' health, this unfavorable environment makes it much more difficult for them to receive rehabilitation and eventually be reintegrated into society (Moore, 2017). Human rights dictate that the way in which prisoners are treated must be in accordance with internationally recognized norms that are intended to protect their human rights and deter cruel treatment. A foundation for guaranteeing that prisoners are treated with dignity and granted basic rights is provided by the Universal Declaration of Human Rights (UDHR) and the United Nations Standard Minimum Rules for the Treatment of Prisoners, also referred to as the Mandela Rules (Latessa and Lovins, 2019). A concept that is closely related to the administration of jail conditions is Article 5 of the UDHR, which expressly forbids torture and cruel, inhuman, or degrading treatment. In a similar vein, the Mandela Rules provide minimal requirements for the treatment of inmates, including clauses pertaining to appropriate housing, healthcare, and access to programs for rehabilitation. Upholding prisoners' rights and guaranteeing that penal procedures adhere to international human rights commitments depend on compliance with these standards (Moore, 2017).

The necessity to strike a balance between security and compassionate treatment within correctional facilities further complicates the relationship between prison conditions and human rights. Although essential for preserving order, security procedures may result in actions that violate the rights of detainees. For example, the use of disproportionate disciplinary measures and solitary confinement, even if they are frequently justified on security grounds, can cause serious psychological injury and breach fundamental human rights standards. The conflict between humane treatment and security highlights the necessity for a balanced strategy that protects inmates' fundamental rights while addressing security issues (Useem & Morrison Piehl, 2008).

Reforming the law, stepping up oversight, and advocating are common steps taken to enhance prison conditions and bring them into compliance with human rights standards. Legal changes that target systemic flaws in correctional facilities—like decreasing overcrowding, improving healthcare delivery, and increasing rehabilitative services—are essential. These changes are required to guarantee that the criminal justice system operates in a way that complies with its duties under international human rights law, in addition to improving the living conditions of prisoners. Furthermore, impartial oversight agencies and human rights groups are essential in determining adherence to global norms and promoting alterations that are required. By ensuring that violations are noted and dealt with, as well as by conducting routine reviews of prison conditions, these organizations help to foster accountability in the criminal justice system (Liebling and Arnold, 2004).

Oversight and monitoring play a critical role in ensuring that jail conditions comply with human rights norms. Independent bodies, like as state human rights institutions and international organizations, play an important role in providing objective assessments of prison conditions and recommending areas for reform.

These groups frequently audit correctional facilities, evaluate policies and practices, and make recommendations for reforms. Their efforts are critical to ensuring that inmates' rights are protected and that any abuses are addressed swiftly (Crewe, 2012).

Furthermore, human rights organizations play an important role in increasing awareness of concerns within the correctional system and advocating for required reforms. These organizations frequently conduct campaigns to expose the situation of prisoners, particularly those detained in terrible conditions, and to encourage governments and prison officials to make improvements. Human rights organizations help to improve jail conditions and guarantee they meet international standards through lawsuits, public awareness campaigns, and lobbying (Sirisutthidacha and Tititampruk, 2014).

In the broader context of penology, understanding the relationship between prison circumstances and human rights is critical to the ethical administration of justice. The treatment of inmates reflects the ideals and concepts that guide a society's approach to punishment and rehabilitation. A correctional system that respects human rights and offers humane living circumstances for inmates is more likely to contribute to positive rehabilitation and reintegration outcomes. In contrast, a system that disregards these principles is likely to perpetuate cycles of violence, recidivism, and social marginalization (Crewe, 2012).

The study of penology requires a thorough grasp of the relationship between prison circumstances and human rights. Ensuring that prison surroundings fulfill accepted standards of humane treatment while properly handling security issues is critical to the ethical administration of justice. Penology can help to create a more just and rehabilitative correctional system by adhering to international human rights standards and pursuing reforms that improve prison circumstances. This, in turn, improves the prospects for inmate and societal reintegration, thereby contributing to the larger aims of justice and social harmony.

5.7. REENTRY PROGRAMS FOR RELEASED INMATES

Reentry programs for released criminals are an important component of modern penology, which seeks not just to punish and reform offenders, but also to rehabilitate and reintegrate them into society. Former convicts encounter numerous and complex challenges upon release, which frequently leads to a vicious cycle of recidivism. Understanding the importance of these programs in the larger context of criminal justice and societal welfare needs an examination of their role, effectiveness, and the problems they seek to solve.

The journey from prison to freedom is one of the most difficult times in an ex-offender's life. While prison life is organized and supervised, the outside world is unpredictable and could lead to a relapse into criminal conduct. The cultural stigma associated with former inmates exacerbates these issues, making it difficult for them to find work, housing, or simply basic social acceptability. Without sufficient support mechanisms in place, many released convicts are forced to return to a life of crime due to a lack of options. Reentry programs are critical in this regard since they provide a systematic road for individuals to repair their lives and reintegrate into society (Fazel et al., 2016).

Employment is a key element of reentry programs. A gainful job is frequently viewed as the foundation of successful reintegration, giving not only financial security but also a sense of purpose and social belonging. Reentry programs that provide vocational training, job placement services, and resume-building workshops aid in the transition from incarceration to employment. These organizations frequently collaborate with local businesses and industries to develop job possibilities expressly for former convicts. This method benefits both ex-offenders and the community, as employed people are less likely to engage in criminal activity. The link between stable employment and lower recidivism rates highlights the significance of these programs (Haney, 2003).

Housing is another important issue addressed by reentry programs. The lack of safe and stable housing might jeopardize the reintegration process, as homelessness or living in locations linked with previous criminal behavior raises the probability of recidivism. Some organizations offer interim housing alternatives, while others collaborate with local agencies to find long-term accommodations. Safe housing not only provides a physical space for former convicts to reconstruct their lives, but it also improves their psychological well-being by lowering the stress and worry associated with instability. Housing is critical to the effectiveness of other reentry services because it provides a secure basis for persons to pursue jobs, education, and family reunification (Fazel et al., 2016).

Many former convicts struggle with mental health issues and substance misuse. Mental health concerns and substance addiction disorders are very common among incarcerated people, and without effective treatment, these problems can become overwhelming following release. Counseling, therapy, and access to support groups are common components of reentry programs, which assist former convicts in coping with these issues. Addressing mental health and substance misuse involves not only healing the person but also limiting the potential harm to society. By offering ongoing care and support, these programs assist reduce the likelihood of relapse, resulting in decreased recidivism rates.

Education is also an important factor in reentry programs. Many inmates lack formal education or vocational skills, which are required for steady employment after release. GED completion programs, vocational training, and even possibilities for further education provide former convicts with the information and abilities needed to succeed in the labor market. Education has been demonstrated to have a direct impact on recidivism, with research showing that offenders who participate in educational programs while in prison are much less likely to re-offend (Davis et al., 2013). The emphasis on education in reentry programs reflects a broader understanding that rehabilitation is more than just addressing behavior; it is also about providing people with the tools they need to thrive in life.

Family reconnection is another key component of reentry programs. For many former inmates, reuniting with family may be both a source of comfort and a big obstacle. During incarceration, family relationships may have been strained or damaged, and repairing these bonds takes time, effort, and, in many cases, professional help. Reentry programs' counseling and family therapy can help restore these ties, providing former convicts with the support network they need for successful reintegration. Strong family relationships can provide emotional support, lessen feelings of isolation, and offer practical assistance with housing and childcare, all of which lead to lower recidivism rates (Williams, 2012).

Life skills training is another important aspect of reintegration programs. Many offenders, especially those who have been detained for a long time, may lack the basic life skills required for daily existence. These can include budgeting, time management, cooking, and other daily duties that non-institutionalized people take for granted. Reentry programs assist former convicts in navigating the complexity of life outside of prison by providing life skills training, minimizing the probability of them feeling overwhelmed and turning to criminal activity as a coping mechanism (Worley et al., 2021).

The many success stories that have been recorded across the nation demonstrate the effectiveness of reintegration programs. Programs that successfully incorporate housing, mental health care, education, job, and family reunions have been demonstrated to significantly lower recidivism rates, proving that ex-offenders may effectively reintegrate into society with the correct assistance. These initiatives improve communities overall and benefit the participants personally, making society safer and more unified (Worley et al., 2021).

Reentry programs signify a change in the direction of a more restorative and rehabilitative approach to criminal justice in the larger framework of penology. These programs recognize the possibility of transformation and the significance of support in the reintegration process, as opposed to concentrating only on punishment. They represent the idea that people who have served their time should be given another shot and that it is the duty of society to give them the resources and chances they need to be successful (Pyrooz et al., 2011).

Reentry programs for released prisoners are a crucial part of the criminal justice system because they help formerly incarcerated individuals with the many obstacles they encounter when reintegrating into society. These programs offer a complete support system that lowers recidivism and fosters successful reintegration by concentrating on work, housing, mental health, education, family reunification, and life skills. The value of funding reintegration programs cannot be emphasized as society struggles with the challenges of prison reform and the need to lower recidivism. These initiatives help build safer, more resilient communities in addition to supporting ex-offenders on their path to a fresh start.

Chapter 6

JUVENILE JUSTICE

Contents

Juvenile justice, as a subfield of penology, focuses on the legal processes and correctional strategies used to deal with people under the age of 18. This field is built around the recognition that juveniles differ from adults in terms of psychological development and rehabilitation potential. Thus, the juvenile justice system frequently emphasizes rehabilitation over punishment, reflecting a belief in youth's malleability and the possibility for positive behavioral change (Burrell, 2000).

Diversion, which redirects offenders away from formal judicial proceedings and toward rehabilitative programs, and the principle of parens patriae, which positions the state as the guardian of juveniles' welfare, are both important concepts in juvenile justice. The effectiveness of these approaches has been debatable, particularly concerning recidivism rates and the long-term impacts of juvenile detention (Cavanagh, 2022).

Academic discussions in penology frequently focus on the debate between punitive measures and rehabilitative efforts in the juvenile justice system, with studies indicating that overly punitive approaches may undermine the developmental needs of young offenders. Furthermore, current research emphasizes the significance of addressing the socioeconomic and environmental factors that contribute to juvenile delinquency, advocating for a more holistic approach to juvenile justice (Cavanagh, 2022).

6.1. HISTORY OF JUVENILE JUSTICE SYSTEM

The juvenile justice system's history is inextricably linked to the evolution of penology as a whole, reflecting shifts in societal attitudes toward youth, crime, and punishment. The juvenile justice system, which began in the late 19th century, was founded on principles that differed from those that govern adult criminal justice, emphasizing rehabilitation over retribution and acknowledging the unique developmental needs of young offenders (Burrell, 2000).

The establishment of the first juvenile court in Cook County, Illinois, in 1899 marked a significant departure from previous practices, which saw children tried and sentenced alongside adults. The Progressive Era's reformist ethos influenced this innovation, which sought to address the social ills of urbanization and industrialization, particularly the plight of children. The juvenile court embodied the principle of parens patriae, which saw the state as a guardian responsible for the well-being of children rather than a punitive force. This approach was based on the belief that juveniles, because of their immaturity and potential for change, should be treated leniently and given opportunities for rehabilitation (Thompson and Morris, 2016). During this time, penological thought emphasized the importance of tailored interventions that focused on the unique circumstances of each juvenile offender. Early juvenile courts emphasized informal, non-adversarial proceedings in which judges exercised broad discretion to determine outcomes deemed to be in the child's best interests. Probation became an important component of this system, allowing juveniles to stay in their communities under supervision rather than being imprisoned. This approach reflected the larger penological shift towards rehabilitative ideals, contrasting with the punitive philosophies that dominated adult criminal justice (Steinberg, 2009).

However, there have been significant tensions and contradictions throughout the history of the juvenile justice system. As the system grew, criticisms arose about the arbitrary nature of juvenile court proceedings and the absence of legal safeguards for young offenders. By the mid-20th century, these concerns had prompted landmark legal reforms, most notably the United States Supreme Court's decisions in In re Gault (1967) and Kent v. United States (1966). These decisions granted juveniles due process rights, including access to legal representation, the right to confront witnesses, and immunity from self-incrimination. The judicial recognition of juveniles' constitutional rights marked a critical shift in the balance between the rehabilitative goals of the juvenile system and the procedural safeguards traditionally associated with adult criminal justice (Burrell, 2000; Steinberg, 2009).

Despite these reforms, the late 20th century saw a growing backlash against the juvenile justice system, fueled by rising crime rates and public concern about juvenile delinquency. Punitive measures resurfaced in the 1980s and 1990s, as states increasingly transferred juveniles to adult courts and imposed harsher sentences. This period reflected a broader penological trend toward retribution and incapacitation, which called into question the rehabilitative ideals that had previously supported the juvenile justice system. Critics argued that this punitive turn overlooked the developmental differences between juveniles and adults, undermining the potential for rehabilitation and contributing to higher recidivism rates among young offenders (Cavanagh, 2022).

In response to these challenges, contemporary penological scholarship has advocated for a rethinking of juvenile justice policies, emphasizing the importance of rehabilitative approaches that take into account the social, economic, and psychological factors that influence juvenile behavior. Recent research has demonstrated the effectiveness of evidence-based interventions such as restorative justice programs and therapeutic jurisprudence, which emphasize accountability, restitution, and reintegration of juveniles into their communities. These approaches are consistent with the original rehabilitative ethos of the juvenile justice system while incorporating modern insights into adolescent development and criminal behavior (Steinberg, 2009).

The history of the juvenile justice system reflects an ongoing struggle to strike a balance between rehabilitation, accountability, and public safety. As societal attitudes toward youth and crime evolve, so does the juvenile justice system, guided by advances in criminology and a growing recognition of the importance of policies that address the root causes of juvenile delinquency. By revisiting the fundamental principles of the juvenile justice system and incorporating contemporary insights, policymakers and practitioners can better meet the challenges of managing juvenile offenders in a way that promotes both justice and social welfare (Thompson and Morris, 2016).

6.2. JUVENILE DELINQUENCY PREVENTION PROGRAMS

Juvenile delinquency prevention programs are important components of the juvenile justice system. These programs are intended to intervene at various stages of a young person's life, with the goal of lowering the likelihood of criminal behavior and its consequences. Prevention efforts are based on the recognition that juvenile delinquency is frequently the result of complex and interconnected factors such as socioeconomic circumstances, family dynamics, educational challenges, and community environments. Penological theories emphasize the importance of early and sustained interventions that address these underlying causes, rather than focusing solely on punitive measures after delinquent behavior has occurred (Burrell, 2000).

One of the most prominent types of prevention programs is early childhood education and intervention initiatives. These programs, such as the HighScope Perry Preschool Project, are based on the idea that providing high-quality educational experiences to young children, particularly those from disadvantaged backgrounds, can have long-term benefits for their development and behavior. The High Scope Perry Preschool Project, for example, targeted African American children from low-income families and offered a structured preschool program with both academic and social-emotional components. Longitudinal studies revealed that participants in this program were less likely to engage in criminal behavior as adolescents and adults than a control group. This suggests that early educational intervention can be an effective means of preventing juvenile delinquency by addressing some of the root causes of later criminal behavior, such as poor academic performance and limited social skills (de Vries et al., 2015).

Another important type of juvenile delinquency prevention program focuses on family-based interventions. These programs are based on the understanding that family dynamics and parenting practices are important predictors of a child's behavior. One well-known example is the Multisystemic Therapy (MST) program, which focuses on families with adolescents who are at high risk of delinquent behavior. MST is a comprehensive and intensive program that involves collaborating with the entire family to improve communication, strengthen relationships, and create more effective parenting techniques. The program is based on the ecological model of human development, which holds that multiple systems, such as the family, school, and community, influence a child's behavior. By addressing issues across these different systems, MST aims to reduce the risk factors for delinquency and promote positive behavioral outcomes. Research has consistently demonstrated that MST is effective in reducing rates of recidivism among juvenile offenders, highlighting the importance of family-centered approaches in delinquency prevention (Petrosino et al., 2005).

Community-based programs are also effective in preventing juvenile delinquency. These programs frequently focus on giving young people positive alternatives to delinquent behavior, such as after-school activities, mentorship, and job training. The Boys & Girls Clubs of America is one such program that has received widespread recognition for its effectiveness in reducing juvenile crime rates. The Boys & Girls Clubs strive to instill a sense of belonging and purpose in at-risk youth by providing a safe and supportive environment in which they can participate in constructive activities and form relationships with positive role models. According to studies, participation in such programs is associated with lower rates of delinquency, as well as improved academic performance and social skills. The success of these programs underscores the importance of community engagement and support in the prevention of juvenile delinquency (Burrell, 2000; de Vries et al., 2015).

In addition to these specific types of programs, school-based initiatives are an important part of juvenile delinquency prevention efforts. Schools are an important part of a young person's life, so they are an ideal setting for interventions aimed at reducing delinquency. Positive Behavioral Interventions and Supports (PBIS) are programs that aim to encourage positive behavior while also creating a safe and supportive school environment. PBIS is a multi-tiered framework that teaches students appropriate behaviors, reinforces positive behavior consistently, and provides targeted support to students who are at risk of engaging in delinquent behavior. The goal of PBIS is not only to reduce problem behavior but also to improve the overall school climate, which can help prevent delinquency. Research has shown that schools that implement PBIS with fidelity tend to have lower rates of disciplinary referrals, suspensions, and expulsions, all of which are risk factors for juvenile delinquency (de Vries et al., 2015).

Restorative justice programs are also an important approach to reducing juvenile delinquency. These programs are founded on the belief that crime is not only a violation of the law, but also a threat to relationships and communities. Restorative justice attempts to repair this harm through processes that involve the offender, the victim, and the community. Restorative justice practices used to combat juvenile delinquency include victim-offender mediation and family group conferencing. Rather than imposing punishment, these programs aim to hold the offender accountable in a way that promotes understanding, empathy, and reconciliation. Research on restorative justice has shown that these programs can be effective in reducing recidivism and improving outcomes for both offenders and victims, particularly when compared to more traditional punitive approaches (Petrosino et al., 2005).

These prevention programs serve not only to reduce the immediate risk of delinquency but also to promote long-term positive development for youth. Effective prevention necessitates a multifaceted approach that addresses the various factors that contribute to delinquency, from individual characteristics and family dynamics to broader community and societal influences. Penological insights emphasize the importance of developmentally appropriate interventions that take into account each young person's specific needs and circumstances. This necessitates a commitment to ongoing assessment and adaptation of prevention programs, as well as collaboration across different sectors, such as education, social services, law enforcement, and community (Steinberg, 2009).

The ability to engage young people and their families in meaningful ways is ultimately what determines the success of juvenile delinquency prevention programs. Programs that are culturally responsive, build on the strengths of individuals and communities, and adhere to evidence-based practices are more likely to yield positive results. Furthermore, prevention efforts must be sustained over time, as short-term interventions frequently fail to address the complex and multifaceted nature of juvenile delinquency. By focusing on prevention rather than punishment, these programs embody the core principles of rehabilitative justice, offering hope and opportunity for young people to avoid the pitfalls of delinquency and reach their full potential (Petrosino et al., 2005; Steinberg, 2009).

6.3. JUVENILE COURT PROCESS

The juvenile court process reflects a penological emphasis on rehabilitation and reintegration rather than punishment, while also acknowledging juvenile offenders' potential for growth and reform. The underlying philosophy is that children and adolescents, due to their ongoing development, should not be subjected to the same punitive measures as adults, but should instead be guided toward positive behavioral change (Rodriguez, 2007) (Figure 6.1).

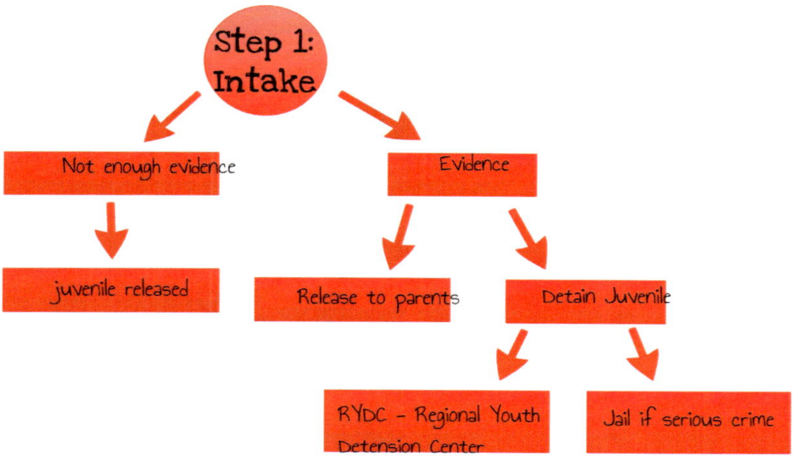

Figure 6.1. *Steps in the juvenile justice process.*

Source: Prezi (2011).

The process typically begins when law enforcement apprehends or arrests the juvenile. In contrast to the adult system, which often focuses solely on the offense, the juvenile process takes into account the juvenile's background, family situation, and the nature of the offense. At this point, the decision to hold or release the juvenile is critical. Detention is typically reserved for serious cases or when there is a risk that the juvenile will flee or commit additional offenses. This initial decision reflects penological insights into the detrimental effects of detention on youth, recognizing that unnecessary detention can exacerbate delinquent behavior and hinder rehabilitation (Pupo and Zane, 2021).

After apprehension, the case is referred to juvenile intake officers, who determine whether formal court proceedings are required. This intake process is critical because it often determines whether the juvenile will enter the court system or be directed to alternative programs. Diversion programs, which may include counseling, community service, or restorative justice practices, are essential to the juvenile justice system. These programs are based on the idea that early and constructive intervention can prevent further escalation of delinquent behavior. Research has shown that diversion can be effective in reducing recidivism, especially when the programs are well-designed and tailored to the juvenile's individual needs (Rodriguez, 2007).

If the case goes to court, the next step is the adjudication hearing, which is the juvenile equivalent of an adult trial. Adjudication hearings are usually less formal and more focused on determining the facts of the case rather than engaging in adversarial proceedings. The judge is central to this process, evaluating evidence and determining whether the juvenile committed the alleged offense. It is important to note that juveniles do not usually have the right to a jury trial; instead, the judge makes the decision based on the evidence presented. This approach reflects the rehabilitative focus of the juvenile justice system, which prioritizes personalized justice over strict adherence to procedural formalities (Emerson, 2017; Pupo and Zane, 2021).

If the juvenile is found responsible for the offense, the case proceeds to the disposition phase, where the court determines the appropriate intervention. The disposition hearing, like sentencing in the adult system, is critical in determining the juvenile's future. Unlike adult courts, where punishment is frequently the primary goal, juvenile courts seek to determine the most effective method of rehabilitating the offender. This could include probation, placement in a juvenile facility, or participation in educational or therapeutic programs. Probation is a common disposition that allows the juvenile to remain in the community while under supervision as long as they meet certain conditions. This approach is informed by penological theories that emphasize the importance of keeping juveniles in their communities and associated with positive influences (Emerson, 2017).

In some cases, the court may order placement in a juvenile detention facility, especially if the offense is serious or the juvenile poses a significant risk to the community. Even in these cases, the focus remains on rehabilitation. Juvenile facilities frequently offer educational and vocational training, counseling, and other programs aimed at addressing the underlying causes of delinquent behavior. The goal is not only to punish but also to provide the juvenile with the skills and support required to lead a law-abiding life after release (de Vries et al., 2015).

The juvenile court process places a strong emphasis on confidentiality and the protection of the juvenile's privacy. Court records are typically sealed, and proceedings are closed to the public, reflecting the belief that young offenders should have the opportunity to reform without the long-term stigma of a public criminal record. This is consistent with penological insights into the importance of protecting juveniles from the long-term negative consequences of their actions, especially those that may impede their ability to successfully reintegrate into society (Emerson, 2017).

Another important aspect of the juvenile court system is the involvement of the juvenile's family. The court frequently requires parents or guardians to participate in the process, whether by attending hearings, participating in family counseling, or ensuring the juvenile's compliance with probation conditions.

This emphasis on family involvement stems from the recognition that family dynamics play an important role in shaping a juvenile's behavior. Penological theories support this approach, emphasizing the need for a holistic strategy that addresses not only the individual but also their larger social environment (de Vries et al., 2015; Emerson, 2017).

The juvenile court process also includes opportunities for appeal and review, which ensure that the juvenile's rights are protected throughout the proceedings. If new evidence emerges or there are concerns about the fairness of the process, the juvenile may request a review of the court's decision. This aspect of the process highlights the system's commitment to justice and fairness, which are important principles in both juvenile justice and penology (Pupo and Zane, 2021).

Restorative justice has received increased attention in recent years within the juvenile court system. Restorative justice practices, which involve bringing together the offender, the victim, and the community to address the harm caused by the offense, are increasingly being incorporated into the juvenile justice system. These practices are consistent with the system's rehabilitative goals, which focus on accountability, making amends, and promoting healing for all parties involved (Rodriguez, 2007).

6.4. REHABILITATION VS. PUNISHMENT FOR JUVENILE OFFENDERS

The debate over rehabilitation versus punishment for juvenile offenders is central to the field of penology, reflecting broader societal concerns about the most effective and ethical approaches to addressing juvenile delinquency. Penological insights emphasize that juveniles, due to their developmental stage, cognitive immaturity, and greater capacity for change, should be treated differently than adults in the justice system. This understanding supports the argument for rehabilitation over punishment, implying that young offenders are more likely to benefit from interventions that focus on their personal development and reintegration into society (Steinberg, 2009).

Rehabilitation for juvenile offenders is based on the belief that criminal behavior in youth is frequently a result of environmental, social, and psychological factors rather than a predetermined disposition. Early intervention programs, education, counseling, and community service are examples of rehabilitative approaches that seek to address the underlying causes of delinquency. These programs aim to provide juveniles with the skills, knowledge, and support they need to avoid future criminal behavior and live productive lives. Research has consistently shown that rehabilitation can help reduce juvenile recidivism.

Studies show that when juveniles are given appropriate resources and guidance, they are less likely to re-offend, indicating that rehabilitation not only benefits the individual but also serves broader societal interests by reducing crime rates (Burrell, 2000).

The rehabilitative approach is also supported by the recognition that the adolescent brain is still developing, particularly in areas such as decision-making, impulse control, and understanding consequences. According to neuroscientific research, juveniles are more vulnerable to peer influence, less capable of foreseeing the long-term consequences of their actions, and more likely to engage in risky behaviors than adults. This developmental perspective contends that juveniles are more adaptable to change and that punitive measures, which frequently fail to address the underlying issues that contribute to delinquent behavior, maybe not only ineffective but also harmful. Incarceration and other forms of punishment can disrupt a juvenile's education, sever family and community ties, and expose them to negative influences within the correctional environment, potentially exacerbating the exact behaviors they are meant to deter (de Vries et al., 2015).

Punishment, on the other hand, is frequently justified on the basis of deterrence, retribution, and incapacitation. From a penological standpoint, the argument for punishment is based on the belief that consequences must be imposed to deter both the individual offender and others in society from engaging in criminal behavior. In the case of juveniles, however, the deterrent effect of punishment is questionable. Juveniles may not fully understand the consequences of their actions due to their developmental stage, and the threat of punishment may not deter them. Furthermore, punitive approaches frequently fail to address the socioeconomic and psychological factors that contribute to delinquency, resulting in higher rates of recidivism after the juvenile is released (Cavanagh, 2022).

The retributive aspect of punishment, based on the concept of "just deserts," is also problematic when applied to juveniles. Retribution assumes a level of moral culpability and intent that young offenders may lack, as they are frequently influenced by factors beyond their control, such as family dynamics, poverty, and exposure to violence. According to penological theories, a one-size-fits-all approach to justice that imposes adult punishment standards on juveniles is both unjust and ineffective (Emerson, 2017).

Incapacitation, another justification for punishment, seeks to protect society by removing dangerous members of the community. While this may be necessary in cases where the juvenile poses a significant risk, it is important to note that long-term incarceration can have negative consequences for a young person's development. Extended periods of confinement can lead to social isolation, mental health issues, and the reinforcement of criminal identities, making it more difficult for the juvenile to reintegrate into society when released (de Vries et al., 2015).

The debate between rehabilitation and punishment in juvenile justice reflects larger philosophical questions about the purpose of the justice system. Should the system prioritize retribution and deterrence, or rehabilitation and reintegration of offenders into society? Given adolescence's unique characteristics and the potential for positive change, penological research is increasingly supporting the latter approach, particularly for juveniles. While punishment may satisfy a societal desire for retribution, it frequently fails to address the underlying causes of delinquency and can lead to more criminal behavior (Cavanagh, 2022).

6.5. JUVENILE DETENTION CENTERS

Juvenile detention institutions, as a key component of the juvenile justice system, play an important role in treating young delinquents. Their function connects with a variety of disciplines, including criminology, penology, psychology, and sociology. From a penological standpoint, juvenile detention facilities represent the penal system's response to child crime, integrating components of punishment, rehabilitation, and social control. As scholars and policymakers debated the effectiveness of these institutions, juvenile detention facilities evolved to reflect shifting societal attitudes toward young offenders, particularly in terms of developmental needs, rehabilitation potential, and the importance of protecting their rights (Figure 6.2).

Figure 6.2. *Juvenile offenders wait to go to the gym inside the Juvenile Detention Center, in Toledo, Ohio.*

Source: Golden (2019).

The traditional objective of juvenile detention centers has been to confine young people who have committed crimes, removing them from situations that could exacerbate their delinquent behavior. However, the conceptual underpinnings of these centers have changed significantly, according to greater penological trends. The early emphasis of the juvenile justice system was on rehabilitation and the offender's moral redemption. However, the system gradually shifted toward a punitive approach, particularly amid the emergence of "get tough on crime" policies in the late 20th century. This transformation resulted in a more carceral approach, with juvenile detention facilities resembling prisons and emphasizing punishment and social control above rehabilitation (Burrell, 2000).

The "new penology" concept, developed in the 1990s, constituted a watershed moment in how penologists and criminologists viewed juvenile incarceration facilities. According to authors such as Steinberg (2009), the new penology prioritizes regulating groups judged at risk of offending over rehabilitating individuals. In this setting, juvenile detention centers are part of a larger risk management system, with the purpose of containing the risk posed by specific parts of the adolescent population rather than reforming them. This approach reflects a growing dissatisfaction with the rehabilitative ideal, as well as a preference for actuarial measurements that favor security and efficiency above personalized care.

Despite this trend, critics of the punitive turn in juvenile justice claim that it fundamentally contradicts young people's developmental needs. They argue that juvenile prison facilities frequently fail to provide the necessary programs and interventions to enable young offenders to be rehabilitated. According to research, juveniles are developmentally distinct from adults, notably in terms of impulse control, vulnerability to peer pressure, and capacity for change. These distinctions need a juvenile justice system that promotes rehabilitation and reintegration into society, rather than one that resembles the adult penal system (de Vries et al., 2015).

Furthermore, the circumstances within many juvenile prison facilities have come under increasing criticism. A rising corpus of literature documents the negative impacts of incarceration on young people's mental health and social development. Research by Tonry, (2016) discovered a significant prevalence of co-occurring mental health illnesses among juveniles in detention centers, implying that these facilities frequently function as de facto mental health institutions without proper therapy services. Another major concern is a lack of access to high-quality education and rehabilitation programs. It has been noted on several occasions that, education in juvenile detention facilities is frequently poor, undermining one of the most important avenues for young people to better their life chances after release (Tonry, 2016). Racial inequities in the juvenile justice system present serious ethical and legal considerations. Research has consistently indicated that minority juveniles, particularly African American and Hispanic teenagers, are overrepresented in juvenile detention facilities. This overrepresentation reflects greater structural racial disparities in the criminal justice system. The role of educators and staff in juvenile detention institutions in addressing these inequities, advocate for a race-conscious pedagogy that can help resist institutional biases that contribute to these results (de Vries et al., 2015).

Efforts to improve juvenile detention centers have centered on lowering the use of incarceration and turning toward community-based alternatives that emphasize restorative justice and therapeutic therapy. Recognizing young people's developmental needs, as well as the role of family and community in their rehabilitation, is a critical component of this approach. Diversion initiatives, mentorship, and restorative justice circles are viable alternatives to detention, with a focus on mending harm and instilling a feeling of responsibility in juvenile offenders (de Vries et al., 2015). These community-based methods challenge the old carceral model and promote a more comprehensive perspective of justice that includes social assistance and prospects for redemption.

The greater ramifications of juvenile detention centers go beyond the immediate treatment of young offenders. These institutions are part of a wider carceral state, which, according to critical criminologists such as Emerson (2017), maintains social order by controlling and managing marginalized communities. According to this viewpoint, juvenile confinement serves not only to address criminal behavior but also to reinforce societal structures and discipline the impoverished and racially excluded. This viewpoint is consistent with the concept of "penal populism," in which public fear and demand for heavy punishments drive policies that may be counterproductive in terms of crime reduction and social fairness (Emerson, 2017).

Juvenile prison facilities are at a crossroads, torn between the opposing goals of punishment and rehabilitation. From a penological standpoint, their evolution mirrors larger trends in criminal justice, such as the increase in risk management and the collapse of the rehabilitative ideal. However, there is a growing realization that juvenile detention, as it currently exists, is frequently destructive to the very people it is intended to help. Addressing these concerns necessitates not just improving conditions in detention facilities, but also rethinking the purpose of custody in the juvenile justice system. By transitioning to a model that emphasizes rehabilitation, community assistance, and restorative justice, society may better address the needs of young offenders and facilitate their successful reintegration into society.

6.6. EDUCATION AND TREATMENT PROGRAMS FOR JUVENILES

Education and treatment programs for adolescents, particularly those involved in the criminal justice system, are crucial in combating delinquency and encouraging rehabilitation. The particular developmental demands of young offenders necessitate specialized techniques that not only address current behavioral concerns but also promote long-term psychological and social progress. These programs, which include community-based efforts, diversion schemes, and positive juvenile development models, aim to provide alternatives to traditional punitive tactics while emphasizing reintegration, prevention, and personal development.

Community treatment programs are an essential component of the rehabilitative landscape for minors in the court system. These projects prioritize juvenile offenders' reintegration into their communities, emphasizing the value of maintaining social connections and reducing the isolation that is common in correctional facilities. According to research, community treatment programs work best when they combine counseling, educational support, and family participation. Counseling is especially important for addressing the psychological and emotional issues that these young people encounter, as many of them have experienced trauma, abuse, or neglect. These programs also collaborate closely with educational institutions to guarantee that juveniles can continue their education, helping them catch up academically and giving them skills that will be necessary for their future success (Latessa and Lovins, 2019).

Family involvement is an important aspect of community treatment programs because it acknowledges the critical role that a stable and supportive home environment plays in the rehabilitation process. Engaging families in counseling and treatment contributes to a more comprehensive approach to rehabilitation, ensuring that the progress established in the program is sustained at home. According to research, juveniles who have good family support are more likely to complete their rehabilitation and prevent recidivism. Programs that attempt to strengthen family relationships offer a key support system for juvenile offenders as they negotiate the hurdles of reintegration (Latessa and Lovins, 2019).

Prevention and early intervention programs provide an additional layer of assistance for juveniles, focusing on at-risk adolescents before they become heavily involved in delinquent behaviors. These programs emphasize teaching social skills, encouraging positive behavior, and offering scheduled activities to keep youth involved in productive activities. Classroom management and behavior modification tactics, for example, have been demonstrated to be successful in helping young people improve their conflict resolution skills and learn how to manage their emotions (Lipsey et al., 2010). By treating behavioral concerns early on, these programs can prevent delinquent behaviors from escalating and lessen the probability of kids coming into contact with the legal system.

Afterschool activities and mentoring initiatives are also important parts of preventative plans. These programs give young people secure places in which to engage in constructive activities, form healthy relationships with peers and mentors, and discover their sense of purpose. According to research, juveniles who participate in afterschool programs are less likely to engage in dangerous behaviors such as substance misuse or violence and are more likely to achieve academic success. Mentorship, in particular, has been found to be an effective technique for assisting adolescents in developing self-esteem, setting goals, and building resilience to negative influences (Rodriguez, 2007).

Diversion programs offer an alternative to traditional legal procedures, allowing minors to obtain education and therapy instead of jail. These programs often involve educational support, substance abuse treatment, and lessons geared toward building empathy and comprehending the consequences of one's choices. Educational and tutorial services are critical components of diversion programs since many youth in the court system struggle academically. These programs help young offenders develop the skills they need to thrive in school while reducing their risk of further participation in the criminal system by offering one-on-one support and individualized learning strategies (Pupo and Zane, 2021).

Substance addiction treatment is another important aspect of diversion programs, as it is a widespread problem among minors in the court system. Addressing these difficulties early can help adolescents develop healthy coping methods and prevent future criminal conduct. Victim awareness programs, which teach adolescents about the repercussions of their conduct and foster empathy for their victims, are also key components of the rehabilitation process. These programs are intended to assist juvenile offenders realize the consequences of their actions on others, instilling a sense of duty and accountability (Petrosino et al., 2005).

Positive youth development programs focus on developing young people's strengths rather than treating their weaknesses. These programs are built on the concept that with the correct chances and support, all adolescents have the capacity to achieve. Engaging youth in community service and leadership positions is an important part of these programs because it helps them develop a sense of purpose and responsibility. These programs encourage constructive social behaviors and assist young people develop a sense of identity that is not oriented toward delinquency by engaging them in meaningful activities that benefit their communities (Leone et al., 2002).

Another important aspect of effective youth development programs is the promotion of educational and career ambitions. Many adolescents involved in the legal system have had substantial disruptions in their education, and helping them define and accomplish academic and occupational goals is critical to their long-term success. According to research, adolescents who receive educational help are more likely to graduate from high school and pursue higher education or work, greatly lowering their odds of recidivism. Programs that provide vocational training and job placement services also provide young people with the skills and resources they need to develop secure and productive lives (Petrosino et al., 2005).

In addition to the immediate benefits of education and treatment programs, these measures have long-term implications for reducing recidivism and enhancing juveniles' life outcomes. According to research, adolescents who participate in educational and treatment programs are less likely to re-offend and more likely to have productive lives. Furthermore, these initiatives contribute to breaking the cycle of poverty and crime by equipping young people with the skills they need to succeed in school and in the workplace (Chung et al., 2005).

However, there are hurdles to successfully executing these initiatives. Limited financing, a lack of skilled staff, and the difficulty of integrating services across numerous organizations can all impede the success of juvenile education and treatment programs. Furthermore, systemic challenges such as racial disparities in the juvenile justice system might impede the efficacy of these programs, as minority adolescents are frequently disproportionately affected by punitive laws and have less access to high-quality assistance (Brown, 2014).

Despite these limitations, research strongly supports the effectiveness of juvenile education and treatment programs. By emphasizing rehabilitation over punishment, these programs assist juvenile offenders in developing the skills and support systems needed to lead successful and meaningful lives. As the juvenile justice system evolves, policymakers and practitioners must prioritize the extension of these programs and ensure that all juveniles have access to the resources they require to succeed.

6.7. FUTURE OF THE JUVENILE JUSTICE SYSTEM

The future of the juvenile justice system is being determined by an expanding amount of scientific information about teenage development, notably the cognitive, emotional, and social differences between adolescents and adults.

This increasing understanding is supported by papers such as the National Research Council's "*Reforming Juvenile Justice: A Maturation Approach*," which recommends legislative solutions to juvenile offending that take into consideration the adolescent brain's maturation stage. This new approach challenges the traditional use of punitive measures like incarceration in favor of initiatives that promote accountability, personal development, and social reintegration.

The developmental approach to juvenile justice recognizes that adolescence is a critical period marked by increased vulnerability to external influences such as peer pressure and a still-developing capacity for impulse control and long-term decision-making. Adolescents are less capable than adults of controlling their actions and evaluating future repercussions, implying that they should not be held to the same accountability standards as adult criminals. The traditional juvenile justice system, which frequently mirrors punitive methods employed in adult courts, fails to account for these developmental distinctions and can harm young offenders' cognitive and emotional well-being (Cavanagh et al., 2022). According to research, punitive confinement can disrupt crucial parts of healthy development by denying youth supportive relationships, pleasant peer interactions, and opportunities for constructive decision-making.

One of the key suggestions of the "*Reforming Juvenile Justice*" study is that juvenile justice systems move from a punitive approach to one that prioritizes rehabilitation, restorative justice, and community-based initiatives. Restorative justice, in particular, presents a viable alternative to conventional punishment. This strategy encourages offenders to accept responsibility for their acts, apologize to those they have wronged, and participate in community service. Restorative justice promotes social reintegration and restores the offender's sense of responsibility by focusing on repairing harm rather than seeking revenge. Furthermore, restorative techniques are targeted to the requirements of the particular offender, providing a more individualized approach that can lead to more positive outcomes than jail (Cavanagh, 2022).

Restorative justice programs have been shown to be more effective in reducing youth recidivism than standard punitive measures. This is largely because restorative justice acknowledges the role of the social environment in determining teenage conduct. Adolescents are more likely to participate in criminal behavior if they lack supportive relationships and positive role models. The existing juvenile justice system, by isolating adolescents from their communities, may unintentionally perpetuate the very issues it aims to remedy. Restorative justice, on the other hand, connects kids to their communities and promotes positive social relationships, both of which are necessary for healthy development and preventing future offending (Rubin, 2019).

Structured risk and needs evaluations are also crucial to the future of juvenile justice reform. These assessments aid in identifying the precise reasons that lead to a youth's offending behavior, such as family dynamics, peer interactions, or mental health difficulties, allowing for targeted treatments that address the underlying causes. By concentrating on each offender's unique requirements, juvenile justice systems can provide more effective rehabilitation and lower the chance of reoffending (Monahan et al., 2015).

However, the effectiveness of these reforms is contingent on a broader reconsideration of how society perceives juvenile criminals. There is a need to shift away from the "tough on crime" approach that dominated juvenile justice policy in the late 20th century, resulting in an increase in the use of incarceration and other punitive measures. Instead, the emphasis should be on developing a system that sees young offenders as individuals in need of guidance and care, rather than irredeemable criminals. This shift in perspective is required for juvenile justice systems to achieve their dual goals of holding adolescents accountable for their acts while also encouraging their long-term growth and reintegration into society (Nellis, 2015).

Furthermore, racial inequities are a problem that needs to be addressed in any juvenile justice system reform. Minority juveniles are overrepresented in all phases of the juvenile justice system, with African American and Hispanic teenagers being the most prevalent. This overrepresentation raises concerns about the fairness of the current system and mirrors larger trends of racial inequality in society. Implementing regulations that guarantee equitable treatment for all adolescents, regardless of race or socioeconomic background, is one way to eradicate these gaps and is a crucial component of efforts to improve juvenile justice. Juvenile justice systems can improve in fairness and equity and better meet the needs of all juvenile offenders by tackling these systemic disparities (Cavanagh, 2022).

In order to treat juvenile delinquency in a more comprehensive manner, it is necessary to incorporate information from other disciplines, such as public health and social work, as juvenile justice systems develop. According to Cavanagh (2022), the public health model perceives delinquency not only as an issue of personal accountability but also as a sign of wider social and environmental problems, including financial hardship, unstable families, and limited access to healthcare and education. Juvenile justice systems are better able to prevent delinquency before it starts and give at-risk adolescents more extensive help when they tackle these core reasons.

The juvenile justice system's future depends on its ability to adapt to new information about adolescent development and incorporate evidence-based approaches that promote rehabilitation, restorative justice, and social equity.

This involves a fundamental adjustment in society's perception of juvenile offenders, as well as a commitment to developing systems that are responsive to young people's developmental needs. By accepting these improvements, juvenile justice systems can better accomplish their role of holding young people accountable, avoiding recidivism, and promoting positive growth (Armstrong, 2001).

The developmental approach to juvenile justice does not come without its obstacles. Implementing these reforms will necessitate considerable modifications to existing laws, regulations, and practices, as well as continual training for juvenile justice personnel. Furthermore, there are also difficulties about how to strike a balance between the necessity for accountability and the purpose of rehabilitation, especially when a youth poses a threat to public safety (Scott and Steinberg, 2008). However, the data suggests that a developmental approach, based on scientific knowledge of adolescent behavior and development, has the best chance of building a more effective and just juvenile justice system (Cavanagh, 2022).

The future of the juvenile justice system will be influenced by a dedication to rehabilitation, restorative justice, and evidence-based strategies that acknowledge adolescents' particular developmental needs. By shifting away from punitive measures and toward programs that foster personal growth and social reintegration, juvenile justice systems can better serve the needs of both young offenders and society as a whole. As the "*Reforming Juvenile Justice*" report makes clear, this is about more than just fairness; it is also about effectiveness. Juvenile justice systems that are aligned with developing knowledge about adolescent development are more likely to succeed in their aims of minimizing recidivism, encouraging accountability, and ensuring that all youth have the opportunity to grow into responsible and productive citizens.

Chapter 7

PROBATION AND PAROLE

Contents

Probation and parole are critical components of penology, reflecting the evolution of criminal justice systems toward rehabilitation and reintegration of offenders. Probation, which is based on modern criminology principles, allows an offender to remain in the community under supervision rather than serving time in prison. Parole, on the other hand, is the conditional release of a prisoner prior to serving their full sentence, also under supervision. Both practices emphasize community-based corrections, with the goal of reducing prison overcrowding, curbing recidivism, and fostering societal reintegration (Miller, 2015).

Penological theories emphasize that probation and parole are more humane alternatives to traditional punitive measures. As part of the rehabilitative framework, they prioritize individualized justice, acknowledging that incarceration may not always be in the best interests of either the offender or the community. Research supports that these alternatives, when properly managed, can result in lower rates of reoffending than institutional confinement (Haqanee et al., 2015) (Figure 7.1).

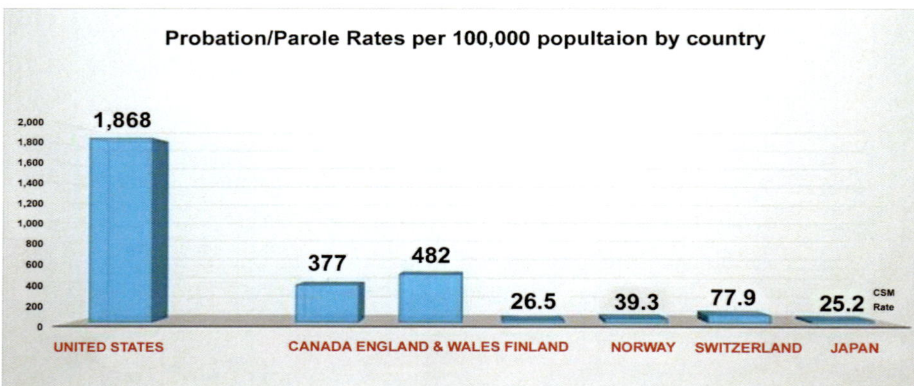

Figure 7.1. *Probation/parole rates by country.*

Source: Porporino (2018).

Key concepts in penology, such as restorative justice and deterrence, interact with probation and parole, emphasizing a balanced approach to punishment and reform. Finally, probation and parole represent an adaptive justice model that considers the social, psychological, and economic dimensions of criminal behavior (Kaeble, 2021).

7.1. ROLE OF PROBATION OFFICERS

Probation officers play a critical role in the criminal justice system, serving as the link between rehabilitation, supervision, and social reintegration. Their contribution is especially important in penology, which is increasingly emphasizing rehabilitative approaches over purely punitive measures. Probation officers represent this shift, serving as the primary agents responsible for balancing the goals of community safety, offender rehabilitation, and the broader societal goal of reducing recidivism (Miller, 2015).

The supervision function is central to probation officers' roles. They are responsible for ensuring that offenders follow the terms of their probation orders, which frequently include keeping a job, attending rehabilitation programs, and refraining from further criminal activity. Supervision is not only a punitive measure; it also allows offenders to demonstrate their ability to self-regulate outside of prison. Probation officers ensure that offenders follow the rules by conducting regular check-ins, home visits, and communicating with other criminal justice agencies. This aspect of their role aligns with the deterrence theory in penology, which contends that the constant threat of re-incarceration acts as a significant deterrent to future offending (Haqanee et al., 2015).

However, probation officers' rehabilitative function may be the most important. Rehabilitation, as a penological concept, seeks to address the root causes of criminal behavior, which range from substance abuse to socioeconomic disadvantage. Probation officers, in their daily work, act as facilitators of this rehabilitation process. They frequently connect probationers with necessary resources such as drug treatment programs, job training, mental health services, and counseling. This approach is consistent with theories of individualized justice, in which the criminal justice system tailors its interventions to the offender's specific needs rather than using a one-size-fits-all punishment model. Probation officers' ability to assess and respond to each offender's unique circumstances helps foster environments conducive to long-term behavioral change, which is a critical component of the rehabilitative ideal in penology (Jones and Kerbs, 2007; Kaeble, 2021).

In addition to these responsibilities, probation officers serve as liaisons between the courts, offenders, and the larger community. Their reports and recommendations have a significant impact on judicial decisions regarding sentencing, probation modifications, and revocations. Judges frequently rely on probation officers' assessments to determine whether an offender is a suitable candidate for probation or parole, giving them a significant influence over the outcomes of specific cases. These assessments typically include not only the offender's criminal history, but also their social circumstances, risk factors, and progress on probation. This aspect of their role emphasizes the importance of professional judgment, because probation officers must navigate complex ethical and legal landscapes while prioritizing both the offender's rights and the safety of the community (Jones and Kerbs, 2007).

Furthermore, probation officers play an important role in the overall penological goal of reintegrating offenders into society. Reintegration is one of the primary goals of probation, as it seeks to return the offender to a law-abiding lifestyle while remaining in the community. This is consistent with restorative justice principles, which view crime as not only a violation of legal norms, but also a threat to relationships and communities. Probation officers help offenders reintegrate into society by facilitating job opportunities, educational advancement, and positive social connections. In many cases, successful reintegration reduces the likelihood of recidivism, improving overall public safety (Andersen and Wildeman, 2015).

Probation officers also play an important role in the administration and enforcement of restorative justice programs, which seek to repair the harm caused by crime. These programs frequently involve mediated interactions between offenders and victims, with the goal of promoting mutual understanding and encouraging offenders to accept responsibility for their actions. The probation officer's role in this context is to ensure that the process is both constructive and supportive, providing guidance to offenders while also meeting the needs of the victim. By facilitating such restorative approaches, probation officers contribute to a larger movement in penology that seeks to reduce reliance on incarceration and emphasize reconciliation and community healing (Miller, 2015).

The changing role of probation officers mirrors broader trends in criminal justice reform. As penological thinking shifts toward decarceration and community-based corrections, probation officers are increasingly viewed as key players in reducing prison populations. This is especially true in jurisdictions where probation is used as an alternative to incarceration for nonviolent offenders. Research has shown that, when adequately supported, probation can be an effective means of reducing recidivism while also alleviating the financial and social costs associated with mass imprisonment (Jones and Kerbs, 2007).

7.2. PROBATION VS. PAROLE

These community-based sanctions aim to humanize punishment and align it more closely with the goals of reintegration, deterrence, and rehabilitation. Probation and parole are both alternatives to traditional incarceration, but they have different applications and legal frameworks. They offer offenders the opportunity to serve part or all of their sentences in the community under supervision, rather than in prison, reflecting the evolving view of crime, punishment, and social responsibility (Kaeble, 2021). Probation is typically granted as an alternative to imprisonment, with the offender placed under the supervision of a probation officer for a set period of time rather than being incarcerated. Probation is based on the assumption that incarceration is not always the best solution for all types of offenders, particularly nonviolent or first-time offenders. Probation emphasizes the concept of individualized justice, a key tenet of penology in which punishment is tailored to both the crime and the perpetrator. Probation aims to reduce the disruptive effects of imprisonment on offenders' social and economic circumstances while still holding them accountable for their actions by allowing them to remain in their community (Paparozzi and Demichele, 2008).

The conditions of probation are frequently strict, requiring offenders to follow certain rules such as maintaining employment, abstaining from substance abuse, participating in rehabilitation programs, or meeting with their probation officers on a regular basis. This reflects the rehabilitative aspect of probation, which seeks to address the underlying issues that led to the offender's criminal behavior, such as substance abuse, a lack of education, or poverty. Successful probation completion without any violations often results in the offender being released from the system with no further legal consequences, whereas violations can result in probation revocation and the imposition of the original sentence. Probation serves as both a rehabilitative tool and a deterrent, with the threat of incarceration serving as a motivator for compliance (Glaze and Bonczar, 2011).

Parole, on the other hand, is the conditional release of an offender from prison before they have completed their full sentence. A parole board determines whether a prisoner has been sufficiently rehabilitated and poses little risk to society. Unlike probation, which is a direct alternative to incarceration, parole follows a period of imprisonment and is designed to help the offender reintegrate into society after serving part of their sentence. Parole recognizes that long-term incarceration can sever offenders' ties to the community, reducing their chances of successful reintegration. In penological terms, parole embodies the idea of conditional freedom, where offenders are allowed to return to society but remain under supervision and must adhere to specific conditions (Paparozzi and Demichele, 2008).

Parole conditions frequently mirror those of probation, such as regular meetings with a parole officer, adherence to a curfew, participation in treatment programs, and refraining from criminal activity. Failure to comply with these conditions may result in parole revocation and the offender's return to prison. The parole system is a critical component of the criminal justice system's overall efforts to balance punishment and rehabilitation. It recognizes that, while imprisonment may be necessary to protect society and punish offenders, it must also take into account offenders' eventual reintegration. In this regard, parole is based on the principle of restorative justice, which seeks to repair the harm caused by crime and return the offender to a productive place in society (Glaze and Bonczar, 2011; McNamara, 2007).

According to penological theories, probation and parole are intended to serve as opportunities for reform rather than punishment mechanisms. Rehabilitation is a primary goal, and the criminal justice system is increasingly aware that many offenders, particularly those convicted of nonviolent crimes, may benefit from interventions that address the underlying causes of their criminal behavior rather than incarceration alone. Research suggests that community-based corrections, when properly implemented, can reduce recidivism rates and promote better outcomes than traditional imprisonment. Studies, for example, have shown that offenders who have access to employment, education, and treatment programs are less likely to reoffend upon release (Kaeble, 2021).

Probation and parole provide significant economic and social benefits as well. Incarceration is costly, and prison overcrowding has been a persistent issue in many countries. Probation and parole are less expensive alternatives to incarceration, relieving the state's financial burden while still holding offenders accountable and providing opportunities for rehabilitation. Furthermore, the societal impact of imprisonment, particularly on marginalized communities, has sparked calls for sentencing reform. Probation and parole help to mitigate the negative effects of imprisonment on families, particularly children, who are often disproportionately affected when a parent is incarcerated (McNamara, 2007).

Despite the benefits of probation and parole, challenges remain. The success of these programs is largely dependent on the resources available to probation and parole officers, who are responsible for managing large caseloads and ensuring that offenders follow their conditions. Officers with high caseloads may struggle to provide the level of supervision and support required for offenders to succeed. Furthermore, the public's perception of probation and parole can be negative, with concerns about community safety and the possibility of reoffending. However, studies show that probation and parole, with proper oversight, are effective tools for reducing recidivism and promoting rehabilitation (Glaze and Bonczar, 2011).

7.3. CONDITIONS OF PROBATION AND PAROLE

Both probation and parole are alternatives to incarceration, allowing offenders to serve their sentences in the community under supervised conditions. The conditions of probation and parole are critical to holding offenders accountable for their actions while also providing opportunities for reform and reintegration into society. Legal frameworks, societal expectations, and penological theories that balance punitive measures with rehabilitative goals all influence these conditions (Paparozzi and Demichele, 2008).

Probation is granted as an alternative to imprisonment and is typically assigned to offenders who are deemed to pose a low risk to the community. Probation conditions are typically stringent in order to ensure that the offender continues on a path of reform. The legal conditions for probation differ depending on the nature of the offense, the offender's criminal history, and the jurisdiction where the probation is granted. Common probation conditions include maintaining regular contact with a probation officer, refraining from committing additional crimes, abstaining from drug and alcohol use, keeping a job, and participating in rehabilitation programs such as drug treatment or counseling. The goal of these conditions is to create a structure within which the offender can address the issues that contributed to their criminal behavior, thereby reducing the likelihood of reoffending (McNamara, 2007).

The conditions of probation reflect broader penological theories like deterrence and restorative justice. The supervision provided by probation officers ensures that offenders are constantly reminded of the consequences of noncompliance, acting as a deterrent to future criminal behavior. At the same time, probation's rehabilitative programs help to restore the offender's position in society, which is consistent with restorative justice's goal of repairing the harm caused by crime. Penology acknowledges that offenders are not always inherently criminal but frequently act out of situational factors, and probation conditions are designed to address these underlying issues through structured supervision and support (Kaeble, 2021).

Parole, unlike probation, is granted after an offender has completed a portion of their prison sentence. It is typically granted to offenders who have demonstrated good behavior while incarcerated and are no longer deemed a significant threat to society. A parole board decides whether to grant parole based on the offender's behavior, criminal history, and likelihood of successful reintegration into society. The conditions of parole frequently resemble those of probation, requiring offenders to follow strict rules and regulations while living in the community under supervision. Common parole conditions include regular meetings with a parole officer, curfews, participation in treatment programs, and travel restrictions. Parolees may also be required to avoid contact with certain individuals or places that may cause the risk of reoffending (Glaze and Bonczar, 2011).

The conditions of parole are intended not only to monitor the offender's behavior, but also to facilitate their successful reintegration into society. In this sense, parole reflects the penological goal of reintegration, which emphasizes that offenders who have served a portion of their sentence should be given the opportunity to demonstrate their ability to live a law-abiding lifestyle. Parole conditions, such as mandatory employment and participation in rehabilitation programs, help to create a structured environment that facilitates the offender's reintegration into society. Research indicates that parolees who receive adequate supervision and support during their reintegration process are less likely to reoffend (Andersen and Wildeman, 2015).

Violations of probation or parole conditions can lead to serious consequences. Probation violations may result in the revocation of probation and the imposition of the original prison sentence. Similarly, parole violations can result in the parolee returning to prison to serve the remainder of their sentence. The severity of the breach, as well as the offender's overall compliance with their conditions, frequently determine the consequences of violations. For example, minor violations such as missing a meeting with a probation or parole officer may result in a warning or an adjustment to the conditions, whereas more serious violations, such as committing a new crime, are likely to result in revocation and reincarceration. This system of graduated sanctions reflects the penological theory of proportionality, which holds that the punishment should be proportional to the offense, taking into account both the seriousness of the violation and the offender's prior behavior (Paparozzi and Demichele, 2008).

The probation and parole rules and regulations are based on both legal statutes and penological theory. The court or parole board often sets probation and parole conditions, which probation and parole officers are responsible for enforcing. These officers play a critical role in the successful implementation of probation and parole by serving as both supervisors and support systems for offenders. The dual role of probation and parole officers as both law enforcement and rehabilitation facilitators reflects the larger tension in penology between punishment and reform. While probation and parole officers are tasked with ensuring that offenders comply with the conditions of their release, they are also responsible for helping offenders access the resources they require to successfully reintegrate into society (Glaze and Bonczar, 2011; McNamara, 2007).

The ability of probation and parole officers to effectively manage their caseloads, as well as the availability of resources, are critical to the successful implementation of these conditions. According to studies, high caseloads and limited resources can make it difficult for officers to provide adequate supervision and support, resulting in higher recidivism rates. This issue emphasizes the importance of investing in community-based corrections to reduce reliance on incarceration while also ensuring that probationers and parolees have access to the support they need to succeed (Paparozzi and Demichele, 2008).

7.4. SUPERVISION OF PROBATIONERS AND PAROLEES

Probation and parole supervision ensure that offenders who are not incarcerated or have been conditionally released from prison follow strict guidelines as they reintegrate into society. The goal of this supervision process is to reduce recidivism, promote public safety, and facilitate offenders' rehabilitation. Probation and parole officers are critical agents responsible for overseeing this process, ensuring compliance with the terms of probation or parole while also providing support to facilitate successful reintegration (Haqanee et al., 2015) (Figure 7.2).

Figure 7.2. *The U.S. probation and parole system.*

Source: Rodriguez (2023).

The concept of deterrence underpins probation and parole supervision. As part of their probation or parole, offenders must follow certain conditions, such as reporting to their supervising officer on a regular basis, maintaining employment, participating in rehabilitation programs, and refraining from criminal activity. The threat of revocation of probation or parole, which could result in incarceration, acts as a deterrent to future criminal behavior. This system of supervision allows offenders to avoid prison while holding them accountable for their actions. The principle of deterrence is based on the idea that consistent monitoring and the potential consequences of noncompliance will discourage offenders from engaging in additional criminal activity (Miller, 2015).

Probation and parole officers play a multifaceted role in supervision, carrying out both enforcement and rehabilitation functions. On the enforcement side, officers ensure that offenders follow the legal terms of their release. This frequently entails routine home visits, workplace visits, and meetings with the offender, as well as collaboration with law enforcement and social service agencies. Probation and parole officers monitor offenders' behavior and report any violations to the court or parole board. In cases where offenders violate the conditions of their supervision, officers may recommend sanctions that range from warnings to revocation and re-incarceration (Phelps and Curry, 2017).

However, the role of probation and parole officers is more than just enforcement. They also play an important role in the rehabilitation of offenders by connecting them to resources such as substance abuse treatment, mental health services, educational programs, and job opportunities. The rehabilitative aspect of supervision is based on penological theories of individualized justice, which advocate for interventions tailored to the offender's specific needs. Research has shown that addressing the underlying causes of criminal behavior, such as addiction or a lack of employment skills, is critical to reducing recidivism. Probation and parole officers, as facilitators of rehabilitation, work to address these issues by ensuring that offenders have access to the needed support services (Gleicher et al., 2013).

One of the most difficult challenges in supervising probationers and parolees is balancing the dual responsibilities of enforcement and rehabilitation. This tension is central to the ongoing debate in criminology about whether criminal justice's primary goal should be punishment or rehabilitation. Probation and parole officers must balance this tension by enforcing legal requirements while also fostering trust and cooperation with offenders. Officers in this dual role must exercise significant discretion when deciding how to respond to violations of supervision conditions. Instead of seeking immediate revocation, an officer may choose to provide additional support services or impose stricter monitoring conditions. This flexibility allows officers to tailor their response to each individual offender's circumstances, reflecting the penological principle of proportionality, which holds that sanctions should be commensurate with the severity of the violation (Haqanee et al., 2015; Phelps and Curry, 2017).

The success of probation and parole supervision is also dependent on the availability of resources and manageable caseloads. Overburdened probation and parole officers with heavy caseloads may struggle to provide adequate supervision, reducing the effectiveness of community-based correctional services. According to studies, high caseloads can result in less frequent contact with offenders, less time for meaningful interventions, and an overreliance on punitive rather than rehabilitative measures. Properly resourcing probation and parole departments is essential for ensuring that officers can effectively balance enforcement with rehabilitation while also providing offenders with the support they need to succeed in the community (Glaze and Bonczar, 2011; Gleicher et al., 2013).

Using risk assessment tools to determine the appropriate level of supervision for each offender is an essential component of effective supervision. Penological research supports the use of evidence-based practices that tailor the level of supervision to the offender's likelihood of reoffending. High-risk offenders require more intensive supervision, such as regular check-ins, electronic monitoring, and increased collaboration with law enforcement. Low-risk offenders, on the other hand, may benefit from less intensive supervision, freeing up officers' time to focus on those who pose a greater risk to public safety. Risk assessment tools assess an offender's criminal history, substance abuse issues, employment status, and social support networks. By using these tools, probation and parole officers can allocate their time and resources more efficiently, thereby enhancing the effectiveness of supervision (Gleicher et al., 2013).

Community involvement is another important aspect of probation and parole supervision. The success of community-based corrections is frequently dependent on the offender's ability to reintegrate into society, which necessitates assistance from a variety of social institutions, including employers, educational institutions, and community organizations. Probation and parole officers frequently serve as liaisons between the offender and the community, advocating for the offender's access to employment, education, and housing while also addressing the community's safety concerns. This role is consistent with the principles of restorative justice, a penological theory that emphasizes the importance of repairing crime-related harm and returning the offender to a productive role in the community. Restorative justice promotes community participation in the rehabilitation process, acknowledging that successful reintegration requires support from multiple stakeholders (Glaze and Bonczar, 2011; Miller, 2015).

Supervision also plays an important role in reducing recidivism, which is a major goal of penology. Research has shown that offenders who receive adequate supervision and access to rehabilitative services are less likely to reoffend than those who are incarcerated without such support. As a result, effective supervision contributes not only to public safety, but also to long-term crime reduction by addressing the root causes of criminal behavior. This reflects the rehabilitative ideal in penology, which holds that the criminal justice system should focus not only on punishing offenders but also on preparing them to successfully return to society (Paparozzi and Demichele, 2008).

Despite its advantages, probation and parole supervision is not without challenges. One of the primary concerns is that supervision may become overly punitive, particularly when violations of conditions result in revocation and re-incarceration. Critics argue that using technical violations, such as missing a probation officer meeting or failing a drug test, can result in disproportionate incarceration, even if the offender poses little risk to public safety. This has led to calls for reform in the use of probation and parole conditions, advocating for a more balanced approach that prioritizes rehabilitation and only uses imprisonment as a last resort (Phelps and Curry, 2017).

7.5. EFFECTIVENESS OF PROBATION AND PAROLE IN REHABILITATION

Probation and parole are critical components of community-based correctional systems that aim to provide alternatives to incarceration while also promoting offenders' rehabilitation. These systems prioritize reintegration, aiming to address the root causes of criminal behavior and reduce recidivism. Both approaches rely on structured supervision and intervention programs designed to reduce criminal behavior. However, the extent to which probation and parole are effective in achieving rehabilitation has been an ongoing debate (Paparozzi and Demichele, 2008).

The rehabilitative ideal that underpins probation and parole focuses on addressing the underlying causes of criminal behavior and assisting an offender's reintegration into society. The key principles are to provide tailored interventions, promote social control, and reduce recidivism. A major challenge is the gap between these systems' rehabilitative goals and the practical realities of their implementation. Insufficient resources frequently result in high caseloads for probation and parole officers, limiting their ability to provide individualized attention and support rehabilitation (Gleicher et al., 2013). The disparity between goals and available resources reduces the overall effectiveness of probation and parole in achieving long-term behavioral change.

One of the most important factors in determining the effectiveness of probation and parole is the risk level of offenders. Rehabilitation programs are typically most beneficial to medium- and high-risk offenders, whereas low-risk offenders may not require intensive supervision or intervention. The Risk-Needs-Responsivity (RNR) model proposes that rehabilitation efforts be proportionate to the offender's risk of recidivism and tailored to their specific criminogenic needs. Despite theoretical support for RNR, its application is inconsistent, limiting the overall effectiveness of probation and parole in reducing criminal behavior (Bhutta, 2010).

The success of probation and parole in promoting rehabilitation is also dependent on the availability and quality of rehabilitative programs. Cognitive-behavioral therapy (CBT), substance abuse treatment, and educational and vocational training are popular interventions for addressing the underlying causes of criminal behavior, such as substance abuse and poor problem-solving skills. However, budgetary constraints, geographic availability, and logistical barriers frequently limit access to these programs, preventing many probationers and parolees from fully participating in rehabilitative services that could facilitate their successful reintegration (Bhutta, 2010; Paparozzi and Demichele, 2008).

Technical violations, which occur when offenders violate the terms of their probation or parole without committing new crimes, pose a significant challenge to the effectiveness of these programs. Common technical violations include failing drug tests, missing appointments, and breaking curfews. These violations account for a significant portion of probation and parole revocations, which frequently result in re-incarceration, disrupting the rehabilitative process and increasing the likelihood of recidivism. To address this issue, a graduated sanctions system—proportional responses to violations based on their severity—has been proposed as a way to reduce revocations and improve compliance with probation and parole conditions (Andersen and Wildeman, 2015).

Another important area of focus is the role of social bonds in the rehabilitation process. According to social control theory, people are less likely to engage in criminal behavior when they are closely connected to traditional social institutions such as family, work, and education. Probation and parole have the potential to strengthen these social bonds by allowing offenders to maintain connections with family and community, as opposed to incarceration, which frequently severes these ties. By keeping offenders in the community, probation and parole facilitate the maintenance of social relationships, which can act as preventative factors against future criminal activity (McNamara, 2007).

Despite their potential for rehabilitation, probation and parole face significant challenges in promoting long-term reintegration. One of the most persistent barriers is the stigma associated with having a criminal record, which can make it difficult for an offender to find work, live in a home, or attend school. These collateral consequences of a criminal conviction make it difficult for offenders to successfully reintegrate, even if they follow the terms of their probation or parole and attend rehabilitation programs. This creates a cycle of marginalization that increases the risk of reoffending and emphasizes the need for broader reforms to address the structural barriers to reintegration (Bhutta, 2010).

Another factor influencing the effectiveness of probation and parole is an overreliance on monitoring and control measures. While supervision is necessary, a focus on monitoring can undermine rehabilitative efforts. Offenders who perceive supervision as punitive rather than supportive may be less likely to participate in rehabilitation programs meaningfully. Increased emphasis on offender agency, which allows them to take more responsibility for their rehabilitation process, may result in better outcomes and deeper engagement with rehabilitative efforts (Andersen and Wildeman, 2015).

7.6. CHALLENGES FACED BY PROBATION AND PAROLE OFFICERS

Probation and parole officers play an important role in the criminal justice system by supervising offenders in the community, assisting with their reintegration, and ensuring legal compliance. However, the nature of their responsibilities, which include balancing rehabilitation and public safety, poses numerous challenges. These challenges can be classified into several categories, including heavy caseloads, limited resources, the complexity of offender needs, legal constraints, and the emotional toll officers face. These elements not only complicate the officers' work, but also have a significant impact on the effectiveness of probation and parole as rehabilitation mechanisms (Paparozzi and Demichele, 2008).

Among the most difficult challenges for probation and parole officers is managing large caseloads. Officers are frequently tasked with supervising large groups of offenders, which limits the amount of time and attention they can give to each individual. This strain jeopardizes the quality of supervision and the officer's ability to provide the necessary rehabilitative services. Probation and parole officers are responsible for monitoring compliance with legal conditions, administering drug tests, ensuring participation in rehabilitation programs, and addressing violations as they arise. However, the sheer volume of cases frequently prevents them from allocating adequate time to individualized case management. The inability to provide tailored support to each offender undermines the rehabilitative potential of probation and parole, as offenders may not receive the necessary guidance and resources to address the underlying causes of their criminal behavior (Haqanee et al., 2015).

Resource constraints exacerbate the difficulties officers face in their jobs. Inadequate funding frequently results in limited access to rehabilitation programs such as substance abuse treatment, mental health services, and vocational training, all of which are critical to reducing recidivism. Probation and parole officers are responsible for referring offenders to these programs, but service availability varies greatly depending on jurisdiction and budget priorities. When such programs are unavailable or underfunded, officers have few options for facilitating offenders' rehabilitation, increasing the likelihood of recidivism. This lack of resources creates a gap between the theoretical objectives of probation and parole, which are to support reintegration and reduce recidivism, and the practical limitations that officers encounter in fulfilling these goals (Kaeble, 2021).

Another challenge arises from the complex and diverse needs of offenders under supervision. Offenders frequently present with a variety of problems, including substance abuse, mental health disorders, housing insecurity, and unemployment, all of which contribute to their criminal behavior. Probation and parole officers must address these diverse needs while also enforcing legal compliance, due to their dual role as law enforcement agents and social workers. This duality can cause tension because officers must balance providing assistance with the need to ensure public safety and respond to violations. This balancing act is especially difficult when dealing with high-risk offenders or individuals with extensive criminal histories, because officers must assess and manage the risk of recidivism while also attempting to rehabilitate the individual (Paparozzi and Demichele, 2008).

The legal constraints imposed on probation and parole officers also pose significant challenges. Officers work within a set of laws and regulations that govern how they respond to violations of probation or parole conditions. In many cases, these violations, such as missed appointments, positive drug tests, or failure to attend mandated programs, result in revocations, which can lead to the offender's re-incarceration. The strict enforcement of these rules can undermine probation and parole's rehabilitative efforts, as offenders may face severe penalties for minor infractions. Officers are frequently caught in a quandary, as they must follow legal protocols while also acknowledging that incarceration may not be the most effective response to minor violations. This issue reflects a broader tension within the criminal justice system, where punitive measures often take precedence over rehabilitative approaches, even though the latter may be more effective in addressing the root causes of criminal behavior (Bhutta, 2010).

Another significant challenge for probation and parole officers is the emotional and psychological toll they face. Officers work in high-stress environments and frequently interact with people who may pose a threat to public safety or are dealing with serious personal issues such as addiction, mental illness, or domestic instability. The emotional burden of managing offenders who may reoffend or violate their conditions, combined with the responsibility of making decisions that can have life-changing consequences for the offenders, puts a significant strain on officers. This stress is exacerbated by the possibility of physical harm, as officers may have to supervise individuals with violent backgrounds or conduct home visits in dangerous environments. The cumulative effects of these stressors can lead to burnout, which in turn affects the officer's ability to effectively perform their duties (McNamara, 2007).

In addition to these operational challenges, probation and parole officers must navigate the broader societal stigma associated with offenders. The stigma associated with a criminal record frequently restricts offenders' access to employment, housing, and social services, making successful reintegration into society challenging. Officers face the challenge of advocating for offenders in a system that may be resistant to giving them second chances. This societal resistance complicates probation and parole's rehabilitative mission, as officers must help offenders overcome barriers to reintegration while also managing public expectations of punishment and accountability. The public's emphasis on punitive measures can pressure officers to prioritize compliance and punishment over rehabilitation, even when the latter would be more beneficial for long-term public safety (Haqanee et al., 2015).

Officer discretion is also a significant factor in the challenges they face. Probation and parole officers are frequently required to make decisions about how to respond to violations or how to handle individual cases. While discretion is necessary, it can lead to inconsistencies in how officers handle similar cases, especially when it comes to revocation or the imposition of sanctions for violations. Officers must weigh the potential risks to public safety against the offender's rehabilitative progress, a difficult decision that may differ depending on the officer's experience, training, and personal philosophy. The challenge is exacerbated by the absence of clear, standardized guidelines for exercising discretion, making it difficult for officers to balance their roles as both enforcers of the law and facilitators of rehabilitation (Paparozzi and Demichele, 2008).

7.7. ALTERNATIVES TO INCARCERATION

Alternatives to incarceration have become a hot topic in penology, as scholars and policymakers seek to address the limitations and negative consequences of traditional imprisonment. Probation, parole, restorative justice programs, and diversion initiatives are examples of alternatives that aim to provide rehabilitative opportunities while lowering the social and economic costs of incarceration. The underlying premise is that not all offenders require incarceration to be rehabilitated or deterred, and in many cases, community-based sanctions can better achieve the dual goals of public safety and offender rehabilitation. Alternatives to incarceration reflect broader shifts in criminal justice policy, moving away from purely punitive approaches and toward more rehabilitative and restorative models (Bonta and Andrews, 2016).

Probation is a popular alternative to imprisonment. Probation allows offenders to serve their sentences in the community instead of in prison, with the goal of promoting reintegration and rehabilitation. The idea behind probation is that many offenders, particularly those convicted of nonviolent or low-level crimes, do not pose a significant threat to public safety and can benefit from structured supervision while remaining connected to family, employment, and community. Probation emphasizes adherence to court-imposed conditions such as regular meetings with a probation officer, participation in treatment programs, and observance of curfews or other restrictions. Probation's rehabilitative potential stems from its ability to address the root causes of criminal behavior, such as substance abuse, unemployment, or mental health issues, while allowing offenders to remain connected to the social structures that can facilitate their reintegration. However, probation also carries risks, particularly when resources are limited or when caseloads for probation officers are high, which can compromise the effectiveness of supervision (Kim, 2018).

Parole, another alternative to incarceration, is the conditional release of an offender from prison before the end of their sentence, with continued community supervision. Parole is based on the idea that gradual reintegration into society under supervision is more effective than immediate release after serving a full prison sentence. Parole boards typically consider an offender's behavior while incarcerated, participation in rehabilitation programs, and the likelihood of successful reintegration when deciding whether to grant parole. Like probation, parole emphasizes a balance of supervision and support, with conditions imposed to reduce the likelihood of recidivism. The effectiveness of parole as a rehabilitative tool depends on the availability of support services, such as job training, housing assistance, and mental health care, which can help parolees navigate the challenges of reentering society after incarceration (Wood, 2015).

Restorative justice is a more transformative alternative to incarceration, focusing on repairing the harm caused by criminal behaviour through processes involving both the offender and the victim. Instead of punishment, restorative justice seeks to address the needs of all parties affected by the crime while also promoting accountability, healing, and reconciliation. Victim-offender mediation, community conferencing, and circle sentencing are all key practices in restorative justice, with the goal of facilitating dialogue between offenders and victims and reaching mutually acceptable resolutions. The underlying philosophy of restorative justice is that crime harms individuals and communities, and that addressing this harm necessitates more than punitive measures. Instead, restorative justice emphasizes offender accountability and personal transformation in order to reduce recidivism and foster community involvement in the justice system. While restorative justice has been primarily used in cases involving juvenile offenders or less serious crimes, it has gained traction as a viable alternative for dealing with a broader range of offenses (Bonta and Andrews, 2016; Kim, 2018).

Diversion programs are an important alternative to traditional incarceration, especially for first-time offenders and those charged with nonviolent crimes. Diversion programs seek to redirect offenders away from the formal criminal justice system and toward community-based treatment or rehabilitation programs. These initiatives are frequently used in cases involving substance abuse or mental health issues, where treating the underlying cause of criminal behavior is more effective than punishing it. Diversion programs can take many forms, such as drug courts, mental health courts, and community service requirements. The benefit of diversion is that it allows offenders to avoid the stigma and long-term consequences of a criminal conviction while receiving the treatment and support they require to address the factors that led to their offending. By providing an alternative path, diversion programs reduce the burden on the criminal justice system and avoid the negative consequences of incarceration, such as disruption of family life, loss of employment, and exposure to more serious criminal influences in prison (Kim, 2018; Wood, 2015).

Fines and community service are less intrusive alternatives to incarceration. Fines, when properly scaled to an offender's ability to pay, can be an effective punishment for minor offenses that do not require imprisonment. Community service, which requires offenders to contribute time and labor to public projects or charitable organizations, is intended to raise offenders' awareness of their social responsibilities while compensating for the harm caused by their actions. These sanctions preserve the punitive aspect of sentencing while avoiding the high social and economic costs associated with incarceration. However, the effectiveness of fines and community service as alternatives depends on the appropriate matching of the sanction to the offense and offender, as well as the availability of compliance monitoring programs (Glaze and Bonczar, 2011).

Electronic monitoring and house arrest have emerged as technological alternatives to incarceration, allowing offenders to serve their sentences under surveillance rather than in prison. Electronic monitoring usually entails the use of ankle bracelets or other tracking devices that allow authorities to track an offender's location and ensure compliance with restrictions like curfews or geographical boundaries. House arrest, in which offenders are confined to their homes except for approved activities such as work, school, or medical appointments, is a non-incarceration punishment option. These alternatives have the advantage of preserving family and community ties while lowering the financial and social costs of incarceration. However, concerns remain regarding the potential for over-surveillance and the stigmatizing effects of electronic monitoring, as well as the effectiveness of house arrest in addressing the underlying causes of criminal behavior (Bonta and Andrews, 2016; Kim, 2018).

Finally, alternatives to incarceration reflect a larger shift in penology toward more rehabilitative and restorative forms of justice. These alternatives recognize that imprisonment is not always the most effective way to combat crime, and that community-based sanctions can offer more meaningful opportunities for rehabilitation and reintegration. The challenge is to ensure that these alternatives are adequately resourced, applied equitably, and supported by evidence-based practices that address the underlying causes of offending behavior. Alternatives to incarceration have the potential to reduce recidivism, promote public safety, and relieve the overburdened prison system by providing a range of sanctions tailored to offenders' needs and the severity of their crimes (Wood, 2015).

Chapter 8

CAPITAL PUNISHMENT

Contents

Capital punishment remains one of the most contentious punitive measures in criminal justice. Penology, or the study of punishment and prison management, investigates the effectiveness, morality, and social implications of capital punishment. Capital punishment, which has its roots in the retributive theory of justice, seeks to provide the ultimate form of retribution for heinous crimes, most notably murder. Scholars have scrutinized its deterrent effect, with studies offering mixed results on whether it significantly reduces crime rates (Zimring, 2004) (Figure 8.1).

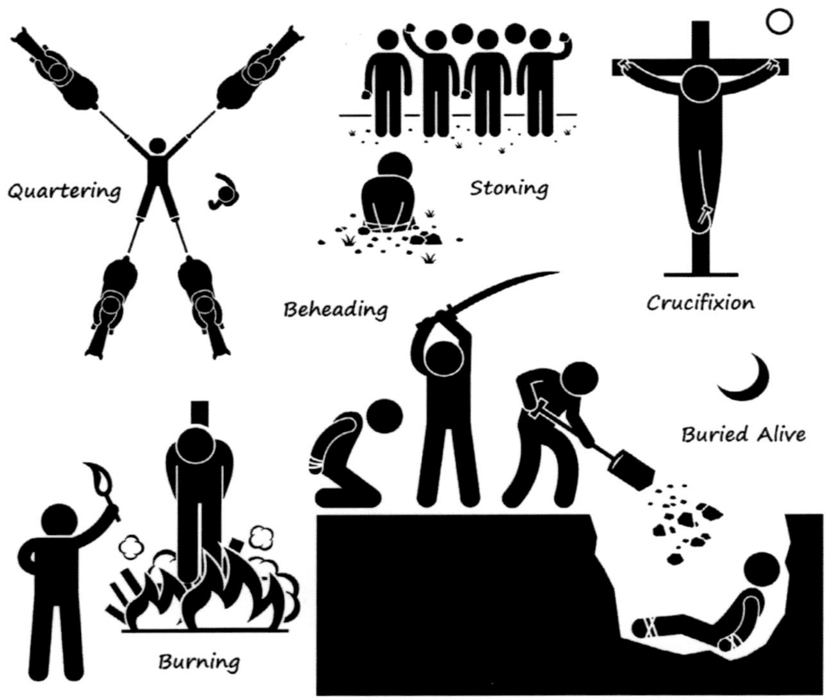

Figure 8.1. *Set of pictograms depicting ancient execution methods: quartering, stoning, crucifixion, burning, beheading, burial.*

Source: Thirst (2020).

When it comes to the death penalty, key penological concepts like deterrence, reformation, and incapacitation frequently collide. Deterrence theory suggests that the threat of capital punishment deters potential offenders, but empirical evidence does not back up this claim. Furthermore, penology emphasizes rehabilitation, a concept that capital punishment inherently negates, raising ethical concerns about its irreversibility and the risk of wrongful executions (Sarat, 2002).

Moreover, numerous academic studies have raised concerns about the social implications of capital punishment, such as racial bias and socioeconomic disparities in its application. Thus, capital punishment poses a significant challenge to contemporary penology, requiring ongoing critical assessment within the context of justice, fairness, and human rights (Edens et al., 2005).

8.1. HISTORY OF CAPITAL PUNISHMENT

The institution of capital punishment has ancient roots that can be traced back to Mesopotamia, Egypt, and Greece. In these societies, the death penalty was frequently used to maintain law and order in the absence of formal policing systems. Execution was used not only to punish individuals for serious crimes such as murder or treason but also as a public spectacle to deter others. This connection between punishment and deterrence, central to the practice of capital punishment, is a theme that has endured throughout history (Sarat, 2002).

The death penalty has its origins in early legal systems such as ancient Mesopotamia's Code of Hammurabi and the 12 tables of Roman law. The death penalty was frequently used in these early legal frameworks for a variety of offenses, including theft and blasphemy, indicating a rigid and often draconian approach to justice. Capital punishment was deemed necessary to instill fear in the population, thereby preventing crime and maintaining social cohesion. This concept of deterrence, though controversial, continues to influence modern debates around the death penalty, particularly in the context of penology (Edens et al., 2005).

The scope and application of the death penalty evolved along with Western legal traditions. During the Middle Ages in Europe, capital punishment became more formalized, particularly in monarchies that saw the death penalty as an essential tool for maintaining royal power. Treason and other crimes against the state were frequently punishable by the harshest penalties, including public executions. Public executions served two functions: they were punitive but also deeply symbolic, reinforcing the sovereign's control over life and death and deterring potential insurgencies or acts of rebellion (Edens et al., 2005).

By the 18th century, the death penalty was under increasing scrutiny from philosophers and legal reformers, particularly during the Enlightenment. Cesare Beccaria, for example, argued in his seminal work On Crimes and Punishments (1764) that capital punishment was ineffective as a deterrent. Beccaria's critique emphasized that the death penalty was frequently arbitrary and contradicted emerging justice ideals that favored proportionality and rational punishment.

His arguments had a significant impact on subsequent legal reforms in Europe, leading to a gradual decrease in the use of capital punishment in the late 18th and 19th centuries (Zimring, 2004).

The rise of penology as an academic discipline fueled further transformations in punishment theory and practice during the 19th century. Penologists began to advocate for a shift away from punitive measures aimed solely at retribution and deterrence, and toward a rehabilitative approach to criminal justice. The prison system, in particular, was viewed as a more humane alternative to the death penalty because it emphasized reforming offenders through isolation, labor, and moral instruction. During this period, many countries restricted or abolished the death penalty due to the increasing number of prisons and growing concerns about the fairness and irreversibility of capital punishment (Sarat, 2002; Zimring, 2004).

Despite the growing opposition to capital punishment, it remained firmly entrenched in many legal systems well into the 20th century. In the United States, for example, the death penalty remained widely used, particularly in the southern states. During this period, racial and economic biases in the application of the death penalty became a major issue, with critics claiming that capital punishment disproportionately affected marginalized populations. These concerns echoed broader debates within penology regarding the role of social inequality in shaping criminal justice outcomes (Edens et al., 2005; Sarat, 2002).

The post-World War II period saw a renewed global push to abolish the death penalty, particularly in light of emerging human rights standards. International treaties, such as the Universal Declaration of Human Rights (1948), began to frame the death penalty as a violation of the right to life, prompting many countries to reconsider its application. The growing emphasis on rehabilitation and restorative justice in penology has pushed the death penalty further out of favor as a legitimate form of punishment. By the late 20th century, a significant number of countries had abolished the death penalty, reflecting larger societal shifts toward more humane and rehabilitative approaches to criminal justice (Sarat, 2002).

Nonetheless, capital punishment remains a contentious issue in the 21st century, particularly in countries like the United States, China, and Iran, where it is still used. In these situations, the death penalty is frequently justified on the basis of deterrence and retribution, particularly for crimes like murder and terrorism. However, within penological discourse, the death penalty is increasingly seen as an anachronistic form of punishment, incompatible with modern notions of justice that prioritize rehabilitation, fairness, and the protection of human rights (Zimring, 2004).

8.2. ARGUMENTS FOR AND AGAINST CAPITAL PUNISHMENT

Penological insights offer a nuanced understanding of the arguments for and against capital punishment, placing these viewpoints within larger theoretical frameworks such as retribution, deterrence, rehabilitation, and human rights. Each of these frameworks provides insights into the ethical, social, and practical dimensions of the death penalty, while also raising critical questions about the values that support modern justice systems (Zimring, 2004).

One of the primary arguments in favor of the death penalty, particularly within the context of retributive justice, is that it responds proportionately to the most heinous crimes. Retribution is based on the idea that punishment should be proportionate to the gravity of the crime; for crimes such as premeditated murder, proponents argue that no punishment other than death can adequately express society's condemnation. This viewpoint emphasizes moral balance and justice for victims, arguing that the death penalty is a necessary form of retribution for the most heinous crimes. Within this framework, the death penalty is viewed not only as a tool of justice but also as a moral obligation to ensure that perpetrators face the punishment they deserve. From a penological standpoint, this approach aligns with traditional concepts of justice that prioritize the notion of punishment as a necessary consequence of wrongdoing (Sarat, 2002).

Another common argument in favor of capital punishment is its alleged deterrent effect. Proponents argue that the threat of the death penalty acts as a powerful deterrent to potential offenders, reducing the likelihood of violent crimes like murder. This argument is based on the classical criminological theory of deterrence, which asserts that the certainty and severity of punishment influence people's decisions to commit crimes. In theory, the ultimate punishment of death should have the greatest deterrent effect because it represents the highest possible cost for criminal behavior. Deterrence is closely related to the utilitarian principle of maximizing social welfare by preventing future crimes. Capital punishment, in this sense, is seen as a means of protecting society by making an example of those who commit the most serious offenses, thereby discouraging others from engaging in similar behavior (Sunstein and Vermeule, 2014; Zimring, 2004).

The incapacitation argument also supports the use of the death penalty to permanently remove dangerous criminals from society. Advocates of this position argue that certain individuals, particularly those who have committed heinous acts of violence, continue to pose a threat to public safety even after being imprisoned. In this context, the death penalty is viewed as the most effective means of neutralizing this threat, as it prevents convicted murderers from committing further crimes, either inside or outside of prison. While life imprisonment without the possibility of parole is occasionally offered as an alternative, proponents of capital punishment argue that it lacks the same level of certainty due to the possibility of escape, parole, or sentence commutation. Penological considerations of incapacitation thus focus on the need to protect society by eliminating the risk posed by individuals who have demonstrated their capacity for extreme violence (Sunstein and Vermeule, 2014).

Despite these proponents' arguments, the death penalty has received significant criticism from both ethical and practical perspectives. One of the most compelling arguments against capital punishment is its irreversible nature. The possibility of wrongful convictions, especially in cases involving circumstantial evidence or prosecutorial misconduct, has raised serious questions about the morality of executing people who may be innocent. Penology, with its emphasis on fairness and justice, emphasizes the possibility of irreversible harm if errors occur in the criminal justice system. The fallibility of legal systems, combined with the finality of death, highlights the inherent dangers of capital punishment. Critics argue that the risk of executing an innocent person outweighs any potential benefits (Unnever et al., 2008).

In addition to concerns about wrongful convictions, opponents of the death penalty claim that it fails to meet the rehabilitative goals of modern criminal justice. Rehabilitation is a central tenet of penology, reflecting the view that the primary goal of punishment should be to reform offenders and reintegrate them into society. Capital punishment, by definition, precludes any possibility of rehabilitation, making it incompatible with the principles of restorative justice. Critics argue that a justice system that values reformation cannot support a punishment that eliminates all opportunities for personal transformation. In this sense, the death penalty constitutes a fundamental contradiction within systems that otherwise embrace rehabilitative approaches to criminal justice (Sarat, 2002; Unnever et al., 2008).

The death penalty has also been criticized for its uneven application, particularly in terms of race, socioeconomic status, and geographic location. Numerous studies have found disparities in how the death penalty is applied, with marginalized groups often overrepresented on death row. From a penological standpoint, this raises serious concerns about the fairness and equity of capital punishment, implying that it may worsen existing social inequalities rather than promote justice. Critics argue that a system of punishment that disproportionately targets certain groups cannot claim to uphold principles of fairness or equality and that the arbitrary nature of the death penalty sentence undermines its legitimacy as a tool of justice (Zimring, 2004).

Furthermore, the argument that the death penalty acts as a deterrent is becoming increasingly contentious in penological discourse. Critics argue that the empirical evidence supporting the deterrent effect of capital punishment is inconclusive at best, with many studies finding little to no link between the death penalty and lower crime rates. This raises concerns about whether the death penalty achieves its stated goal of preventing future crimes, especially since alternative forms of punishment, such as life imprisonment without parole, can serve the same incapacitating function without the moral and practical risks associated with execution. The deterrence debate emphasizes the complex interplay between theory and practice in penology, as well as the need for evidence-based approaches to criminal justice policy (Unnever et al., 2008).

Finally, the death penalty is frequently considered a violation of human rights, particularly the right to life. International human rights organizations have increasingly condemned capital punishment as a form of cruel and inhumane treatment that violates the dignity of the individual. From a penological standpoint, this raises serious concerns about the ethical basis of punishment and the limits of state power in administering justice. Critics argue that the death penalty is an outdated and morally indefensible form of punishment that undermines the overarching goals of a humane and just society (Sunstein and Vermeule, 2014).

8.3. METHODS OF EXECUTION

Hanging is one of the most historically significant methods of execution, dating back to ancient times and widely used in many parts of the world. Hanging was widely regarded as a relatively simple and efficient method of carrying out capital punishment, requiring little equipment and allowing for public executions. The public nature of these hangings was an important factor, as penology has frequently emphasized the performative aspect of punishment, particularly its deterrent function. By making executions visible, authorities hoped to reinforce social norms and discourage criminal behavior through the fear of death. Hanging, however, carries the risk of extreme suffering, particularly when improperly performed, which has led to its decline in many modern legal systems as societies have moved toward less visible violent methods of execution (Garland, 2011).

The development of the guillotine during the French Revolution marked a significant shift in the mechanics and ideology of capital punishment. Unlike earlier methods, the guillotine was specifically designed to provide a quick and painless death. From a penological standpoint, the guillotine was consistent with Enlightenment ideals that sought to reduce the cruelty of punishment while retaining its effectiveness. The guillotine's rapid decapitation was regarded as more humane than methods such as hanging or sword beheading, which could be slow and gruesome. Nonetheless, as with earlier forms of execution, the guillotine became a symbol of state power and control, and its use in public executions continued to serve the dual purpose of punishment and social deterrence (Zimring, 2004).

In the 20th century, electrocution became the most common method of execution in several countries, particularly the United States. Electrocution was introduced as part of a larger trend in penology toward developing execution methods that were less overtly violent and more "scientific" in their application. The electric chair represented progress in the realm of capital punishment, as it was perceived to provide a more controlled and modern method of carrying out death sentences. However, this method has received significant ethical and practical criticism as a result of reports of botched executions that caused the condemned to suffer for an extended period of time. These issues have highlighted ongoing concerns within penology regarding the balance between administering justice and minimizing unnecessary pain, a dilemma that persists in modern debates over the death penalty (Haag and Conrad, 2013).

The gas chamber emerged as another method of execution in the 20th century, with the goal of providing a more sanitary and humane way to carry out death sentences. Drawing on technological advancements, the gas chamber was designed to cause death by inhaling lethal gas, allowing for a quick and painless end. Penologically, the introduction of the gas chamber reflected a growing emphasis on reducing the visible violence associated with executions, as well as an increased concern for the psychological well-being of both the condemned and the executioners. However, as with other methods, the gas chamber has been criticized for having the potential to cause severe pain if the procedure does not go as planned. The tension between the desire for humane punishment and the practical difficulties of achieving a painless death continues to influence discussions around the gas chamber's use in capital punishment (Garland, 2011; Haag and Conrad, 2013).

Lethal injection, which is now the most common method of execution in many countries that still use the death penalty, was introduced as part of a larger penological trend to medicalize the execution process. Lethal injection was intended to be a more humane alternative to electrocution and gas chambers, with a series of drugs administered to cause unconsciousness, paralysis, and death. Lethal injection reflects the modern desire to reduce both physical pain and the visibility of violence in executions. Its clinical nature eliminates many of the more visceral aspects of previous methods, resulting in its acceptance as a more civilized form of capital punishment. However, lethal injection, like previous methods, has sparked controversy. Cases of botched executions, where the drugs did not function as intended, have reignited debates about the ethical and practical implications of the death penalty. These incidents highlight the ongoing challenges in finding a method of execution that aligns with the penological ideals of justice, humanity, and efficiency (Haag and Conrad, 2013; Zimring, 2004) (Figure 8.2).

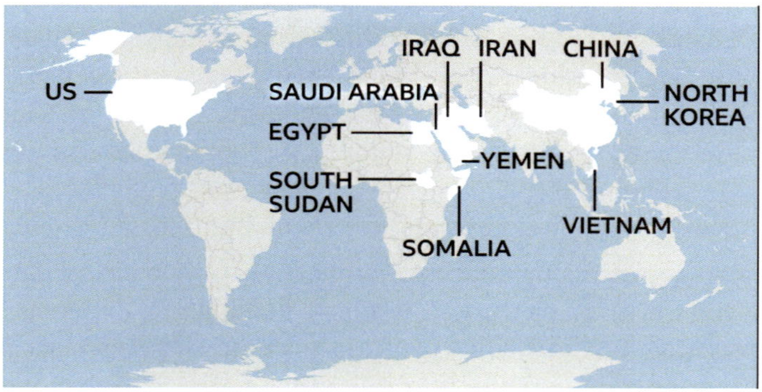

Figure 8.2. *Countries still having the death penalty.*

Source: (BBC News (2024).

In addition to these more formalized methods, firing squads are still used in some jurisdictions, often as an alternative method for individuals who choose it over lethal injection. The firing squad is one of the oldest methods of execution, historically associated with military justice. It consists of a group of shooters who fire at the condemned person at the same time, usually aiming for the heart. While less common in modern times, the firing squad is notable for its transparency and reliance on human action, as opposed to the mechanized or medicalized methods more commonly used today. Penologically, the firing squad raises important questions about the role of human agency in execution and the psychological impact on those tasked with carrying out the sentence. It also underscores the symbolic power of state-sanctioned violence, which continues to be a critical element in discussions surrounding capital punishment (Garland, 2011).

The balance between retribution and humanity has been a central concern in penology throughout these methods. While the death penalty is intended to be the most severe form of punishment for the most serious crimes, the methods used to carry it out have evolved in response to changing societal attitudes toward pain, suffering, and the dignity of the condemned. Modern penological thought emphasizes the importance of minimizing unnecessary suffering in punishment, even when the death penalty is considered a justifiable response to certain crimes. This has led to a growing preference for methods perceived as more humane, such as lethal injection, even as debates about the morality and efficacy of capital punishment itself continue (Haag and Conrad, 2013).

8.4. DEATH ROW INMATES

Death row inmates hold a unique and highly scrutinized position in the criminal justice system, representing people who have been sentenced to death but are awaiting the final imposition of their punishment. From a penological standpoint, the study of death row inmates includes an examination of the psychological, social, and legal aspects of their confinement, as well as the broader implications of capital punishment (Cunningham and Vigen, 2002).

One of the most pressing concerns in the study of death row inmates is the time they spend awaiting execution. In many jurisdictions, inmates can spend years, if not decades, on death row, often due to lengthy legal appeals, procedural delays, and the inherent complexities of capital cases. This prolonged period of uncertainty presents significant challenges, both for the inmates and for the institutions responsible for their confinement. The prolonged nature of death row confinement raises concerns about the psychological toll of such conditions, as inmates are frequently isolated, subjected to strict security measures, and constantly reminded of their impending execution. This phenomenon, sometimes referred to as "death row syndrome," reflects the intense mental strain that can result from living in the shadow of death, compounded by the monotony and isolation of life on death row (Cunningham and Vigen, 2002).

Death row inmates typically face more restrictive confinement conditions than other prisoners. Because of the severity of their sentences, death row inmates are frequently housed in maximum-security facilities, where they may be subjected to extended periods of solitary confinement, limited contact with other inmates, and restricted access to programs and activities. These conditions are justified by security concerns, as people on death row are often thought to be more likely to commit violence or flee. However, penological critics of this approach argue that such isolation has a negative impact on inmates' mental and emotional well-being. The use of solitary confinement, in particular, has been the subject of growing scrutiny, as research increasingly suggests that prolonged isolation can exacerbate mental health problems, lead to feelings of hopelessness, and contribute to a sense of dehumanization (Heflick, 2005; Zimring, 2004).

The legal and procedural aspects of managing death row inmates pose significant challenges. The appeals process in capital cases is frequently lengthy and complex, with multiple layers of judicial review to ensure that the sentence is fair and that no legal errors have occurred. While this procedure is intended to protect the rights of the condemned and reduce the risk of wrongful execution, it can also contribute to the long periods of time inmates spend on death row. Penologists argue that the delay undermines both the retributive and deterrent functions of capital punishment, as the punishment is not carried out quickly enough to serve as an effective deterrent or to provide victims and their families with prompt justice. Additionally, the uncertainty surrounding the outcome of these appeals can exacerbate the psychological stress experienced by death row inmates, who must endure the possibility of reprieve or execution for years on end (Heflick, 2005).

The demographic characteristics of death row inmates raise important questions about the fairness and equity of the death penalty. In many jurisdictions, studies have found that death row populations are disproportionately made up of people from marginalized racial, ethnic, and socioeconomic groups. This has led to criticisms of the death penalty for being biased in its application, with certain groups receiving more death sentences than others. Penologists have investigated how race, class, and geography affect the likelihood of receiving a death sentence, highlighting systemic inequalities in the criminal justice system. These disparities raise concerns about the legitimacy of capital punishment as a tool of justice, especially when it appears to be applied discriminatorily or arbitrarily (Sarat, 2002).

In addition to concerns about bias, the risk of executing innocent people is high in discussions about death row inmates. Advances in forensic science, particularly DNA testing, have resulted in the exoneration of people who were wrongfully convicted and sentenced to death. This has raised awareness of the possibility of error in the justice system, with penologists citing the irreversible nature of the death penalty as a particularly troubling aspect of its implementation. The possibility of wrongful conviction casts a shadow over the entire process, fueling debates about the morality and practicality of keeping death row in modern justice systems (Sunstein and Vermeule, 2014).

Another important aspect of death row inmates' lives is their interaction with the outside world. In many cases, death row inmates maintain contact with family members, friends, and supporters despite the restrictions on their activities. These relationships can provide crucial emotional and psychological support, providing a sense of connection and humanity in the midst of isolation on death row. Studies have investigated the role of these social ties in assisting inmates in coping with the stresses of confinement, noting that the restrictive conditions of death row frequently limit access to visitors, correspondence, and legal counsel. The ability to keep some semblance of a personal life even while facing execution raises important questions about the role of compassion and rehabilitation in the treatment of death row inmates (Cunningham and Vigen, 2002).

Finally, the prospect of clemency or commutation provides a glimmer of hope for some death row inmates, though this is extremely rare. Governors or other high-ranking officials typically grant clemency in cases where there are compelling reasons to show mercy, such as doubts about guilt, mitigating circumstances, or concerns about the trial's fairness. The availability of clemency reflects the tension between the finality of capital punishment and the possibility of redemption or rehabilitation. While clemency can provide relief for individual inmates, its rarity highlights the harsh and inflexible nature of the death penalty system (Heflick, 2005).

8.5. WRONGFUL CONVICTIONS AND EXONERATIONS

Wrongful convictions and exonerations are an important topic in penology because they highlight basic errors in the criminal justice system that lead to miscarriages of justice. Wrongful convictions occur when someone is found guilty of crimes they did not commit, which can result in lengthy sentences or even death penalties. These mistakes are corrected by exonerations, which occur when fresh evidence, frequently DNA-based, demonstrates the innocence of the mistakenly condemned. The convergence of erroneous convictions and the broader discipline of penology, which focuses on offenders' punishment and rehabilitation, raises serious concerns about the justice system's effectiveness, fairness, and humanity.

The breadth of wrongful convictions is much greater than commonly assumed. While high-profile DNA exonerations garner public attention, many erroneous convictions go unnoticed because DNA evidence is not always available. The National Registry of Exonerations records hundreds of such cases in the United States, illustrating the systemic nature of the problem. These unjust convictions are frequently caused by a combination of factors, including eyewitness misidentification, false confessions, police and prosecutorial misconduct, and weak legal defense. Each of these issues highlights deeper systemic faults within the judicial system, highlighting the need for reform to prevent future miscarriages of justice (Cunningham and Vigen, 2002).

The use of flawed forensic evidence is a key contributor to erroneous convictions. Forensic techniques that were originally thought to be flawless, such as bite mark analysis or hair comparison, have been undermined by fresh scientific discoveries. In several cases, erroneous forensic conclusions resulted in false convictions that could only be overturned years later with DNA evidence. This emphasizes the importance of tighter scientific standards in the courts and more rigorous regulation of forensic labs and practitioners (Garrett, 2020).

Eyewitness misidentification is another prominent contributing factor to false convictions, especially in violent crimes. According to psychological research, human memory is highly fallible, and witnesses frequently accidentally misidentify suspects as a result of stress, bad lighting conditions, or suggestive police lineups. These misidentifications are especially troubling because they are often the only evidence linking a suspect to a crime. The penological ramifications are considerable, as individuals convicted on such untrustworthy evidence may spend decades in prison for crimes they did not commit, fundamentally undermining the purpose of punishment in the criminal justice system.

False confessions are yet another unpleasant aspect of erroneous convictions. Despite the contrary, a large majority of wrongful convictions involve people who confessed to crimes they did not commit. Psychological pressure, tiredness, anxiety, and even manipulation by law enforcement can lead to innocent persons confessing, especially among minors or those with cognitive disabilities. The penological system's reliance on such confessions, even in the lack of supporting evidence, indicates a long-standing problem with interrogation procedures and emphasizes the necessity for legal measures to protect vulnerable individuals from forced questioning.

The role of race in unjust convictions cannot be ignored. Research repeatedly shows that ethnic minorities, particularly African Americans, are overrepresented among persons mistakenly convicted and later exonerated (Garrett, 2020). This racial discrepancy reflects greater issues of systemic racism in the criminal justice system, including biased police, racial profiling, and discriminatory jury selection. When racial minorities are unfairly convicted, the consequences go beyond the individuals themselves, leading to a greater sense of distrust in the legal system and hindering efforts to foster rehabilitation and reintegration into society (Tonry, 2016).

In recent years, the introduction of DNA testing has proved critical in obtaining exonerations for falsely condemned people. Organizations such as the Innocence Project have used DNA evidence to challenge convictions based on weak or circumstantial evidence, proving hundreds of people's innocence. While DNA testing has been an effective tool in correcting some unjust convictions, it is only available in a small number of cases, especially in older cases where biological evidence may no longer be maintained. This constraint highlights the need for more comprehensive criminal justice changes that go beyond DNA-based exonerations (Norris et al., 2020).

Wrongful convictions have significant repercussions both for the individuals involved and for society as a whole. Individuals who have been wrongfully convicted frequently suffer significant challenges following release, such as stigmatization, psychological trauma, and difficulty finding work or housing. The experience of being falsely convicted can leave lasting psychological scars, as many exonerees serve years or even decades in jail before their innocence is established. Furthermore, the financial recompense offered to exonerees is sometimes insufficient to remedy the long-term harm inflicted by years of incarceration (Westervelt and Cook, 2010).

From a penological standpoint, unjust convictions call into question the criminal justice system's entire purpose. Penology, which deals with the punishment and rehabilitation of criminals, assumes that people being punished are guilty. When innocent people are imprisoned, the entire penological system crumbles, with punishment becoming arbitrary and rehabilitation impossible. Wrongfully punishing innocent people undermines the credibility of the criminal justice system and erodes public belief in its ability to achieve justice (Zimring, 2004).

Furthermore, unjust convictions have far-reaching consequences for crime prevention and public safety. When innocent people are imprisoned for crimes they did not commit, the genuine culprits roam free, posing a continuing threat to society. This failure to arrest actual offenders undermines the criminal justice system's deterrent effect by sending the message that the system is incapable of effectively identifying and punishing criminals. Furthermore, the resources used to prosecute and imprison innocent people could be better spent on crime prevention and rehabilitation programs that address the underlying reasons for criminal behavior (Zimring, 2004).

The systemic nature of wrongful convictions has sparked calls for criminal justice reform on both the procedural and institutional fronts. Reforms designed to improve the accuracy of criminal investigations, such as the use of blind lineups and video-recorded interrogations, have been demonstrated to lessen the likelihood of false convictions. Furthermore, the creation of conviction integrity units within prosecutors' offices has proven effective in examining previous convictions and identifying probable cases of erroneous convictions. These teams, which operate independently of the police and prosecution, play an important role in ensuring that justice is served, even when initial convictions are based on defective evidence (Useem & Morrison Piehl, 2008).

Therefore, unjust convictions represent a substantial challenge to the penological goals of the criminal justice system. Wrongful convictions can be caused by a variety of factors, including inaccurate forensic evidence, eyewitness misidentification, false confessions, and racial bias. These miscarriages of justice have far-reaching implications, hurting not just those falsely convicted, but also society's belief in the legal system. Addressing this issue requires a holistic approach, which includes criminal justice changes targeted at boosting investigative accuracy, strengthening legislative protections for vulnerable people, and encouraging system transparency and accountability. Only by resolving these fundamental concerns will the criminal justice system be able to achieve its dual duty of protecting society and ensuring that justice is fairly administered.

8.6. PUBLIC OPINION ON CAPITAL PUNISHMENT

Public opinion on death punishment is deeply divided, and impacted by geographical, cultural, and demographic considerations. This question has long been a source of debate in penology, with emphasis on its usefulness as a deterrent and its ethical consequences. When examining changing public sentiment toward the death penalty, particularly in the United States and the United Kingdom, scholarly sources suggest that support for capital punishment is not only declining but also being shaped by concerns about miscarriages of justice, ethical concerns, and the efficacy of deterrence. These variations in public opinion reflect broader penological arguments about the role of punishment in society, with many wondering whether the death sentence has any justifiable purpose in a modern justice system.

In the United States, where death punishment is still allowed in some states, public support has declined significantly over the last few decades. According to a Gallup poll conducted in 2023, around 53% of Americans approve of the death penalty, the lowest level of support since 1972. This drop reflects increased worries about erroneous executions and the effectiveness of capital punishment as a deterrence to crime. According to studies, high-profile exonerations of death row inmates have influenced public opinion, drawing attention to the possibility of irreversible errors in the judicial system. This pattern suggests that, while a small majority of Americans still support the death penalty, there is a rising awareness of its inherent hazards and a shift toward life imprisonment without parole as a more appealing alternative (Sarat, 2002).

In contrast, the United Kingdom banned death punishment in 1965, and public support for its resumption has been low ever since. Despite periodic appeals for the restoration of the death sentence, particularly in cases of severe crimes, the majority of the British public remains opposed. Concerns about false convictions, ethical issues, and the belief that the death sentence violates human rights have all played important roles in maintaining opposition. According to Sunstein & Vermeule's (2014) research, British society's opposition to capital punishment is formed by a long-standing dedication to justice reform and rehabilitation, ideas that have been important to the country's modern penological practices. The abolition of the death penalty in the UK is frequently viewed as part of a larger shift toward more humanitarian and restorative forms of punishment (Garland, 2005).

One of the main arguments against capital punishment, especially in democratic cultures, is the ethical and moral consequences of state-sanctioned executions. Legal academics like Sarat (2004) have suggested that if people were better educated about the facts of the death sentence, it would most likely be rejected. This concept, known as the "Marshall hypothesis," holds that popular support for the death sentence stems from a lack of understanding of the procedure and the possibility of errors. As more people become aware of unjust executions and the excessive use of the death sentence based on race and socioeconomic status, public opinion is shifting toward abolition (Unnever et al., 2008).

Furthermore, public opinion on the death penalty can vary dramatically among populations. In the United States, for example, some groups, such as the elderly, conservatives, and residents of southern states, are more likely to support the death penalty. However, younger generations, liberals, and persons of color are more likely to oppose the death penalty. This demographic division reflects larger ideological divides over the function of punishment in society. For example, retributive justice models that emphasize punishment for transgression tend to correspond with support for the death sentence, whereas rehabilitative models focusing on reintegration and change are frequently opposed to it (Cullen, Fisher, and Applegate, 2000).

The issue of whether the death penalty is a successful deterrent to crime is another important one that shapes public opinion. The death penalty's supporters frequently claim that it deters would-be offenders from committing heinous crimes like murder. Empirical evidence on this assertion is equivocal, nevertheless. Compared to other kinds of punishment, studies have not found much evidence that the death sentence significantly lowers crime rates. Indeed, as noted by criminologists, nations that do not have the death penalty, including several in Western Europe, frequently have lower crime rates than those that do. This lack of deterrent, combined with worries about the financial implications of capital punishment, has weakened support for its continued usage (Garland, 2003).

Another factor influencing public opinion is the cost of keeping the death sentence in place. In the United States, capital punishment is much more expensive than life imprisonment with no chance of parole. The costs of long trials, appeals, and keeping death row inmates frequently outweigh the price of life imprisonment. This fiscal cost has prompted some governments to reassess the sustainability of the death sentence, with many moving toward abolition or moratoriums (Garland, 2005).

In addition to these concerns, racial and socioeconomic inequality in the use of the death sentence has emerged as significant issues in the discussion. According to studies, people from minority origins, particularly Black men, are more likely to be condemned to death than their white counterparts. This racial imbalance in sentencing has prompted efforts to reexamine the justice system's fairness and impartiality, with many claiming that capital punishment perpetuates systemic disparities. The public's awareness of these inequities has contributed to a decline in support for the death sentence, particularly among progressive groups promoting criminal justice reform (Unnever et al., 2005).

Public opinion on capital punishment is a fluid and changing issue that reflects larger societal disputes about justice, morality, and the function of punishment in society. While some regions and demographic groupings continue to support the death penalty, the overall trend, particularly in Western democracies, is toward abolition or limited implementation. This movement is driven by concerns about botched executions, racial and socioeconomic disparities, a lack of deterrents, and the financial expenses involved with the death sentence. As society continues to wrestle with these challenges, it is expected that support for the death penalty will continue to fall, particularly as alternative kinds of punishment, such as life imprisonment without parole, become more universally accepted. Public opinion, influenced by ethical considerations and empirical study, has a significant impact on the future of capital punishment and its place in modern penology (Garland, 2003).

8.7. INTERNATIONAL PERSPECTIVE ON CAPITAL PUNISHMENT

The international perspective on capital punishment demonstrates a complex interplay of ethical, legal, and cultural elements, showing a wide range of opinions about its continued usage. Over the last few decades, a global trend toward abolition of the death sentence has evolved, as more countries have embraced human rights and dignity-based concepts. This rising agreement supports the identification of the right to life as a fundamental human right. Currently, more than 70% of the world's nations have abolished capital punishment, either in law or in practice, thanks to evolving legal norms and the influence of international agreements like the International Covenant on Civil and Political Rights (ICCPR) and its Second Optional Protocol. However, the abolitionist movement is far from consistent, with substantial regional, political, and cultural disparities around the world.

One of the most significant pushing causes behind the universal abolition of capital punishment is the international human rights framework, which increasingly sees the death penalty as incompatible with the fundamental dignity of the individual. The ICCPR, enacted by the United Nations in 1966, provided the framework for the global discussion of the right to life, emphasizing that "every human being has the inherent right to life" (Article 6). Although the ICCPR allows the death sentence in nations where it has not been abolished, it only applies to the "most serious crimes" and discourages its usage. The Second Optional Protocol to the ICCPR, ratified in 1989, takes a step further by specifically calling for the abolition of the death sentence, establishing a key legal milestone for human rights activism. Over 90 countries have accepted or acceded to this treaty, demonstrating their commitment to not executing anyone within their borders. This paradigm demonstrates how international law influences domestic legal procedures and advances the abolitionist movement (Dyer, 2023).

Despite the rising worldwide consensus for abolition, there are significant regional variances in the practice of capital punishment. European countries, most notably members of the European Union, have totally abolished the death sentence, as entrenched in the European Convention on Human Rights (ECHR). Protocol No. 6 of the ECHR, which prohibits the death penalty in times of peace, and Protocol No. 13, which extends this prohibition to all circumstances, reaffirm Europe's commitment to a death-free continent. Similarly, Latin American countries such as Brazil and Mexico have abolished the death penalty, demonstrating the region's dedication to human rights ideals and constitutional safeguards of life. However, capital punishment is prevalent throughout Asia, the Middle East, and portions of Africa, especially in countries with huge populations, authoritarian governments, or legal systems that prioritize retributive justice. China, Iran, Saudi Arabia, and Egypt continue to account for the vast majority of global executions, highlighting the pervasiveness of capital punishment in these regions (Dieter, 2019).

In countries where the death sentence is still used, there is ongoing discussion about its efficacy, fairness, and moral justification. Proponents of the death penalty believe that it serves as a deterrence to serious crimes such as murder and terrorism and that its existence secures justice for victims while also protecting society. However, a growing amount of evidence challenges the veracity of these claims. According to studies, there is no compelling evidence that capital punishment is more successful at deterring crime than life imprisonment or other forms of harsh punishment. Furthermore, worries about false convictions, racial and socioeconomic disparities in sentencing, and the possibility of human error in the justice system all undercut the legitimacy of the death sentence as a fair and just form of retribution (Bakura, 2020).

Human rights organizations and the United Nations have been outspoken in their opposition to the death sentence, citing it as a breach of the right to life and a potential form of harsh, inhumane, or humiliating treatment or punishment. The United Nations General Assembly has voted on many resolutions asking for a moratorium on executions with the goal of eventually abolishing the death penalty, reflecting a growing international agreement that it has no place in modern society. One of the primary reasons presented by abolitionists is that the death penalty necessarily carries the possibility of murdering innocent people, as proven by the exoneration of several death row inmates in various countries owing to new evidence, DNA testing, or court errors. The permanent nature of capital punishment makes such blunders especially devastating, reinforcing calls for its abolition (Garland, 2003).

The United States stands out as a striking outlier among Western democracies, with the death penalty still authorized in some states and actively used. Despite its status as a global human rights advocate, the United States faces significant international criticism for its continued use of capital punishment, particularly in light of documented racial biases in sentencing, disproportionate executions of marginalized communities, and the widespread use of the death penalty for crimes committed by people with intellectual disabilities or mental illnesses. In contrast, certain states in the United States have pushed for abolition or set moratoriums on executions, underscoring the country's internal divides on the topic. While several administrations have imposed a moratorium on federal executions, others have resumed them, confusing the United States' stance on the matter (Dyer, 2023).

The broader argument over capital punishment interacts with debates about justice, revenge, and rehabilitation. Penology, the study of punishment and its applications in the criminal justice system, provides several perspectives on the role of the death sentence. From a retributive stance, capital punishment is viewed as a justifiable response to severe crimes, maintaining moral order by guaranteeing that the punishment is proportionate to the gravity of the transgression. However, rehabilitative and restorative justice advocates believe that the death sentence fails to address the underlying reasons of criminal conduct and does not provide opportunity for offender transformation or social healing. These opposing penological frameworks underscore the contradictions between retribution and rehabilitation, justice and mercy, in the debate about the death penalty's position in modern society (Haag and Conrad, 2013).

As a result, the international perspective on death punishment shows a clear trend toward abolition, driven by changing human rights values, legal frameworks, and increased awareness of all individuals' intrinsic dignity. While great progress has been made in many parts of the world, particularly in Europe and Latin America, the death sentence continues widely used in other areas, particularly in countries with huge populations and authoritarian administrations. The continued use of capital punishment poses serious ethical and legal concerns, particularly about its effectiveness, fairness, and conformity with contemporary human rights standards. As the world grapples with these concerns, the abolitionist movement is expected to strengthen, reflecting a growing commitment to the right to life and a rejection of state-sanctioned executions.

Chapter 9

EMERGING ISSUES IN PENOLOGY

Contents

Emerging issues reflect the changing nature of crime, punishment, and societal approaches to rehabilitation. One important area is the incorporation of technology into correctional facilities. Electronic monitoring, predictive analytics, and AI-driven security systems are transforming prison management and inmate behavior monitoring. However, these technologies raise ethical concerns regarding privacy and the possibility of surveillance overreach (Jonathan, 2013).

Another critical development is the privatization of prisons, which has sparked intense debate. Proponents argue that privatization increases efficiency and lowers costs, but critics point to the possibility of profit-driven motives jeopardizing the quality of inmate care and rehabilitation efforts (Scott, 2008). This issue highlights the conflict between market incentives and justice-based penal philosophies.

Additionally, drug rehabilitation programs within the prison system are gaining popularity as public opinion shifts toward treatment rather than punishment for nonviolent drug offenders. Evidence-based interventions, such as cognitive-behavioral therapy and medication-assisted treatment, are increasingly being used to reduce recidivism rates (Clear et al., 2013).

Overcrowding, racial disparities, and the impact of long-term solitary confinement are all relevant issues that continue to challenge contemporary penology and call for holistic, reform-oriented approaches (Lipsey and Cullen, 2007).

9.1. TECHNOLOGY IN CORRECTIONAL SYSTEMS

The incorporation of technology into correctional systems is changing how prisons operate and how punishment and rehabilitation are administered. Technology's role in these environments is multifaceted, encompassing inmate monitoring, security enhancement, rehabilitation programs, and prison administration. While these innovations offer many advantages, there are several ethical, legal, and practical challenges that accompany their adoption, necessitating a careful balance between operational efficiency and human rights protection (Clear et al., 2013).

Inmate surveillance and monitoring is one of the most common applications of technology in correctional facilities. Electronic monitoring devices, such as ankle bracelets, enable real-time tracking of offenders on parole or probation, reducing the need for physical confinement in some cases. This technology offers a cost-effective method of managing offenders outside of prison walls while still ensuring their legal compliance. However, the widespread use of electronic monitoring raises ethical concerns about privacy and individual autonomy. Critics argue that continuous digital surveillance can create an environment of persistent observation, similar to the concept of a "digital panopticon," potentially infringing on individual liberties even after offenders leave physical confinement (Lipsey and Cullen, 2007).

In terms of prison security, technology is critical to the safe operation of correctional facilities. High-tech security measures, such as biometric scanning, facial recognition, and predictive algorithms, are now widely used to track inmate behavior, prevent violence, and detect threats. Predictive algorithms, for example, help authorities predict potential incidents based on analyzed patterns. These tools improve safety for both inmates and staff by allowing authorities to respond to potential risks proactively. However, the use of these algorithms raises concerns about bias and fairness. These technologies are built on datasets that may contain societal biases, particularly regarding race and class, which raises the risk of perpetuating discrimination within the justice system (Wortley, 2002).

Digital technology has also helped to improve rehabilitation and education programs in prisons. Inmates can now access educational content, vocational training, and therapy through online platforms, giving them more flexibility and access to resources that would otherwise be limited in prisons. These digital programs enable more personalized approaches to rehabilitation, tailored to the specific needs and abilities of each inmate. The potential for technology to improve inmate outcomes through education and rehabilitation is significant, but issues of access and inequality remain. Inmates in underfunded facilities or from disadvantaged backgrounds may have less access to these digital resources, resulting in disparities in the benefits of technological innovations (Wortley, 2002).

The intersection of privatization and technology in correctional systems raises additional concerns. Private prison companies frequently use technology to streamline operations and cut costs. While this approach has the potential to improve prison efficiency, the underlying profit-driven motivations may jeopardize inmates' well-being. There is concern that private companies will prioritize cost-cutting measures, such as automated security systems, over critical investments in mental health services and rehabilitation programs. This dynamic poses a critical question: is technology being used to improve the quality of inmate care, or simply to maximize profits in privatized settings? (Clear et al., 2013; Scott, 2008).

Another emerging issue is cybersecurity. As correctional facilities rely more on digital systems to manage inmate data, surveillance, and communications, they become more vulnerable to cyberattacks. Breaches in these systems could expose sensitive inmate information such as legal records, health data, and personal histories, posing privacy concerns and potential security risks. In the event of a cyberattack, compromised data or security systems could be exploited to manipulate prison operations or facilitate illegal activities, emphasizing the urgent need for strong cybersecurity measures in prisons (Lipsey and Cullen, 2007).

While technology clearly improves prison security, efficiency, and rehabilitation efforts, its use has controversial implications for the balance of efficiency and justice. Technological advancements can undoubtedly improve safety and reduce costs, but they can also exacerbate inequalities, infringe on individual rights, and obscure accountability. This is especially troubling when profit motives, as seen in privatized prison models, drive the adoption of new technologies. As technological innovations continue to influence the future of correctional systems, policymakers must engage in thoughtful discussions about the ethical, legal, and social implications of these advancements (Clear et al., 2013; Lipsey and Cullen, 2007).

9.2. PRIVATIZATION OF PRISONS

Privatization is the process of contracting out the management, operation, or construction of correctional facilities to private, for-profit companies. This shift in penal policy reflects broader trends toward neoliberal governance, in which state functions are increasingly outsourced to private entities with the goal of cost savings and improved service delivery. While supporters argue that privatization offers solutions to the challenges of overcrowding, resource shortages, and bureaucratic inefficiencies, critics raise significant concerns about accountability, ethics, and the impact of profit motives on the humane treatment of inmates (Lukemeyer and McCorkle, 2006) (Figure 9.1).

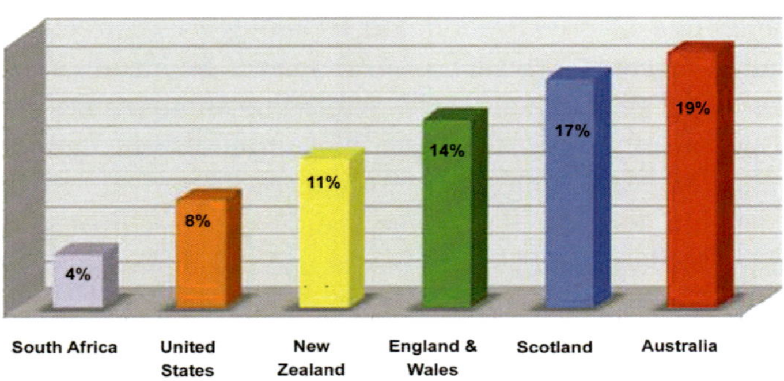

Figure 9.1. *Global trends in the utilization of private prisons.*

Source: Byrne et al. (2015).

One of the primary arguments in favor of prison privatization is its ability to reduce the financial burden on governments. Supporters argue that private companies, motivated by market competition, can manage prisons more effectively than public-sector institutions. This efficiency is thought to stem from the private sector's ability to streamline operations, reduce bureaucratic red tape, and implement cost-cutting measures. Proponents also argue that private firms can frequently build and operate prisons faster than the government, addressing issues such as overcrowding, which has long been a pervasive problem in many correctional systems (Clear et al., 2013).

Furthermore, privatization is viewed as a practical solution to relieve pressure on governments struggling to meet the rising costs of incarceration. The growing number of inmates in many countries has put a strain on public finances, prompting governments to look for alternatives to reduce these fiscal burdens. Private prison companies frequently offer contracts promising cost savings by running prisons at lower daily rates than their public counterparts. These cost savings are viewed as advantageous to taxpayers and are frequently cited as a key justification for the privatization of correctional services (Lundahl et al., 2009).

However, the central tension in the privatization debate stems from the inherent contradiction between private companies' profit motives and the state's ethical obligations in administering justice. Critics of privatization argue that for-profit prisons put financial gain over inmate rehabilitation and humane treatment. When a private company's primary goal is to generate profit, there are concerns that cost-cutting measures will result in insufficient staffing, poor living conditions, and reduced access to essential services such as healthcare, mental health support, and educational programs. These concerns are exacerbated by the fact that inmates, as a captive population, have limited means to advocate for their rights or seek recourse for substandard treatment (Jonathan, 2013).

Accountability is also an important issue in prison privatization. Prisons in public correctional systems are overseen by the government, which, in theory, ensures transparency and accountability. Public prisons are ultimately accountable to the voters, and their operations are governed by public law and policy. Private prisons, on the other hand, operate under contracts that may lack rigorous oversight mechanisms, raising concerns about their operational transparency. The relationship between government agencies and private prison contractors is frequently governed by legal agreements that focus on meeting specific performance metrics, such as cost per inmate or the maintenance of certain security standards. However, these metrics may not adequately capture important factors such as rehabilitation program quality or inmate well-being.

The lack of comprehensive oversight in some privatized systems has led to instances where private prisons have been criticized for poor management practices, mistreatment of inmates, and failure to comply with contractual obligations (Lukemeyer and McCorkle, 2006).

Furthermore, the privatization of prisons raises complex issues regarding incentives. In a public system, the state is responsible for balancing punishment and rehabilitation, reflecting broader societal goals such as reducing recidivism and facilitating former offenders' reintegration into society. However, the profit motive in private prisons can create perverse incentives that undermine these objectives. Private prison companies may benefit financially from higher incarceration rates and longer sentences, as their profits are frequently linked to the number of inmates they house. This creates an inherent conflict of interest, as the financial success of private prison operators may be dependent on policies that promote mass incarceration rather than those that seek to reduce it. Consequently, critics argue that privatization can perpetuate a "prison-industrial complex," where the demand for prison services drives the expansion of incarceration, undermining efforts to reform the criminal justice system and reduce reliance on imprisonment (Scott, 2008).

The ethical implications of prison privatization include questions about the role of the state in administering justice. Punishment is frequently viewed in a democratic society as a core function of the state, inextricably linked to its monopoly on the legitimate use of force. By delegating prison management to private companies, the state loses some direct control over how punishment is administered, raising serious concerns about the commodification of justice. Individual imprisonment, a significant exercise of state power, has the potential to become commercialized when driven by private entities whose primary obligation is to shareholders rather than the public. This shift may erode public trust in the justice system, especially if private prisons are perceived to prioritize profit over public safety and inmate welfare (Lukemeyer and McCorkle, 2006; Lundahl et al., 2009).

Moreover, privatizing prisons has implications for the professionalization of prison personnel. Private prisons may employ lower-wage workers with less training than public facilities, potentially resulting in poorer inmate management and rehabilitation outcomes. Working conditions in private prisons have frequently been criticized as substandard, with staff reporting high levels of stress, insufficient support, and a lack of professional development opportunities. These conditions can lead to high staff turnover rates, further destabilizing the prison environment and undermining efforts to maintain safety and order (Jonathan, 2013).

Despite the concerns raised, privatization remains a popular option for many governments, particularly those dealing with budget constraints and overcrowded prison systems. The challenge is to ensure that the privatization of correctional services does not jeopardize the principles of justice, fairness, and human dignity that should govern the operation of all prisons. Addressing this issue requires strong legal frameworks, comprehensive oversight mechanisms, and a commitment to transparency and accountability. Contracts between governments and private prison companies must include stringent performance standards that address not only operational efficiency but also the quality of inmate care, access to rehabilitation programs, and human rights. Furthermore, governments must resist the temptation to use imprisonment as a means of addressing broader social issues such as poverty, addiction, and mental health, that contribute to crime (Lundahl et al., 2009).

9.3. MENTAL HEALTH TREATMENT IN PRISONS

Mental health treatment in prisons is a critical issue in criminology, reflecting the larger challenges of meeting psychological and psychiatric needs in a punitive setting. The high prevalence of mental illness among incarcerated people, combined with the limitations of prison infrastructure, creates a complicated dynamic in which correctional institutions are frequently ill-equipped to provide adequate care. Addressing mental health in prisons entails not only providing treatment but also understanding the structural factors that exacerbate mental health issues, such as overcrowding, isolation, and the inherently coercive nature of imprisonment (Fazel et al., 2016).

Individuals with mental health disorders are overrepresented in prison systems, which is a major source of concern. Many inmates enter the correctional system with pre-existing mental health issues, which are often exacerbated by substance abuse, trauma, and socioeconomic disadvantages. The justice system, which is primarily designed for punishment rather than rehabilitation, frequently serves as a de facto mental health provider when other aspects of the social welfare system fail to adequately support people with psychiatric needs. As a result, prisons are now responsible for managing large numbers of mentally ill individuals, a task for which they were not initially designed (Nurse et al., 2003).

The majority of prison environments can exacerbate mental health issues. Prisons are inherently stressful environments that can exacerbate psychiatric symptoms. Overcrowding, which is a common problem in many prison systems, causes tensions among inmates, increases the risk of violence, and limits the capacity for individualized care. Inmates with mental health issues are especially vulnerable in such settings, as they may struggle to cope with the constant stress, aggression, and sensory deprivation. Furthermore, the use of solitary confinement, which is frequently used as a disciplinary measure, has been widely condemned for its negative impact on mental health. Prolonged isolation can exacerbate pre-existing conditions such as depression, anxiety, and psychosis, and in some cases, cause these conditions in previously healthy people. The use of solitary confinement for individuals with mental health disorders is particularly problematic, as the isolation tends to aggravate their symptoms and impede their recovery (Fazel et al., 2016).

Resource constraints make it more difficult to provide adequate mental health treatment in prisons. Prisons are typically underfunded and understaffed, especially in terms of mental health care. Many facilities lack enough trained mental health professionals, such as psychologists, psychiatrists, and social workers, to meet the needs of their incarcerated populations. Furthermore, correctional officers frequently receive insufficient training in recognizing and responding to mental health crises, which can result in the mismanagement of inmates with psychiatric conditions. In some cases, inmates with mental illnesses are perceived as disciplinary problems rather than individuals who require treatment, resulting in punitive rather than therapeutic responses (Kupers, 2005).

Another issue complicating mental health care in prison is the criminalization of mental illness. Individuals who have untreated psychiatric conditions are more likely to engage in criminal justice-related behaviors. For example, people suffering from severe mental illnesses may exhibit disruptive or erratic behavior, which can be misinterpreted as criminal behavior rather than a symptom of their psychiatric disorder. As a result, rather than receiving treatment in mental health facilities, these people are incarcerated, where their conditions are frequently untreated or inadequately addressed. This creates a cycle in which individuals with mental health disorders are repeatedly incarcerated, their conditions left untreated, and their prospects for rehabilitation reduced (Kupers, 2005).

Efforts to address mental health issues in prison necessitate a multifaceted approach. One of the most difficult challenges is ensuring that people with mental illnesses receive the necessary treatment and support while incarcerated. This includes providing access to psychiatric care, such as medication, therapy, and crisis intervention services. Mental health treatment must be integrated into the prison system's overall rehabilitative framework. Rehabilitation programs that address both mental health and behavioral issues are essential for lowering recidivism rates among mentally ill offenders. By emphasizing recovery over punishment, these programs aim to provide inmates with the tools they need to manage their conditions and reintegrate into society upon release (Kupers, 2005; Nurse et al., 2003).

In addition to direct treatment, prisons must create environments that promote mental health. This includes addressing the structural issues that contribute to the decline of mental health, such as overcrowding, violence, and isolation. Reducing the use of solitary confinement, particularly for people with mental illnesses, is an important step toward minimizing harm. Alternative disciplinary measures, such as therapeutic interventions and conflict resolution programs, may prove more effective in managing inmate behavior without exacerbating mental health symptom (Fazel et al., 2016).

Mental health treatment in prison necessitates collaboration between correctional systems and outside mental health providers. Continuity of care is critical, especially as inmates return to the community following release. Many people with mental illnesses struggle to reintegrate, especially if they do not have consistent access to psychiatric care, housing, or social support. Ensuring that inmates have access to community-based mental health services before they are released can help prevent recidivism and promote long-term recovery. Furthermore, diversion programs, which direct individuals with mental health disorders away from the criminal justice system and into treatment, provide an alternative approach that prioritizes care over punishment (Fazel et al., 2016; Nurse et al., 2003).

The ethical implications of mental health treatment in prisons are significant. Incarcerated people, regardless of their crimes, have the right to adequate medical and psychiatric care. Failure to provide such care is a violation of fundamental human rights, raising serious concerns about the state's role in the treatment of vulnerable populations. Furthermore, increasing awareness of the high rates of mental illness in prisons has prompted calls for broader reforms to the criminal justice system, with advocates arguing that prisons are unsuitable as mental health facilities. This has fueled a movement to decriminalize mental illness and create alternative models of care that prioritize treatment over incarceration (Kupers, 2005).

9.4. DRUG REHABILITATION PROGRAMS IN PRISONS

The high prevalence of substance abuse among incarcerated people necessitates the implementation of comprehensive rehabilitation programs that address both the underlying addiction issues and their relationship to criminal behavior. From a penological standpoint, these programs' primary goals are to reduce recidivism, promote rehabilitation, and facilitate reintegration into society. Drug rehabilitation in prisons is thus not only about treatment; it is a broader part of the effort to transform the criminal justice system from one focused on punishment to one that incorporates principles of recovery and social reintegration (Taxman et al., 2007) (Figure 9.2).

Figure 9.2. *Women prisons offering gender responsive substance abuse programming.*

Source: CDCR (2022).

One of the central concepts in prison drug rehabilitation is the therapeutic approach, which sees addiction as a health issue rather than a criminal one. This viewpoint advocates for treating incarcerated people with substance use disorders through medical and psychological interventions rather than relying solely on punitive measures. Therapeutic approaches frequently include a combination of behavioral therapies, counseling, and medication-assisted treatment (MAT), all tailored to each inmate's unique needs. Behavioral therapies, such as cognitive-behavioral therapy (CBT), are widely used to assist individuals in recognizing and changing harmful thought patterns and behaviors associated with drug use. These therapies aim to provide inmates with the skills necessary to avoid relapse and make healthier life choices, both during and after incarceration (Bahr et al., 2012).

Medication-assisted treatment is another important aspect of drug rehabilitation in prison. This method entails administering medications such as methadone or buprenorphine to alleviate withdrawal symptoms and cravings associated with opioid addiction. When combined with counseling and behavioral therapy, MAT has proven to be effective in promoting long-term recovery. However, access to MAT in prison settings is frequently restricted due to logistical, financial, and ideological constraints. The stigma around addiction and the perception of drug use as a moral failing continue to influence prison policies, with some correctional systems resisting the implementation of MAT despite its acknowledged benefits (Taxman et al., 2007).

The continuity of care is an important component of effective drug rehabilitation in prisons. For many inmates, substance abuse is a chronic condition that necessitates ongoing treatment. The transition from prison to the community is a particularly vulnerable time for individuals, as they face a variety of challenges that can lead to relapse, including reintroduction to environments that may trigger substance use. Effective rehabilitation programs recognize the importance of post-release support, ensuring that inmates have access to treatment services once released. This may include enrollment in outpatient programs, support groups, or halfway houses that offer a structured environment conducive to recovery (Dolan et al., 2007).

The therapeutic community (TC) approach is another important model for prison drug rehabilitation. In this model, a group of inmates voluntarily joins a highly structured, peer-led community that emphasizes mutual support and accountability. The TC model prioritizes personal responsibility, social learning, and the development of prosocial behaviors. Participants in therapeutic communities engage in daily activities aimed at addressing both their substance use and broader behavioral and emotional issues. This holistic approach sees addiction as a symptom of deeper psychological and social problems that must be addressed to facilitate long-term recovery (Bahr et al., 2012).

Therapeutic communities in prisons frequently have a hierarchical structure, with inmates progressing through different levels of responsibility and privilege as they improve their recovery. This structure reflects societal norms, aiming to prepare inmates for life outside of prison by encouraging them to take on responsible, law-abiding roles. One of the therapeutic community model's main strengths is its emphasis on peer support, which encourages people in recovery to help one another, reinforcing their own commitment to sobriety. However, the effectiveness of therapeutic communities is heavily dependent on the prison's culture, staff training, and the availability of resources to support these programs (Dolan et al., 2007; Taxman et al., 2007).

Drug rehabilitation programs must also consider the co-existence of mental health issues among inmates with substance use disorders. Many people who struggle with addiction also have mental health issues like depression, anxiety, and post-traumatic stress disorder (PTSD). This phenomenon, known as dual diagnosis, poses unique challenges for treatment. Effective rehabilitation programs must take an integrated treatment approach that addresses both the substance use disorder and the underlying mental health issues. Failure to address co-occurring disorders can undermine the success of rehabilitation efforts, as untreated mental health problems can drive individuals back into substance use as a form of self-medication (Bahr et al., 2012).

Staff training and education play a critical role in the success of prison-based drug rehabilitation programs. Correctional officers and other staff members who interact with inmates play an important role in creating an environment conducive to recovery. However, many prison personnel are not adequately trained to understand or respond to substance use disorders, which can result in misunderstandings and punitive responses rather than therapeutic interventions. Training staff to recognize addiction symptoms, understand rehabilitation principles, and assist inmates in their recovery is critical for the successful implementation of drug rehabilitation programs. Furthermore, staff must be trained to handle the unique challenges posed by inmates with co-occurring mental health and substance use disorders (Taxman et al., 2007).

One of the most challenging aspects of implementing drug rehabilitation programs in prisons is the conflict between security and treatment. Prisons are fundamentally designed to control and contain populations, and the security protocols in place may occasionally conflict with inmates' therapeutic needs. For example, prison's strict schedules, lack of privacy, and limited autonomy can undermine the principles of personal responsibility and self-motivation that are central to many drug rehabilitation programs. Balancing the institutional security needs with the therapeutic needs of the inmate population requires careful planning and collaboration between correctional staff, healthcare providers, and policymakers (Bahr et al., 2012; Dolan et al., 2007).

9.5. RESTORATIVE JUSTICE INITIATIVE

Restorative justice has developed as a prominent project in modern criminology, indicating a trend away from punitive policies and toward more inclusive and reparative solutions to crime and conflict. Unlike the traditional criminal justice system, which focuses on punishment as a tool of deterrence and retribution, restorative justice stresses mending harm and encouraging accountability via discourse and collaborative decision-making. This approach provides a more compassionate and socially constructive option by addressing the concerns of all parties involved, including the victim, the offender, and the community as a whole (Zehr, 2002). Restorative justice is increasingly viewed as an effective and ethical way to achieve justice, having applications in diverse institutional settings such as courts, schools, and communities (Johnstone & Van Ness, 2007).

Restorative justice is based on the principles of connection and shared accountability. Restorative justice shifts the focus of justice systems toward healing and transformation by understanding crime as harm done to people and relationships rather than a violation of the law. Victims, offenders, and community members are all asked to participate in a conversation and reconciliation process in which the root causes of harm are investigated and remedies are found jointly. This method stresses the needs of the wounded while also empowering offenders to accept responsibility for their acts, understand the consequences of their behavior, and actively participate in making apologies. Restorative justice differs significantly from traditional retributive justice systems in that it imposes punishment without regard for the broader social and emotional dynamics at play (Zehr, 2015).

Restorative justice places a strong emphasis on discussion and participatory decision-making. Peacemaking, circles, and conferencing processes, which are typically influenced by Indigenous customs, bring together all people affected by specific damage to address the nature of the wrongdoing, its consequences, and potential paths forward. In contrast to the one-size-fits-all punitive tactics that characterize many legal systems, these mechanisms provide a more tailored and context-specific reaction to harm. Victims, especially, gain from the ability to express their sentiments, explain their demands, and take an active role in establishing what justice should look like in their instance. For offenders, the procedure promotes accountability and remorse since they must address the real-life repercussions of their acts and seek to rectify the harm they have caused (Johnstone, 2011).

The origins of restorative justice can be found in prehistoric Indigenous dispute settlement techniques that prioritized reestablishing social harmony and attending to communal needs. Indigenous techniques like peacemaking and circle processes serve as a solid basis for contemporary restorative approaches and offer insightful knowledge about how justice may be attained by communication, reaching consensus, and sharing accountability. According to Zehr (2002), justice is viewed in these traditions not as a punitive measure for transgression, but rather as a way to fortify social relationships and promote a feeling of shared responsibility. Modern restorative justice projects aim to reinvigorate these community-based approaches to justice, emphasizing empathy, understanding, and healing above punishment and exclusion, by relying on these indigenous frameworks (Johnstone & Van Ness, 2007).

The criminal court system, educational institutions, and community organizations are just a few of the arenas in which restorative justice has found use in modern times. Restorative justice is frequently employed in the criminal justice system as an alternative to traditional court proceedings. Victims and offenders can participate in a dialogue and jointly choose a course of action that addresses the harm in these restorative processes. Recidivism has been demonstrated to be decreased by this strategy because criminals who engage in restorative processes are less likely to commit crimes again than those who go through traditional penal systems. Furthermore, victims frequently report higher levels of satisfaction with restorative justice processes because they are given a voice and agency in the justice system, which is typically missing in traditional systems (Latimer et al., 2005).

Restorative justice is also widely used in schools to address conflict and reduce occurrences of damage. In contrast to zero-tolerance rules that have resulted in the criminalization of student behavior and the so-called school-to-prison pipeline, restorative practices provide a more constructive and compassionate approach to discipline. Restorative circles or conferences can help schools foster a healthy culture of respect, responsibility, and accountability among students, teachers, and parents. Rather than just penalizing children for their wrongdoing, restorative justice tries to understand the root causes of conflict, restore damaged relationships, and reintegrate students into the school community. This method not only minimizes suspensions and expulsions but also encourages social-emotional learning and contributes to the development of stronger, more supportive school settings (Gavrielides, 2017).

The emphasis on community engagement and collective responsibility is one of restorative justice's most significant contributions to the area of penology. In contrast to traditional judicial systems, which frequently separate offenders from their communities, restorative justice acknowledges crime as a societal problem that necessitates a collaborative response. Restorative justice strives to harness the power and knowledge of the larger community by incorporating them into the justice process in order to address the root causes of harm and establish conditions that encourage safety and well-being. This greater emphasis on community responsibility challenges the conventional assumption that justice is entirely the responsibility of the state and its legal institutions, calling for a more holistic approach that includes the voices and perspectives of all those affected by harm (Zehr, 2015).

Additionally, restorative justice also challenges the established power structures in the criminal justice system. Structural injustices, such as systemic racism, class inequality, and other types of oppression, have long distorted traditional judicial systems, resulting in disproportionately harsh penalties for underprivileged communities. Restorative justice aims to promote more fair power dynamics within the legal system by focusing on discussion and participatory decision-making. It helps disenfranchised voices to be heard and recognized, resulting in chances for empowerment and healing. Restorative justice appeals to individuals seeking to eliminate the systematic prejudices found in many criminal justice systems because of its capacity to address structural inequities (Zehr, 2015). However, some have expressed doubts regarding the efficacy of restorative justice in addressing severe crimes, including violent ones. Because restorative justice does not rely on the formal punishment processes that are essential to retributive justice, some contend that it is either too mild or does not provide an appropriate deterrent. Additionally, issues regarding the possibility of coercion in restorative procedures have been brought up, especially in situations where victims and offenders have unequal power relations. Restorative justice advocates, however, contend that these worries are outweighed by the benefits of the approach, which are especially seen in terms of victim satisfaction, offender accountability, and community involvement. They contend that restorative justice is a more ethical and socially responsible approach to dealing with injustice, emphasizing healing and transformation over punishment and exclusion (Johnstone & Van Ness, 2007).

Restorative justice is an important developing problem in penology. Its emphasis on conversation, participatory decision-making, and collective accountability indicates a shift towards more inclusive and reparative forms of justice. Restorative justice continues to gain popularity as a creative and revolutionary approach to justice, despite ongoing obstacles in its application to major crimes and promise for resolving structural injustices. As society struggles to overcome the limitations of retributive justice, restorative justice efforts provide a path to a more compassionate and just future.

9.6. REENTRY PROGRAMS FOR EX-OFFENDERS

Reentry programs for ex-offenders are a significant and rising subject in penology, reflecting broader changes in the criminal justice system's approach to rehabilitation, reintegration, and crime prevention. These programs are intended to help persons transition from incarceration to life after prison by providing a structured framework for effective reintegration into society. Reentry programs are intended to minimize recidivism, improve public safety, and lessen the social and economic costs of crime and imprisonment. By addressing the numerous challenges that ex-offenders face upon release, such as obtaining employment, overcoming substance abuse issues, and re-establishing social ties, these programs attempt to disrupt the cycle of re-offending that has historically characterized much of the criminal justice system. In studying the function of reintegration programs in modern penology, it is critical to investigate their objectives, components, problems, and potential future paths (Alper et al., 2018).

The fundamental goal of reentry programs is to reduce recidivism by providing ex-offenders with the tools they need to live productive, law-abiding lives. Numerous studies have shown that people who are released from prison without receiving enough support are considerably more likely to re-offend and return to the criminal justice system. According to a 2019 analysis by the United States Department of Justice, around 68% of freed inmates were rearrested within three years, emphasizing the difficulty of breaking the cycle of recidivism. Reentry programs address this issue by offering services that address the underlying causes of criminal conduct. These services include vocational training, educational opportunities, substance addiction treatment, and mental health care, all of which try to reduce the conditions that contribute to re-offending. Reentry programs aim to smooth the transition back into society by assisting ex-offenders in developing the skills and resources required to get jobs, maintain stable housing, and form supportive connections (Latessa and Lovins, 2019).

Education and vocational training are key components of effective reentry programs. Research has consistently demonstrated that ex-offenders who learn marketable skills while incarcerated are much more likely to find permanent jobs after their release. Employment is an important aspect of reducing recidivism since it provides individuals with financial security and promotes a feeling of purpose and belonging. A RAND Corporation research discovered that offenders who engaged in educational programs were 43% less likely to return to prison than those who did not. Many successful reentry programs incorporate job training and placement services to assist ex-offenders navigate the labor market and overcome hurdles to employment. These programs frequently collaborate with local businesses and organizations to give possibilities for apprenticeships, internships, and full-time employment, allowing participants to establish a positive work history and a strong support network in their communities (Davis et al., 2013).

In addition to educational and vocational training, reintegration programs must treat the mental health and substance addiction concerns that frequently lead to criminal activity. A sizable proportion of incarcerated people suffer from mental illnesses or substance misuse disorders, which are usually exacerbated by the strains of imprisonment and the difficulties of reintegration. According to the Bureau of Justice Statistics, more than 40% of state prisoners and over 30% of federal convicts have had mental health issues. Without appropriate treatment and support, these people are more likely to re-offend. Many reentry programs provide counseling, therapy, and support groups to assist ex-offenders with their mental health and addiction difficulties. Such programs hope to lessen the likelihood of relapse and recidivism by addressing the underlying causes (James, 2015).

However, reentry programs encounter numerous serious challenges that can jeopardize their efficacy. One of the most significant concerns is a lack of financing and resources to support these projects. Many reentry programs are underfunded and understaffed, which limits the services available and the number of people they can help. As a result, ex-offenders may not receive the necessary support required to properly reintegrate into society. Furthermore, the fragmented nature of reentry programs can cause gaps in assistance, making it difficult for individuals to navigate the system and receive the support they need. For example, an ex-offender may obtain employment training in one program but not have access to housing or mental health services in another, resulting in a fragmented and incomplete reintegration process (Eddy and Burraston, 2018).

Stigma and discrimination are also significant hurdles to successful reintegration for ex-offenders. Many people experience societal discrimination because of their criminal history, making it harder to find work, housing, and social acceptance. Employers and landlords frequently discriminate against people with criminal records, severely restricting their chances for steady employment and housing. The stigma associated with being an ex-offender can also damage relationships with family members and friends, denying individuals the social support they require during the reintegration process. To address these societal impediments, reentry programs must advocate for policy changes that lessen discrimination and assist ex-offenders in rebuilding their social networks (James, 2015).

Legal and policy impediments impede the reintegration process. Individuals with criminal records suffer employment restrictions in many jurisdictions, especially in industries such as healthcare, education, and law enforcement. These restrictions can severely hinder ex-offenders' ability to find meaningful employment, even if they possess the requisite skills and certifications. Furthermore, rules prohibiting individuals with felony convictions from accessing public housing or receiving some sort of government aid can increase the obstacles to reintegration, particularly for those who come from low-income homes. To address these concerns, reentry reform activists have asked for the erasure of criminal records in certain situations, as well as the removal of legal barriers that prohibit ex-offenders from obtaining jobs, housing, and other crucial services (Latessa and Lovins, 2019).

In response to these issues, several reentry programs are implementing novel techniques to provide more comprehensive and effective support. One such strategy is to create holistic models that handle numerous parts of a person's life at once, rather than focusing on single issues like job or housing. Holistic reentry programs acknowledge that effective reintegration necessitates a multifaceted approach that addresses mental health, substance misuse, education, family ties, and other issues. These programs provide a more comprehensive and supportive framework for those moving out of prison (Eddy and Burraston, 2018).

Collaboration among government agencies, non-profit organizations, and private corporations is also critical for the success of reintegration programs. Collaborations between these organizations can help leverage resources and experience to provide more effective and comprehensive assistance. Some reentry programs, for example, collaborate with local employers to generate job possibilities for ex-offenders, while others work with community-based organizations to provide housing and mental health services. By encouraging teamwork and coordination, reintegration programs can better fulfill the diverse requirements of ex-offenders and lower the chance of recidivism (Alper, 2018).

As reentry programs evolve, future efforts must center on pushing for legislative reform and raising public awareness about the issues that ex-offenders face. Policy improvements that remove barriers to employment and housing, like as record expungement and anti-discrimination legislation, can dramatically improve the efficacy of reentry programs. Furthermore, increasing public knowledge of the necessity of reintegration might serve to eliminate stigma and increase support for reentry projects. Public awareness of the advantages of successful reintegration, such as lower crime rates and jail costs, can help shift attitudes and create a more welcoming atmosphere for ex-offenders (James, 2015).

9.7. GLOBALIZATION OF PENOLOGICAL PRACTICES

The globalization of penological practices is an important and ongoing subject in the study of penology, reflecting countries' increasing interconnection and the spread of penal ideas, reforms, and practices across boundaries. As nations become more economically, politically, and culturally intertwined, their approaches to criminal justice, particularly punishment, become more global in scope. These changes are frequently driven by international collaboration, knowledge exchange through comparative studies, and the adoption of best practices from other countries. While the globalization of penology allows for the dissemination of progressive and effective criminal reforms, it also raises concerns about how local cultural, legal, and historical settings influence the application of these global models.

International cooperation has been a major driving force behind the globalization of penological techniques. Organizations such as the International Union of Criminal Law and the International Prison and Penitentiary Congresses have encouraged governments to communicate and collaborate in order to promote criminal reforms that are consistent with international human rights norms (Scott, 2008). These organizations offer platforms for practitioners, scholars, and politicians to address difficulties in criminal justice systems and share ideas on how to improve prison conditions, reduce recidivism, and promote more compassionate ways of punishment. International agreements, such as the United Nations Standard Minimum Rules for the Treatment of Prisoners (the Nelson Mandela Rules), have an impact on national penal systems by encouraging countries to adopt practices that prioritize the dignity and rights of incarcerated people. These achievements demonstrate how international collaboration contributes to a more standard framework for penal practices around the world, albeit the degree of influence differs according to each country's political and legal circumstances (Nelken, 2010).

Comparative studies are an important component of the globalization of penological procedures. By analyzing different countries' correctional systems, scholars and practitioners get insight into which policies and methods are most effective in lowering crime and improving prison operations. Comparative penology identifies successful models that can be applied to local circumstances while also providing a greater understanding of the many ideologies that govern criminal systems around the world. Scandinavian countries, such as Norway and Sweden, are frequently highlighted as examples of progressive penal reform due to their emphasis on rehabilitation, reintegration, and humane treatment of convicts. These systems, which have low incarceration rates and a focus on prisoners' social reintegration, have been praised for their success in reducing recidivism. As a result, other countries, particularly in Europe and North America, have attempted to adapt components of similar approaches into their own criminal justice systems (Bosworth, 2011).

At the same time, the internationalization of penological practices presents some obstacles. The idea of "new penology," coined by researchers Malcolm Feeley and Jonathan Simon in 2002, represents a significant shift in the focus of prison institutions from individual rehabilitation to population and risk management. Modern penal methods are more focused on analyzing and managing the risks posed by offenders, rather than on their moral or social rehabilitation. This risk management strategy has led to the widespread adoption of actuarial methodologies, such as risk assessment tools, to forecast the possibility of recidivism. These strategies, which were first developed in the United States, have since been transferred to other countries and implemented into their parole and probation programs. The global development of these tactics reflects a larger tendency toward managing crime through surveillance, control, and confinement rather than individualized treatment and support (Nelken, 2010).

However, the "new penology"'s emphasis on risk management has been criticized for depersonalizing offenders and contributing to the growth of the carceral state. Critics claim that the emphasis on statistical prediction models and population management reduces people to risk categories, ignoring human responsibility, social context, and the potential of rehabilitation. Furthermore, global acceptance of these techniques frequently occurs without proper consideration for the diverse social, economic, and cultural variables that determine crime and punishment in different countries. In some situations, this can lead to the implementation of criminal policies that are inappropriate for local contexts, resulting in unintended consequences such as jail overcrowding, increasing incarceration rates, and marginalization of vulnerable people (Nutz, 2005).

One of the most important features of penological practice globalization is the adoption of best practices from other nations. The exchange of knowledge and experience among criminal justice professionals has resulted in the widespread implementation of novel punitive reforms. Restorative justice techniques, which originated in indigenous communities and gained popularity in nations such as New Zealand and Canada, have expanded to other parts of the world. Restorative justice seeks to repair the harm caused by criminal action via communication and reconciliation among the victim, the offender, and the community. This method contrasts with traditional punitive models and has been adopted by several countries as a successful technique of lowering recidivism and creating social cohesion. Similarly, community-based alternatives to incarceration, including probation, parole, and electronic monitoring, are gaining popularity around the world as governments seek to decrease the financial and social costs of imprisonment (Scott, 2008).

While the globalization of penological practices aids the spread of new reforms, it is critical to remember that local cultural, legal, and historical circumstances have a significant impact on how these policies are implemented. While the Scandinavian model of criminal reform has been hailed for its efficacy in encouraging rehabilitation and lowering recidivism, attempting to replicate it in nations with differing legislative traditions or cultural attitudes toward punishment may present considerable problems. Progressive changes may face opposition in countries where the judicial system is more punitive or when public opinion strongly advocates harsh consequences for criminals. In such instances, criminal changes that prioritize rehabilitation and reintegration may be perceived as unduly soft or incompatible with public ideals of justice (Nelken, 2010).

Furthermore, different countries' legal systems take quite varied approaches to punishment, reflecting greater historical and political settings. Many countries with colonial legacies, for example, have had their criminal procedures affected by the entry of European legal systems during the colonial period, which may not be consistent with local customs or values. The implementation of foreign legal frameworks can lead to contradictions between global penal trends and local practices, as demonstrated in places where Indigenous justice systems coexist with formal criminal justice organizations. These processes underline the necessity of understanding the individual cultural and legal contexts in which criminal systems are anchored, even as countries become more involved in global penology trends (Bosworth, 2011).

The globalization of penological practices is a complex and rising problem that reflects the increasing interconnection of criminal justice systems around the world. Countries are rapidly adopting prison reforms that are in line with global trends in human rights, risk management, and rehabilitation thanks to international cooperation, comparative research, and the sharing of best practices. However, the effectiveness of these changes is dependent on countries' capacity to tailor them to their specific cultural, legal, and historical settings. While the globalization of penology has the potential to significantly improve criminal justice systems, it also raises critical challenges regarding how these global models may be reconciled with local practices and beliefs.

Chapter 10

ETHICS AND PROFESSIONALISM IN PENOLOGY

Contents

Ethics and professionalism are essential for ensuring that correctional systems function fairly and humanely. Penology, which deals with the management, rehabilitation, and reintegration of offenders, necessitates adherence to moral principles and professional standards that protect the rights and dignity of both inmates and staff (Bonner and Vandecreek, 2006).

The concept of human dignity is central to ethical penology because it requires all individuals, regardless of criminal status, to be treated with respect and fairness. This is consistent with international human rights frameworks such as the United Nations Standard Minimum Rules for the Treatment of Prisoners (the Nelson Mandela Rules), which call for humane treatment, medical care, and the prohibition of torture and cruel punishment.

Professionalism in criminology entails following clear guidelines in order to reduce abuse, corruption, and discrimination. Correctional personnel are expected to maintain high ethical standards, demonstrating impartiality, integrity, and accountability in their interactions. Ethical quandaries frequently arise in areas such as solitary confinement, force, and rehabilitative programming, requiring practitioners to balance security concerns with rehabilitative goals (Webb, 2012).

Academic research emphasizes the importance of creating ethical frameworks in corrections (Scott, 2008), recognizing that a professional and ethical approach strengthens the correctional system's legitimacy, reduces recidivism, and fosters societal trust.

10.1. CODE OF ETHICS FOR CORRECTIONAL OFFICERS

The code of ethics for correctional officers is critical in guiding behavior and practices in the correctional setting. Correctional officers, who are responsible for overseeing incarcerated people, face unique ethical challenges that require strict adherence to ethical standards and professionalism. These ethical principles help to balance the dual responsibilities of ensuring security and supporting rehabilitative processes within correctional facilities (Webb, 2012).

The concept of human dignity is central to the correctional officers' code of ethics. Regardless of the crimes committed by incarcerated individuals, officers must treat them with dignity and protect their fundamental human rights. This is consistent with larger ethical frameworks in penology, such as the United Nations Standard Minimum Rules for the Treatment of Prisoners (also known as the Mandela Rules). These guidelines emphasize the prohibition on torture, inhumane treatment, and punishment, as well as the provision of necessary healthcare and social services to inmates. The code of ethics for correctional officers enshrines similar values, emphasizing the importance of not subjecting prisoners to cruelty, degrading treatment, or unnecessary hardships (Bonner and Vandecreek, 2006).

Correctional officers are expected to be impartial and fair while upholding human dignity. This is an important ethical principle that requires officers to treat all inmates equally, regardless of their background, race, or the nature of their crimes. Impartiality is especially important in environments where officers must navigate complex interpersonal dynamics among inmates, which may include racial, ethnic, or gang-related tensions. Ethical codes require officers to avoid favoritism and discrimination, ensuring that all inmates receive the same level of protection, access to services, and disciplinary responses. In this regard, the penological perspective emphasizes that fairness in the treatment of inmates increases the legitimacy of the correctional system and fosters an environment conducive to rehabilitation (Souryal and Whitehead, 2019).

The code of ethics for correctional officers also emphasizes integrity and accountability. Officers are given significant authority over the lives of incarcerated people, which raises the possibility of abuse or corruption. The ethical mandate of integrity requires officers to carry out their duties honestly and in accordance with the law, even when pressured to compromise their values. This includes refraining from engaging in or facilitating contraband smuggling, using excessive force, and reporting any instances of misconduct among their peers. Accountability also implies that officers are accountable for their actions and decisions, particularly when using force or disciplinary measures. Ethical codes often include guidelines for reporting and addressing instances of unethical behavior, which is essential for maintaining the credibility and transparency of the correctional system (Bonner and Vandecreek, 2006).

Another ethical issue that correctional officers frequently face is the use of force. Many correctional facilities allow officers to use force as needed to maintain order and security. However, the ethical use of force requires officers to exercise restraint and use the least amount of force necessary to accomplish their goals. Ethical codes emphasize the importance of using force only as a last resort and training officers to de-escalate situations whenever possible. Penology literature emphasizes the possibility of force being used inappropriately in correctional facilities, where tensions between inmates and staff can quickly escalate. Ethical guidelines, therefore, play a critical role in ensuring that officers are mindful of their power and exercise it judiciously to prevent harm to inmates and avoid excessive or retaliatory actions (Souryal and Whitehead, 2019).

Confidentiality is another important concept in the ethical framework for correction officers. Officers frequently have access to sensitive information about inmates, such as their criminal records, medical conditions, and psychological profiles. Ethical codes require officers to respect inmates' privacy by keeping this information confidential, unless disclosure is legally required or necessary to prevent harm. This principle applies to interactions with external entities such as the media or law enforcement agencies, where officers must exercise caution not to share confidential information without proper authorization. Maintaining confidentiality is essential for building trust between officers and inmates, especially in the context of rehabilitation and reintegration efforts (Webb, 2012).

Furthermore, correctional officers are expected to be professional in all aspects of their duties. Professionalism includes a variety of behaviors such as following established policies and procedures, treating colleagues and inmates with respect, and committing to ongoing training and development. Penology emphasizes the value of ongoing education for correctional officers, particularly in areas such as crisis intervention, mental health awareness, and conflict resolution. Officers are frequently required to participate in such training under ethical codes in order to improve their ability to respond to the diverse and complex needs of the inmate population. Officers must also maintain emotional stability and resilience since correctional work can be highly stressful and emotionally taxing (Scott, 2008).

The principle of rehabilitation is also incorporated into the ethical code for correctional officers. While security is their primary responsibility, correctional officers also play an important role in the correctional system's rehabilitative efforts. Ethical codes frequently encourage officers to promote positive behavior among inmates, facilitate access to educational and vocational programs, and serve as role models for pro-social behavior. This is consistent with the broader penological shift toward viewing incarceration as an opportunity for rehabilitation and reintegration into society, rather than simply a means of punishment. By promoting a culture of rehabilitation, ethical officers help to reduce recidivism and successfully reintegrate offenders (Bonner and Vandecreek, 2006; Souryal and Whitehead, 2019).

10.2. ETHICAL DILEMMAS IN PENOLOGICAL PRACTICES

Ethical dilemmas in penological practice stem from inherent tensions between the goals of security, punishment, rehabilitation, and humane treatment of incarcerated people. Penology, as a field inextricably linked to justice administration, must navigate complex moral landscapes in which prisoners' rights frequently conflict with institutional imperatives of control and public safety. The ethical issues that arise from these tensions necessitate ongoing reflection on the principles governing correctional institutions and the behavior of those who work within them (Webb, 2012).

One of the most prominent moral dilemmas in penology concerns the use of solitary confinement. Solitary confinement is frequently used as a disciplinary measure to maintain order in prisons, but its use raises serious ethical concerns. Extensive periods of isolation can cause severe psychological distress, and many scholars believe that such treatment is an example of inhumane punishment. Penological frameworks based on human rights emphasize that correctional practices must respect prisoners' dignity and avoid actions that cause unnecessary suffering. This presents a dilemma for correctional administrators, who must strike a balance between the need to control disruptive or dangerous inmates and the ethical obligation to avoid causing harm. Solitary confinement thus forces penological practitioners to weigh the demands of institutional security against the mental and physical well-being of individuals in their care (Dubler, 2014).

Similarly, the use of force in correctional facilities raises another complex ethical concern. Correctional officers are frequently called upon to deal with volatile situations involving violence or threats of violence. The ethical question is how much force is justified, and when does its use become excessive or abusive. Ethical codes typically require that force be used as a last resort and in proportion to the threat posed. However, in practice, it can be difficult to distinguish between legitimate and excessive force, especially in high-stress situations requiring split-second decisions. The potential for abuse of power in these situations emphasizes the importance of strong ethical guidelines, training, and oversight to prevent officers from resorting to unnecessary violence. Moreover, the abuse of force undermines the legitimacy of correctional institutions, eroding trust and potentially exacerbating tensions between staff and inmates (Bonner and Vandecreek, 2006; Dubler, 2014).

The issue of healthcare provision in correctional facilities also raises significant ethical concerns. Incarcerated people frequently face a variety of health challenges, including mental illness, substance abuse disorders, and chronic physical conditions. Ethical penology requires that prisoners receive adequate medical care, a right protected by international human rights law. However, healthcare in many correctional facilities is frequently insufficient due to limited resources, overcrowding, or intentional neglect. This raises ethical concerns about the state's responsibilities to care for those incarcerated. Inadequate healthcare not only violates prisoners' rights, but it also contributes to deteriorating prison conditions, making the environment dangerous for both inmates and staff. The challenge for penological practitioners is to advocate for better healthcare services while managing the logistical and financial constraints that often limit the quality of care available in correctional facilities (Bouagga, 2014).

Another major ethical quandary in penology is the disproportionate impact of incarceration on marginalised groups, particularly racial and ethnic minorities. The overrepresentation of certain groups in prison populations raises serious ethical concerns about the fairness of the criminal justice system, as well as the role of correctional institutions in perpetuating social inequality. In many countries, racial minorities are disproportionately targeted by law enforcement and sentenced to longer prison terms for similar crimes than their white counterparts. This systemic bias persists within correctional facilities, where minorities may face harsher treatment, limited access to rehabilitative programs, and discrimination by staff or other inmates. Penology, from an ethical standpoint, must address these disparities and strive for a more equitable system that does not reinforce social divisions. Addressing these issues requires not only changes in correctional practices but also broader reforms in the criminal justice system to ensure that incarceration is not used as a tool of social control over marginalized populations (Dubler, 2014; Scott, 2008).

Rehabilitation, a central concept in penology, raises ethical concerns, especially when weighed against the punitive aspects of incarceration. The rehabilitative ideal holds that prisons should be places where offenders can reform and learn the skills they need to reintegrate into society. However, the punitive nature of most correctional systems frequently undermines this goal, resulting in ethical debates over the true purpose of incarceration. Many prison systems prioritize security and punishment over rehabilitation, creating environments that are more likely to exacerbate criminal behavior than to promote reform. This raises ethical concerns about the state's responsibility to provide opportunities for personal growth and rehabilitation to those incarcerated. When prisoners are denied access to educational programs, vocational training, or psychological support, the system fails to live up to its ethical obligation to facilitate their reintegration into society (Bouagga, 2014).

Another important issue in penology is how to treat mentally ill inmates ethically. Prisons have increasingly become institutions where people with severe mental illnesses are housed, often in environments that are inadequate to meet their needs. Ethical quandaries arise when correctional officers, lacking proper training, use punitive measures such as isolation or physical restraint to manage mentally ill inmates. These actions can exacerbate inmates' conditions and raise concerns about the efficacy of incarceration as a response to mental illness. From a penological standpoint, the ethical treatment of mentally ill prisoners necessitates a shift to more therapeutic approaches that prioritize mental health care and rehabilitation over punishment. This poses a significant challenge to correctional systems that are primarily designed for security rather than treatment (Levinson, 2002).

Finally, the privatization of prisons raises additional ethical concerns in penological practice. The involvement of private companies in correctional facility management frequently prioritizes profit over inmate welfare, raising concerns about the commodification of incarceration. Ethical concerns arise when cost-cutting measures jeopardize the quality of inmates' care, rehabilitation, and living conditions. Furthermore, the financial incentives inherent in privatization may result in conflicts of interest, as private companies profit from higher incarceration rates and longer sentences. Penology, as a discipline concerned with justice and rehabilitation, must critically examine the influence of private interests on correctional practices and policies. The ethical challenge is to ensure that the pursuit of profit does not undermine the fundamental principles of humane and just treatment in the penal system (Dubler, 2014).

10.3. PROFESSIONAL STANDARDS IN PENOLOGY

Professional standards are critical for ensuring that correctional institutions operate efficiently, ethically, and in accordance with societal values of justice and rehabilitation. These standards guide correctional staff, particularly officers, in their interactions with incarcerated people, decision-making processes, and approach to managing the complex dynamics of penal environments. Central to these standards is the need to balance security and order with the humane treatment of prisoners, reflecting both ethical principles and penological goals (Scott, 2008).

One of the most important professional standards in penology is impartiality and fairness. Correctional officers are in charge of managing a population that is frequently diverse in terms of ethnicity, background, and the type of offense committed. Ensuring fair treatment of all inmates, regardless of status, is critical to the correctional system's legitimacy. Professional standards require correctional staff to avoid discriminatory practices based on race, gender, or other characteristics, and to ensure that all inmates are treated equally under institutional rules. This also includes carrying out disciplinary actions in a fair and consistent manner, without any appearance of bias or favoritism. The principle of impartiality is critical for reducing tensions within prisons and fostering an environment where rehabilitation can occur (Meško et al., 2011).

Commitment to integrity and accountability is another important aspect of professional penology standards. Correctional staff have significant authority over the lives of incarcerated people, so it is critical that they use their authority responsibly. Officers who are committed to integrity must follow legal and institutional guidelines, be transparent in their actions, and avoid corrupt practices such as contraband smuggling or abuse of authority. Accountability is closely related because it requires correctional staff to be held accountable for their actions, particularly when using force or disciplinary measures. Professional standards frequently include protocols for reporting and investigating incidents of misconduct, which ensures that those who violate ethical norms are held accountable. This not only protects the rights of inmates but also enhances the credibility and trustworthiness of the correctional institution (Cullen and Gendreau, 2007; Dubler, 2014).

Professional standards play a critical role in guiding correctional officers' behavior when using force. Officers in correctional facilities may be required to use force to maintain order or to protect themselves and others. However, professional standards require that force be used only as a last resort and that it always be proportionate to the threat. These guidelines emphasize the importance of training officers in conflict resolution techniques, which will allow them to manage potentially volatile situations without resorting to excessive violence. The principle of proportionality ensures that correctional officers do not abuse their authority and is an important factor in maintaining the institution's ethical standards. Inadequate training or lax enforcement of these standards can lead to the mistreatment of inmates, undermining the ethical foundation of penological practice (Webb, 2012).

The provision of healthcare and mental health services in correctional facilities is another critical area governed by professional standards. Individuals who are incarcerated frequently face a variety of physical and mental health issues, many of which are exacerbated by their confinement. Professional standards require prisons to provide adequate healthcare services, ensuring that inmates receive medical treatment and support as needed. This includes correctional staff's ethical responsibility to treat mentally ill inmates with compassion and appropriate care, rather than subjecting them to punitive measures. Inadequate healthcare in prisons not only violates inmates' rights but also contributes to the deterioration of the overall correctional environment, increasing the likelihood of unrest and complicating rehabilitation efforts (Cullen and Gendreau, 2007).

Penology's professional standards also emphasize the importance of confidentiality. Correctional officers frequently have access to sensitive information about inmates, such as their criminal histories, medical records, and psychological profiles. Maintaining the confidentiality of this information is critical to protecting inmates' privacy and building trust within the correctional environment. Breach of confidentiality can have serious consequences for both inmate safety and institutional integrity. Professional standards ensure that officers are aware of their responsibilities concerning sensitive information and that such data is handled in accordance with legal and ethical guidelines (Cullen and Gendreau, 2007; Meško et al., 2011). Finally, professional standards in penology highlight the importance of rehabilitation and reintegration. While the primary function of correctional facilities is frequently viewed as maintaining security and order, modern penological thought increasingly recognizes rehabilitation as a key goal. Professional standards require correctional officers to support rehabilitative programs aimed at assisting inmates in acquiring the skills and education required for successful reintegration into society. This includes giving people access to vocational training, educational programs, and psychological counseling, all of which are critical for reducing recidivism and promoting positive outcomes after release. Correctional officers are expected to act as change facilitators, contributing to a culture that prioritizes rehabilitation over punishment alone (Meško et al., 2011).

10.4. BALANCING PUNISHMENT AND REHABILITATION ETHICALLY

Correctional officers are responsible for striking a delicate balance between punishment and rehabilitation. This balance is fraught with ethical complexities, as the dual goals of ensuring security and facilitating offenders' reintegration are frequently incompatible. However, ethical guidelines and professional standards emphasize the importance of managing both dimensions in a way that is consistent with the principles of justice, fairness, and human rights. This dual responsibility reflects broader penological debates about the purpose of incarceration and the role of correctional institutions in punishing offenders while also preparing them for eventual reintegration into society (Webb, 2012).

Correctional officers are responsible for maintaining the security and order of penal institutions, which is a primary function of punishment in the penal system. Punishment, defined as the legal consequence of breaking societal laws, necessitates that correctional staff enforce rules and maintain discipline within correctional facilities. This responsibility frequently includes the implementation of disciplinary measures such as segregation or restricted privileges, which are intended to reinforce the punitive aspect of incarceration. Correctional officers must ensure that these measures are applied fairly and proportionately, avoiding unnecessary harm or punishment. The principle of proportionality is essential here, as it requires that punitive actions correspond to the severity of an inmate's infractions, thus preventing the overuse of punitive measures that may degrade the dignity of prisoners (Dubler, 2014; Scott, 2008)

While security must be maintained at all times, correctional officers are also expected to support the correctional system's rehabilitative goals. Rehabilitation seeks to reform offenders by addressing the root causes of criminal behavior and providing them with the necessary skills and support for reintegration into society. This shift reflects the modern penological perspective, which sees incarceration not only as a means of retribution, but also as a chance for behavioral change and societal integration. Correctional officers must create environments that promote rehabilitation, such as facilitating access to educational programs, vocational training, and psychological support. This role requires officers to engage with inmates in a way that promotes positive behavior, rather than just controlling or disciplining them (Bouagga, 2014).

The tension between these two roles is the source of the ethical dilemma. On the one hand, correctional officers must ensure that justice is served by enforcing the punishments prescribed by the legal system. On the other hand, they are responsible for assisting inmates with their personal development in order to reduce recidivism rates. Penology emphasizes the difficulties of reconciling these goals, especially in settings where punitive practices dominate institutional culture. When correctional officers focus solely on punishment, they may unintentionally create conditions that are detrimental to rehabilitation, instilling hostility and resentment in inmates rather than encouraging behavioral change. This conflict highlights the significance of ethical training and professional standards, which assist officers in effectively managing these competing goals (Meško et al., 2011).

Ethical penology emphasizes the humanization of correctional practices. Inmates must be treated with dignity and respect, even in a punitive setting, to ensure that incarceration does not dehumanize offenders. This approach is consistent with international human rights frameworks such as the Mandela Rules, which advocate for humane treatment and the protection of prisoners' rights regardless of the offense committed. Correctional officers must navigate this ethical imperative by ensuring that disciplinary measures do not diminish the humanity of those incarcerated. Promoting an environment that balances security with opportunities for personal growth is crucial for striking an ethical balance between punishment and rehabilitation(Webb, 2012).

The role of discretion is especially important in how correctional officers balance their competing responsibilities. Officers frequently face situations that require them to use their discretion in determining the best balance between maintaining order and promoting rehabilitation. For example, they may have to decide when to impose punitive sanctions and when to encourage participation in rehabilitative programs. The ethical use of discretion ensures that officers do not resort to punitive measures unnecessarily or allow institutional rules to overshadow the opportunity for personal development(Bonner and Vandecreek, 2006).

Finally, ethical penology requires correctional officers to see punishment and rehabilitation as interconnected components of the correctional system's larger mission rather than as mutually exclusive. By ensuring that punitive actions are administered fairly and with respect for inmates' dignity, officers contribute to a correctional environment that holds individuals accountable while also preparing them for successful reintegration. This dual responsibility reflects a dedication to justice, not only in terms of retribution, but also in creating conditions for reform and societal reintegration. Ethical frameworks in penology provide correctional officers with the tools to navigate this balance, ensuring that correctional practices are both humane and effective in meeting the long-term goals of the penal system (Dubler, 2014).

10.5. CULTURAL COMPETENCE IN CORRECTIONAL SETTINGS

Cultural competency in correctional settings has recently been established as an essential component of penology ethics and professionalism. Correctional institutions, which contain a diverse population of jailed people, face unique problems in creating an atmosphere that is not only safe but also respectful of the many cultural backgrounds of both inmates and staff. The term cultural competency in this context relates to correctional professionals' capacity to effectively engage with people from various cultural, ethnic, and socioeconomic backgrounds. This is crucial not only for preserving ethical standards in the treatment of inmates but also for increasing professionalism in the corrections industry.

Cultural competence refers to a collection of abilities, attitudes, and knowledge that professionals use to effectively comprehend, communicate, and interact across cultures. In correctional environments, where tensions may already be high owing to the nature of incarceration, cultural competence is critical to ensuring that convicts are treated with decency and respect. Ethical considerations in penology require correctional officers and administrators to prevent discriminatory actions, promote inclusivity, and recognize the unique requirements that may result from cultural differences. The fact that correctional institutions frequently hold disproportionate numbers of racial and ethnic minorities, who may already be marginalized in society, emphasizes the ethical requirement for justice and equality in treatment (Scott, 2008a).

Understanding how cultural differences may influence behaviors and perceptions of authority is a crucial component of cultural competence in correctional settings. For example, correctional officers may come across cultural norms that diverge from their own, which could result in misunderstandings or conflicts. In certain cultures, for instance, making direct eye contact with authority figures can be seen as disrespectful, while in others, it can be seen as an indication of honesty. If correctional staff members are unaware of these differences, they may misinterpret an inmate's behavior, which could result in unfair disciplinary actions. This highlights the significance of training correctional officers to identify and respect cultural differences, preventing unintentional biases from affecting their professional judgment (Nutz, 2005).

Additionally, encouraging successful communication between prisoners and correctional workers requires cultural competence. In correctional settings, language problems can present serious difficulties, especially when convicts do not speak the staff's primary language fluently. This may result in misconceptions about the policies, practices, or even medical treatment provided by the institution. Correctional facilities must thus take action to close these gaps and guarantee that all prisoners have access to the information they need, such as by hiring bilingual employees or offering translation services. Ignoring language difficulties jeopardizes not only the moral treatment of prisoners but also raises the possibility of safety hazards because miscommunication in correctional facilities can intensify hostilities and spark violence (Latessa and Lovins, 2019).

Cultural competence is essential for meeting the unique demands of different prison populations, in addition to communication. For example, people from a variety of religious backgrounds who may need special accommodations for their religious practices—like dietary restrictions or prayer times—are frequently housed in correctional facilities. Correctional staff members must uphold these religious customs and make sure that institutional policies do not unduly restrict an inmate's freedom of expression. This is a requirement of ethical professionalism. When such needs are not met, prisoners' rights may be violated, and the prison population may become resentful and hostile (Latessa and Lovins, 2019).

Furthermore, cultural competence in correctional settings includes understanding the influence of historical and structural injustices that may affect specific inmate populations. Many jailed people originate from marginalized communities that have long faced systemic racism and socioeconomic inequality. Culturally competent correctional staff are more likely to comprehend the larger sociopolitical environment that has molded these convicts' lives, and as a result, they may be better prepared to manage the complexity of their rehabilitation and reintegration into society. This understanding is critical for correctional officers, who are responsible for not only keeping order but also supporting the rehabilitation process (Nelken, 2010).

Therefore, cultural competence and professionalism in the field of penology are inextricably linked. This is because correctional officers and administrators have to strike a careful balance between upholding institutional policies and honoring the cultural identities of the people under their supervision. A lack of cultural competence can result in a number of ethical problems, such as racial profiling, unequal access to services, and the perpetuation of stereotypes. These problems can undermine the integrity of the correctional institution and increase tensions between staff and inmates, creating an environment that is more volatile and unsafe (Tonry, 2016).

Correctional institutions that stress cultural competence create a more compassionate and just environment. This is accomplished through regular training programs that teach employees about cultural understanding, sensitivity, and anti-bias procedures. Such training programs are critical for helping correctional staff realize their own potential prejudices and understand how they may affect their interactions with inmates. As a result, this contributes to a more ethical and professional work environment in which staff members are held accountable for their actions and encouraged to treat all convicts fairly and respectfully, regardless of cultural background (Scott, 2008a).

Cultural competency also plays an important role in minimizing recidivism. According to research, convicts who feel understood and valued by correctional staff are more likely to participate in rehabilitation programs and demonstrate constructive behavior. When offenders face cultural insensitivity or discrimination, they may become alienated from the rehabilitation process, reducing their prospects of successful reintegration into society after release. Correctional institutions that promote cultural competency can assist create an environment that supports convicts' rehabilitation efforts, ultimately contributing to the larger goal of lowering recidivism rates (Useem & Morrison Piehl, 2008).

Given that the demographics of the incarcerated population are constantly changing, correctional institutions must adjust by making sure that their policies, procedures, and staff training reflect a deep understanding and respect for cultural diversity. As a result, the ethical framework in which they operate must include a commitment to cultural competence. This commitment is not only necessary for the fair and equitable treatment of inmates but also a reflection of broader societal values regarding diversity and inclusion (Latessa and Lovins, 2019).

As a result, cultural competence is an essential component of ethics and professionalism in correctional settings. Correctional staff must engage with convicts in a way that respects their cultural identities while adhering to the concepts of fairness and justice. Correctional institutions that stress cultural competence are better able to manage the challenges of a diverse inmate population, reduce conflict, and foster a more rehabilitative environment. Ethical professionalism in penology requires correctional officials to not only enforce rules and maintain order, but also to treat all inmates with the decency and respect they deserve as humans, regardless of cultural origin.

10.6. ADVOCACY FOR INMATES RIGHTS

Inmate rights within the framework of ethics and professionalism are a key field of research, emphasizing the contradiction between maintaining societal order and preserving individuals' fundamental human rights when incarcerated. Advocacy for inmates' rights aims to achieve a balance between safeguarding the safety and security of the larger community and ensuring that prisoners' dignity and rights are not violated. This subject addresses the ethical responsibilities of people working in the criminal justice and correctional systems, as well as broader considerations regarding the professionalism and moral responsibility of those in charge of jailed populations.

The concepts of justice, human dignity, and fairness are central to penology ethics. While prisoners may have some of their liberties taken away from them as part of their sentence, they nevertheless have fundamental rights guaranteed by national and international human rights frameworks, such as the right to healthcare, the right to humane treatment, and the prohibition against cruel and inhumane punishment. The ethical argument in favor of prisoners' rights is based on the belief that people should not be denied their humanity or forced to live in conditions that are degrading or humiliating (Bonner and Vandecreek, 2006).

The historical context of inmate rights reveals a troubling past in which prisoners were frequently treated as less than human, subjected to harsh conditions, and denied basic legal safeguards. However, throughout time, legal reforms, human rights campaigning, and changes in public attitudes have resulted in a shift in how inmates are treated. International treaties, such as the United Nations norm Minimum Rules for the Care of Prisoners (the Nelson Mandela Rules), have established a global norm for ethical prisoner care. These standards define values such as the right to healthcare, access to legal resources, freedom from torture, and living situations that respect the individual's inherent dignity (Cullen and Gendreau, 2007).

Correctional officers, jail administrators, and other professionals involved in the penal system are held to professional standards that demand them to act with integrity and fairness. It is their ethical duty to guarantee that the rights of inmates are respected even in restrictive settings. They also have an obligation to acknowledge the humanity of inmates and endeavor to establish conditions that promote rehabilitation rather than punishment, which entails attending to the physical, mental, and emotional needs of prisoners while simultaneously safeguarding their legal rights (Dubler, 2014; Scott, 2008b).

However, despite developments in legal frameworks and ethical requirements, inmates' experiences frequently fall short of these expectations. Correctional institutions continue to face issues such as overcrowding, poor access to medical care, abuse by prison staff, and racial and socioeconomic inequities in the criminal justice system. These situations provide considerable ethical issues for professionals working in the system, as they frequently face a conflict between adhering to institutional regulations and fighting for inmates' rights and well-being (Bonner and Vandecreek, 2006).

The concept of dual loyalties is an important topic in penology ethics, particularly for medical professionals who work in correctional facilities. Dual allegiance is defined as the conflict between a professional's duty to care for their patient (the convict) and their obligations to the institution or state. For example, a prison doctor may be pressured to prioritize the facility's security concerns over the inmate's health needs, leading to ethical quandaries. This raises concerns about how far a professional's commitment to safeguard human rights goes in the face of institutional constraints (Scott, 2008).

Furthermore, professionalism in penology includes advocating for systemic reforms. Advocates for inmates' rights argue that ethical penology should include more than just individual treatment, but also broader systemic changes. These reforms include efforts to reduce mass incarceration, abolish solitary confinement, improve prison conditions, and address racial disparities in the system. Such reforms necessitate the involvement of system professionals in advocacy efforts, challenging existing practices and policies that perpetuate injustice and inhumanity (Dieter, 2019).

The rights of women, juveniles, and LGBTQ+ people have been the focus of increased advocacy for inmates' rights in recent years. Women in prison, for example, frequently face particular challenges linked to healthcare, sexual abuse, and being separated from their children. Juveniles, despite being incarcerated, are still developing and need different interventions than adults to support their rehabilitation. LGBTQ+ people are more likely to experience sexual violence and discrimination in prison, so targeted advocacy efforts are crucial. Ethical professionalism requires that correctional institutions and those working within them adopt policies and practices that address the unique needs of these vulnerable groups (Dyer, 2023). Despite the hurdles, there are numerous examples of successful lobbying initiatives that resulted in improvements to inmates' rights and prison circumstances. Legal cases such as Estelle v. Gamble, which proved that purposeful disregard for inmates' critical medical requirements violates the Eighth Amendment, have produced important legal precedents. Similarly, grassroots organizations, legal advocacy groups, and human rights organizations have all played important roles in drawing attention to the situation of convicts and advocating for reform. These initiatives underline the significance of external oversight and lobbying in holding correctional institutions accountable and ensuring that ethical standards are met (Cullen and Gendreau, 2007).

Professional ethics for people working in penology extend beyond their direct interactions with inmates. Ethical penology also includes the responsibility to encourage restorative justice techniques that aim to rehabilitate and reintegrate offenders into society. Rehabilitation, rather than punishment, is consistent with ethical concepts that acknowledge the opportunity for personal growth and change. Advocacy for rehabilitation includes ensuring that inmates have access to educational programs, vocational training, and mental health services to help them reintegrate into society. Ethical professionalism, therefore, includes a commitment to minimizing recidivism and supporting offenders' well-being during and after incarceration (Souryal and Whitehead, 2019).

Advocating for inmates' rights in the context of ethics and professionalism in penology is a critical component of a just and compassionate legal system. While inmates are stripped of certain liberties as part of their punishment, they still have fundamental human rights that must be respected and preserved. Correctional professionals have an ethical obligation to defend these rights, despite the difficulties and limits that come with working in correctional facilities. Furthermore, ethical professionalism in penology necessitates fighting for structural reforms that address the underlying causes of unfairness in the prison system, as well as aiding inmates' rehabilitation and reintegration into society. Progress toward a more compassionate and just correctional system is possible with persistent activism and respect for ethical principles.

10.7. CONTINUING EDUCATION AND TRAINING FOR PENOLOGICAL PROFESSIONALS

Continuing education and training for penological experts is critical to maintaining high levels of professionalism in the discipline of penology. Correctional officers, prison administrators, probation officers, and other members of the criminal justice system serve critical roles in ensuring the safety, security, and rehabilitation of inmates in correctional facilities. Their work is extremely dynamic, and the issues they face necessitate a thorough awareness of legal frameworks, human rights, psychological concepts, security protocols, and ethical norms. As a result, the value of continuing education and training in retaining professionalism cannot be emphasized.

Professionalism in penology entails more than just using taught abilities; it also necessitates a dedication to ethical practices, personal integrity, and adherence to legal and human rights principles. Given the increasing complexities of the criminal justice system, which includes concerns such as overcrowding, inmate mental health, and prison violence, penological practitioners must stay current on the newest research, regulations, and best practices. Continuing education is a means for ensuring that these professionals are well-prepared to face such problems and carry out their obligations with competence and moral clarity (Monahan et al., 2015).

A primary justification for continuing education for penological professionals is that it improves their competency in specialized fields. Since offender rehabilitation, psychological support, and reintegration programs are now part of modern penology, professionals need to have a broad understanding of issues like trauma-informed care, addiction treatment, and restorative justice. Specialized training in these fields gives correctional staff the skills and knowledge they need to address the wide range of needs of the incarcerated population. In addition, continuing education promotes a culture of learning and adaptation, in which penological professionals are not just adhering to established protocols but actively engaging with new knowledge and concepts to enhance institutional practices (Scott, 2008).

Furthermore, by promoting career promotion and personal development, ongoing education aids in the professional development of penological staff. Because correctional facilities are inherently hierarchical, advancement prospects frequently hinge on an individual's educational background and training qualifications. Professionals can show their dedication to their field and improve their skills for higher-level roles by continuing their education. This helps the organization as a whole as well as the individual because highly educated and trained employees are better suited to assume leadership positions, guide less experienced employees, and participate in the formulation of policies (Moore, 2017).

The rapidly changing legal and ethical environment in which penological professionals work is another important reason for continuing education in the field. Changes in legislation pertaining to sentencing, prisoner rights, and privatization can have a profound impact on the working environment of penological professionals. Additionally, attitudes toward punishment and rehabilitation can change over time, reflecting broader shifts in public policy and criminal justice reform movements. As new laws are passed and existing ones are reformed, professionals must update their knowledge and practice accordingly to ensure compliance with legal standards and to support the rights of inmates. Continuing education offers the training staff needs to stay abreast of these developments and to apply them successfully in their day-to-day operations (Hurowitz, 2021).

Penology's ethical components necessitate ongoing introspection and learning. Moral conundrums, such as striking a balance between the rights of prisoners and their rights and dignity and the necessity for security, are common in correctional settings. Experts in this domain need to be prepared to handle these difficulties in a morally sound, law-abiding, and compassionate manner. A crucial part of continuing education is ethical training, which enables professionals to assess their choices and behaviors critically in light of justice, equity, and human rights. Maintaining professionalism in such a delicate and high-stakes sector requires cultivating a feeling of accountability and moral duty, which is what this educational component does (Dubler, 2014).

Furthermore, continuing education in penology can assist address and reducing concerns such as job burnout, stress, and emotional exhaustion, which are common in correctional facilities. Correctional officers frequently operate in high-pressure situations where they are exposed to violence, anger, and mental suffering. Over time, this can lead to burnout and decreased job performance, jeopardizing both staff well-being and institutional safety. Stress management, emotional intelligence, and mental health awareness training programs are critical for assisting professionals in dealing with the demands of their jobs. Continuing education can help to create a more stable and successful workforce by teaching employees how to manage their emotional health, thereby improving institutional performance (Souryal and Whitehead, 2019).

In addition to addressing individual professional development and legal duties, continuing education fosters a culture of responsibility and transparency in correctional settings. When employees receive regular training and updates on best practices, there is less room for wrongdoing or neglect. Furthermore, a commitment to learning demonstrates an institution's adherence to ethical norms and professionalism. This not only improves internal operations but also increases public faith in correctional institutions, which are frequently inspected for their treatment of inmates and adherence to legal and moral standards (Latessa and Lovins, 2019).

Technology plays an important role in today's custodial environment, and continuing education is essential for keeping workers up to date on the latest technology innovations. From security systems and surveillance tools to digital record-keeping and data management, technical literacy is critical to ensuring that correctional institutions run smoothly and securely. Continuous education programs that focus on technology teach penological experts how to successfully use these tools, enhancing the overall functionality of correctional institutions (Scott, 2008).

Furthermore, ongoing education promotes a better grasp of the social, cultural, and psychological influences on criminal behavior. Understanding the underlying reasons for crime, such as poverty, trauma, or substance misuse, enables correctional officers to approach their work with more empathy and insight. This can lead to more successful rehabilitation efforts and lower recidivism rates. Training in criminology, psychology, and sociology provides penological practitioners with the information they need to better understand the people in their care and adopt techniques that address the root causes of their behavior rather than relying solely on punishment (Bonner and Vandecreek, 2006; Dubler, 2014).

In an ever-changing area, continuing education ensures that professionals are prepared to face the difficulties of their jobs, from legal compliance and ethical decision-making to technology literacy and stress management. Furthermore, it encourages personal and professional development, allowing individuals to advance their careers while also improving the overall performance of their institutions. Given the high stakes involved in custodial employment, the value of a well-educated and constantly trained workforce cannot be emphasized. Such a dedication to learning benefits not just the professionals, but also the convicts under their care, the institutions they serve, and the criminal justice system as a whole.

BIBLIOGRAPHY

1. Akers, R. L. (2011). Rational choice, deterrence, and social learning theory in criminology: The path not taken. In *Crime Opportunity Theories*. Routledge.
2. Alper, M., Durose, M. R., & Markman, J. (2018). *2018 Update on Prisoner Recidivism: A 9-Year Follow-up Period (2005–2014)* (p. 2). US Department of Justice, Office of Justice Programs, Bureau of Justice Statistics.
3. Andersen, L. H., & Wildeman, C. (2015). Measuring the effect of probation and parole officers on labor market outcomes and recidivism. *Journal of Quantitative Criminology, 31*(4), 629–652. https://doi.org/10.1007/s10940-014-9243-4.
4. Arbach-Lucioni, K., Martinez-García, M., & Andrés-Pueyo, A. (2012). Risk factors for violent behavior in prison inmates: A cross-cultural contribution. *Criminal Justice and Behavior, 39*(9), 1219–1239. https://doi.org/10.1177/0093854812445875.
5. Armstrong, G. S. (2001). Book review: Forms of constraint: A history of prison architecture. *Criminal Justice Review, 26*(1), 98, 99. https://doi.org/10.1177/073401680102600113.
6. Bahr, S. J., Masters, A. L., & Taylor, B. M. (2012). What works in substance abuse treatment programs for offenders? *The Prison Journal, 92*(2), 155–174. https://doi.org/10.1177/0032885512438836.
7. Bakura, J. (2020). Book review: Terry Allen Kupers, *Solitary:* The inside story of supermax isolation and how we can abolish it. *Theory in Action*, 140–147. https://doi.org/10.3798/tia.1937-0237.2041.

8. BBC News. (2024). *How Many Countries Still Have the Death Penalty, and How Many People are Executed*? https://www.bbc.com/news/world-45835584 (accessed on 4th October 2024).

9. Bennett, C. (2010). Punishment and rehabilitation. In J. Ryberg & J. A. Corlett (Eds.), *Punishment and Ethics* (pp. 52–71). Palgrave Macmillan UK. https://doi.org/10.1057/9780230290624_4.

10. Bernburg, J. G. (2019). Labeling theory. In *Handbooks of Sociology and Social Research* (pp. 179–196). https://doi.org/10.1007/978-3-030-20779-3_10.

11. Bernfeld, G. A., Farrington, D. P., & Leschied, A. W. (2003). *Offender Rehabilitation in Practice: Implementing and Evaluating Effective Programs*. John Wiley & Sons.

12. Bhutta, M. H. (2010). *Community-Based Rehabilitation of Offenders; An Overview of Probation and Parole System in Pakistan.*

13. Bond, M. (2017). *Criminology: Social Learning Theory Explained*. e-Roll Call Magazine. https://andragogytheory.com/2017/01/21/criminology-social-learning-theory-explained/ (accessed on 4th October 2024).

14. Bonner, R., & Vandecreek, L. D. (2006). Ethical decision making for correctional mental health providers. *Criminal Justice and Behavior, 33*(4), 542–564. https://doi.org/10.1177/0093854806287352.

15. Bonta, J., Wallace-Capretta, S., Rooney, J., & Mcanoy, K. (2002). An outcome evaluation of a restorative justice alternative to incarceration. *Contemporary Justice Review, 5*(4), 319–338. https://doi.org/10.1080/10282580214772.

16. Bosworth, M., Franko, K., & Pickering, S. (2018). Punishment, globalization and migration control: 'Get them the hell out of here'. *Punishment & Society, 20*(1), 34–53. https://doi.org/10.1177/1462474517738984.

17. Bouagga, Y. (2014). Prison counselors in France: A changing profession and its moral dilemmas. *Configurações, 13*, 79–87. https://doi.org/10.4000/configuracoes.2416.

18. Burrell, S. (2000). *Special Education and the Juvenile Justice System*. US Department of Justice, Office of Justice Programs, Office of Juvenile Justice and Delinquency Prevention.

19. Byrne, J. M., Pattavina, A., & Taxman, F. S. (2015). International trends in prison upsizing and downsizing: In search of evidence of a global rehabilitation revolution. *Victims & Offenders, 10*(4), 420–451. https://doi.org/10.1080/15564886.2015.1078186.

20. Cavanagh, C. (2022). Healthy adolescent development and the juvenile

justice system: Challenges and solutions. *Child Development Perspectives, 16*(3), 141–147. https://doi.org/10.1111/cdep.12461.

21. Centre for Mental Health. (2024). *The Future of Prison Mental Health Care in England.* https://www.centreformentalhealth.org.uk/publications/future-prison-mental-health-care-england/ (accessed on 4th October 2024).
22. Chamberlain, A. W. (2012). Offender rehabilitation: Examining changes in inmate treatment characteristics, program participation, and institutional behavior. *Justice Quarterly, 29*(2), 183–228. https://doi.org/10.1080/07418825.2010.549833.
23. Clear, T., Cole, G., Reisig, M., & Petrosino, C. (2013). *American Corrections in Brief.*
24. Crewe, B. (2012). *The Prisoner Society: Power, Adaptation and Social Life in an English Prison*. OUP Oxford.
25. Crime Museum, LLC. (2024). *Origins of Capital Punishment.* Crime Museum. https://www.crimemuseum.org/crime-library/execution/origins-of-capital-punishment/ (accessed on 4th October 2024).
26. Cullen, F. T., & Gendreau, P. (2007). From nothing works to what works: Changing professional ideology in the 21st century. In *Clinical Forensic Psychology and Law*. Routledge.
27. Cunningham, M. D., & Vigen, M. P. (2002). Death row inmate characteristics, adjustment, and confinement: A critical review of the literature. *Behavioral Sciences & the Law, 20*(1, 2), 191–210. https://doi.org/10.1002/bsl.473.
28. Davis, L. M. (2013). *Evaluating the Effectiveness of Correctional Education: A Meta-Analysis of Programs That Provide Education to Incarcerated Adults*. RAND.
29. de Vries, S. L. A., Hoeve, M., Assink, M., Stams, G. J. J. M., & Asscher, J. J. (2015). Practitioner review: Effective ingredients of prevention programs for youth at risk of persistent juvenile delinquency – Recommendations for clinical practice. *Journal of Child Psychology and Psychiatry, 56*(2), 108–121. https://doi.org/10.1111/jcpp.12320.
30. Dieter, R. C. (2019). Introduction: International perspectives on the death penalty. In C. S. Steiker & J. M. Steiker (Eds.), *Comparative Capital Punishment*. Edward Elgar Publishing. https://doi.org/10.4337/9781786433251.00008.
31. Distributor. (2022). *New CDCR Women's Substance Abuse Program.* Inside CDCR. https://www.cdcr.ca.gov/insidecdcr/2010/02/04/cdcr-

opens-trauma-informed-substance-abuse-program-for-women-at-three-additional-prisons/ (accessed on 4th October 2024).

32. Dolan, K., Khoei, E. M., Brentari, C., & Stevens, A. (2007). *Prisons and Drugs: A Global Review of Incarceration, Drug use and Drug Services.* Report 12 [Reports and papers]. The Beckley Foundation. http://www.beckleyfoundation.org/policy/reports.html (accessed on 4th October 2024).
33. Dubler, N. (2014). *Ethical Dilemmas in Prison and Jail Health Care.* https://doi.org/10.1377/forefront.20140310.037605.
34. Dyer, O. (2023). Global number of executions hit five-year high in 2022, says Amnesty International. *BMJ,* 1145. https://doi.org/10.1136/bmj.p1145.
35. Eddy, J. M., & Burraston, B. O. (2018). Programs promoting the successful reentry of fathers from jail or prison to home in their communities. In C. Wildeman, A. R. Haskins, & J. Poehlmann-Tynan (Eds.), *When Parents are Incarcerated: Interdisciplinary Research and Interventions to Support Children* (pp. 109–131). American Psychological Association. https://doi.org/10.1037/0000062-006.
36. Edens, J. F., Colwell, L. H., Desforges, D. M., & Fernandez, K. (2005). The impact of mental health evidence on support for capital punishment: Are defendants labeled psychopathic considered more deserving of death? *Behavioral Sciences & the Law, 23*(5), 603–625. https://doi.org/10.1002/bsl.660.
37. Emerson, R. M. (2017). *Judging Delinquents: Context and Process in Juvenile Court*. Routledge. https://doi.org/10.4324/9780203787854.
38. Fagan, J., & Meares, T. L. (2008). Punishment, deterrence and social control: The paradox of punishment in minority communities. *Ohio State Journal of Criminal Law, 6*, 173.
39. Faqir, R. (2015). *The Philosophy of Punishment: A Study to the History of Classical and Positive Schools of Penology, 1*(6), 8.
40. Farr, K. A. (2000). Classification for female inmates: Moving forward. *Crime & Delinquency, 46*(1), 3–17. https://doi.org/10.1177/0011128700046001001.
41. Fazel, S., Hayes, A. J., Bartellas, K., Clerici, M., & Trestman, R. (2016). Mental health of prisoners: Prevalence, adverse outcomes, and interventions. *The Lancet Psychiatry, 3*(9), 871–881. https://doi.org/10.1016/S2215-0366(16)30142-0.
42. Garland, D. (2011). Modes of capital punishment: The death penalty in

historical perspective. In D. Garland, R. McGowen, & M. Meranze (Eds.), *America's Death Penalty: Between Past and Present* (pp. 30–71). New York University Press. https://doi.org/10.18574/nyu/9780814732663.003.0002.

43. Garland, D. (2018). *Punishment and Welfare: A History of Penal Strategies*. Quid Pro Books.
44. Garrett, B. L. (2020). Wrongful convictions. *Annual Review of Criminology, 3*(1), 245–259. https://doi.org/10.1146/annurev-criminol-011518-024739.
45. Gavrielides, T. (2017). *Restorative Justice: Ideals and Realities* (1st edition). Taylor and Francis.
46. Glaze, L. E., & Bonczar, T. P. (2011). *Probation and Parole in the United States, 2010*. Nove m Be r.
47. Gleicher, L., Manchak, S. M., & Cullen, F. T. (2013). Creating a supervision tool kit: How to improve probation and parole. *Federal Probation, 77*, 22.
48. Goel, S., Shroff, R., Skeem, J., & Slobogin, C. (2021). The accuracy, equity, and jurisprudence of criminal risk assessment. In R. Vogl (Ed.), *Research Handbook on Big Data Law*. Edward Elgar Publishing. https://doi.org/10.4337/9781788972826.00007.
49. Golden, H. (2019, December 23). *Seattle is on a Road Map to Zero Youth Detention – So Why is it Opening a Huge New Prison?* The Guardian. https://www.theguardian.com/us-news/2019/dec/23/seattle-youth-detention-opening-new-facility (accessed on 4th October 2024).
50. Griffin, M. L., Hogan, N. L., Lambert, E. G., Tucker-Gail, K. A., & Baker, D. N. (2010). Job involvement, job stress, job satisfaction, and organizational commitment and the burnout of correctional staff. *Criminal Justice and Behavior, 37*(2), 239–255. https://doi.org/10.1177/0093854809351682.
51. Haag, E. V. den, & Conrad, J. P. (2013). *The Death Penalty: A Debate*. Springer Science & Business Media.
52. Haney, C. (2003). Mental health issues in long-term solitary and "supermax" confinement. *Crime & Delinquency, 49*(1), 124–156. https://doi.org/10.1177/0011128702239239.
53. Haqanee, Z., Peterson-Badali, M., & Skilling, T. (2015). Making "what works" work: Examining probation officers' experiences addressing the criminogenic needs of juvenile offenders. *Journal of Offender Rehabilitation, 54*(1), 37–59. https://doi.org/10.1080/10509674.2014.980485.
54. Heflick, N. A. (2005). Sentenced to die: Last statements and dying on death row. *OMEGA – Journal of Death and Dying, 51*(4), 323–336. https://doi.org/10.2190/96X8-FLUT-TCLH-EL71.

55. Hurowitz, N. (2021). *El Chapo: The Untold Story of the World's Most Infamous Drug Lord* (First Atria Books hardcover edition). Atria Books.
56. James, N. (2014). *Offender Reentry: Correctional Statistics, Reintegration into the Community, and Recidivism* (Vol. 37). Congressional Research Service.
57. Johnstone, G. (2011). *Restorative Justice: Ideas, Values, Debates* (2nd ed.). Routledge.
58. Johnstone, G., & Van Ness, D. W. (2007). *Handbook of Restorative Justice*. Willan.
59. Jonathan, S. (2013). The new penology: Notes of the emerging strategy of corrections and its implications. In *Crime, Law and Society*. Routledge.
60. Kaeble, D. (2021). *Probation and Parole in the United States, 2020.*
61. Kim, M. E. (2018). From carceral feminism to transformative justice: Women-of-color feminism and alternatives to incarceration. *Journal of Ethnic & Cultural Diversity in Social Work, 27*(3), 219–233. https://doi.org/10.1080/15313204.2018.1474827.
62. Kuhn, J. R., Courtney, J. F., & Morris, B. (2014). A theory of complex adaptive inquiring organizations: Application to continuous assurance of corporate financial information. *The Knowledge Engineering Review, 30*(3), 265–296. https://doi.org/10.1017/s0269888913000428.
63. Kupers, T. A. (2005). Toxic masculinity as a barrier to mental health treatment in prison. *Journal of Clinical Psychology, 61*(6), 713–724. https://doi.org/10.1002/jclp.20105.
64. Lanfear, C. (2021). *Rational Choice and Deterrence.* https://clanfear.github.io/SOC371/lectures/06_deterrence/soc371_lecture_06_deterrence_1.html#1 (accessed on 4th October 2024).
65. Latessa, E. J., & Lovins, B. (2019). *Corrections in the Community* (7th edition). Routledge.
66. Latimer, J., Dowden, C., & Muise, D. (2005). The effectiveness of restorative justice practices: A meta-analysis. *The Prison Journal, 85*(2), 127–144. https://doi.org/10.1177/0032885505276969.
67. LeBel, T. P., Burnett, R., Maruna, S., & Bushway, S. (2008). The `Chicken and egg' of subjective and social factors in desistance from crime. *European Journal of Criminology, 5*(2), 131–159. https://doi.org/10.1177/1477370807087640.
68. Levinson, D. (2002). *Encyclopedia of Crime and Punishment*. SAGE.
69. Liebling, A., & Arnold, H. (2004). *Prisons and Their Moral Performance:*

A Study of Values, Quality, and Prison Life. Oxford University Press. https://doi.org/10.1093/oso/9780199271221.001.0001.

70. Lipsey, M. W., & Cullen, F. T. (2007). The effectiveness of correctional rehabilitation: A review of systematic reviews. *Annual Review of Law and Social Science, 3*(1), 297–320. https://doi.org/10.1146/annurev.lawsocsci.3.081806.112833.
71. Lowenkamp, C. T., Latessa, E. J., & Smith, P. (2006). Does correctional program quality really matter? The impact of adhering to the principles of effective intervention. *Criminology & Public Policy, 5*(3), 575–594. https://doi.org/10.1111/j.1745-9133.2006.00388.x.
72. Lukemeyer, A., & McCorkle, R. C. (2006). Privatization of prisons: Impact on prison conditions. *The American Review of Public Administration, 36*(2), 189–206. https://doi.org/10.1177/0275074005281352.
73. Lundahl, B. W., Kunz, C., Brownell, C., Harris, N., & Van Vleet, R. (2009). Prison privatization: A meta-analysis of cost and quality of confinement indicators. *Research on Social Work Practice, 19*(4), 383–394. https://doi.org/10.1177/1049731509331946.
74. Marsh, I., Cochrane, J., & Melville, G. (2004). *Criminal Justice: An Introduction to Philosophies, Theories and Practice*. Routledge. https://doi.org/10.4324/9780203412657.
75. Martí, M. (2021). Prisoners in the community: The open prison model in Catalonia. *Nordisk Tidsskrift for Kriminalvidenskab, 106*(2), 211–231. https://doi.org/10.7146/ntfk.v106i2.124777.
76. Matsueda, R. L., Kreager, D. A., & Huizinga, D. (2006). Deterring delinquents: A rational choice model of theft and violence. *American Sociological Review, 71*(1), 95–122. https://doi.org/10.1177/000312240607100105.
77. McNamara, A. (2007). The special needs of prison, probation, and parole. *New York University Law Review, 82*, 209.
78. Meško, G., Fields, C., & Smole, T. (2011). A concise overview of penology and penal practice in Slovenia: The unchanged capacity, new standards, and prison overcrowding. *The Prison Journal, 91*(4), 398–424. https://doi.org/10.1177/0032885511424389.
79. Miller, J. (2015). Contemporary modes of probation officer supervision: The triumph of the "synthetic" officer? *Justice Quarterly, 32*(2), 314–336. https://doi.org/10.1080/07418825.2013.770546.
80. Misra, A. (2024). *Latin America: Several Countries Look to Combat Gang Violence by Fighting Fire with Fire.* The Conversation. https://theconversation.com/latin-america-several-countries-look-to-combat-

gang-violence-by-fighting-fire-with-fire-228941 (accessed on 4th October 2024).

81. Monahan, K., Steinberg, L., & Piquero, A. R. (2015). Juvenile justice policy and practice: A developmental perspective. *Crime and Justice, 44*(1), 577–619. https://doi.org/10.1086/681553.
82. Moore, R. (2017). *An Analysis of Michelle Alexander's The New Jim Crow: Mass Incarceration in the Age of Colorblindness*. Macat International Ltd: Routledge.
83. Nagin, D. S. (2013). Deterrence in the twenty-first century. *Crime and Justice, 42*, 199–263. https://doi.org/10.1086/670398.
84. Nelken, D. (2016). *Comparative Criminal Justice and Globalization*. Routledge.
85. Nurse, J., Woodcock, P., & Ormsby, J. (2003). Influence of environmental factors on mental health within prisons: Focus group study. *BMJ, 327*(7413), 480. https://doi.org/10.1136/bmj.327.7413.480.
86. Nutz, T. (2005). Global networks and local prison reforms: Monarchs, bureaucrats and penological experts in early 19th-century Prussia. *German History, 23*(4), 431–459. https://doi.org/10.1191/0266355405gh353oa.
87. Paparozzi, M., & Demichele, M. (2008). Probation and parole: Overworked, misunderstood, and under-appreciated: But why? *The Howard Journal of Criminal Justice, 47*(3), 275–296. https://doi.org/10.1111/j.1468-2311.2008.00522.x.
88. Petrosino, A., Petrosino, C. T., & Buehler, J. (2005). "Scared straight" and other juvenile awareness programs for preventing juvenile delinquency. *Campbell Systematic Reviews, 1*(1), 1–62. https://doi.org/10.4073/csr.2004.2.
89. Phelps, M. S., & Curry, C. (2017). Supervision in the community: Probation and parole. In *Oxford Research Encyclopedia of Criminology*. https://oxfordre.com/criminology/display/10.1093/acrefore/9780190264079.001.0001/acrefore-9780190264079-e-239 (accessed on 4th October 2024).
90. Porporino, F. J. (2018). Developments and challenges in probation practice: Is there a way forward for establishing effective and sustainable probation systems? *European Journal of Probation, 10*(1), 76–95. https://doi.org/10.1177/2066220318764713.
91. Pratt, T. C., Cullen, F. T., Sellers, C. S., Jr, L. T. W., Madensen, T. D., Daigle, L. E., Fearn, N. E., & Gau, J. M. (2010). The empirical status of social learning theory: A meta analysis. *Justice Quarterly*. https://doi.org/10.1080/07418820903379610.

92. Prezi, M. M. O. (2011). *Steps in the Juvenile Justice Process.* prezi.com. https://prezi.com/xsp1gmxkotm_/steps-in-the-juvenile-justice-process/ (accessed on 4th October 2024).

93. *Prison Life for Inmates – What is Prison Like.* (2023). Zoukis Consulting Group. https://federalcriminaldefenseattorney.com/prison-life/ (accessed on 4th October 2024).

94. Pupo, J. A., & Zane, S. N. (2021). Assessing variations in juvenile court processing in urban versus rural courts: Revisiting "justice by geography." *Youth Violence and Juvenile Justice, 19*(3), 330–354. https://doi.org/10.1177/15412040211009585.

95. Pyrooz, D., Decker, S., & Fleisher, M. (2011). From the street to the prison, from the prison to the street: Understanding and responding to prison gangs. *Journal of Aggression, Conflict and Peace Research, 3*(1), 12–24. https://doi.org/10.5042/jacpr.2011.0018.

96. Rodriguez, I. (2023). *Changing the Culture of Community Supervision.* The Crime Report. https://thecrimereport.org/2019/12/10/760473/ (accessed on 4th October 2024).

97. Rodriguez, N. (2007). Juvenile court context and detention decisions: Reconsidering the role of race, ethnicity, and community characteristics in juvenile court processes. *Justice Quarterly, 24*(4), 629–656. https://doi.org/10.1080/07418820701717144.

98. Rubin, A. T. (2019). Heather Ann Thompson, blood in the water: the Attica prison uprising of 1971 and its legacy. *Punishment & Society, 21*(1), 131–137. https://doi.org/10.1177/1462474517724175.

99. Sarat, A. (2002). *When the State Kills: Capital Punishment and the American Condition*. Princeton University Press.

100. Scott, D. (2008). *Penology*. SAGE Publications.

101. Sirisutthidacha, W., & Tititampruk, D. (2014). Patterns of inmate subculture: A qualitative study of Thai inmates. *International Journal of Criminal Justice Sciences, 9*(1). https://ijcjs.com/menu-script/index.php/ijcjs/article/view/151 (accessed on 4th October 2024).

102. Solakoglu, O., & Yuksek, D. A. (2020). Delinquency among Turkish adolescents: Testing Akers' social structure and social learning theory. *International Journal of Offender Therapy and Comparative Criminology, 64*(5), 539–563. https://doi.org/10.1177/0306624X19897400.

103. Souryal, S. S., & Whitehead, J. T. (2019). *Ethics in Criminal Justice: In Search of the Truth* (7th ed.). Routledge. https://doi.org/10.4324/9780429400278.

104. Souryal, S. S., & Whitehead, J. T. (2020). *Ethics in Criminal Justice: In Search of the Truth* (7th edition). Routledge, Taylor & Francis Group.
105. Staphan, J. (2008). *Census of State and Federal Correctional Facilities, 2005*.
106. Steinberg, L. (2009). Adolescent development and juvenile justice. *Annual Review of Clinical Psychology, 5*, 459–485. https://doi.org/10.1146/annurev.clinpsy.032408.153603.
107. Strickland, T. (2024). *Role of a Correctional Officer: Job Description and Duties*. Job Descriptions WIKI. https://jobdescriptionswiki.com/correctional-officer-job-description/ (accessed on 4th October 2024).
108. Sunstein, C. R., & Vermeule, A. (2014). *Is Capital Punishment Morally Required? Acts, Omissions, and Life-Life Tradeoffs*. In Deterrence. Routledge.
109. Taxman, F. S., Perdoni, M. L., & Harrison, L. D. (2007). Drug treatment services for adult offenders: The state of the state. *Journal of Substance Abuse Treatment, 32*(3), 239–254. https://doi.org/10.1016/j.jsat.2006.12.019.
110. *The Problem of Prison Overcrowding | Law Paper Example*. (2024). LawBirdie. https://lawbirdie.com/the-problem-of-prison-overcrowding/ (accessed on 4th October 2024).
111. Thirst, L. (2020). *Capital Punishment: Evolution, Delay and Need for Balance*. Legal Thirst. https://legalthirst.com/capital-punishment-evolution-delay-and-need-for-balance/ (accessed on 4th October 2024).
112. Thompson, K. C., & Morris, R. J. (2016). History of the juvenile justice system. In K. C. Thompson & R. J. Morris (Eds.), *Juvenile Delinquency and Disability* (pp. 55–72). Springer International Publishing. https://doi.org/10.1007/978-3-319-29343-1_5.
113. Tonry, M. H. (2016). *Sentencing Fragments: Penal Reform in America, 1975-2025*. Oxford University Press.
114. Unnever, J. D., Cullen, F. T., & Jonson, C. L. (2008). Race, racism, and support for capital punishment. *Crime and Justice, 37*, 45–96. https://doi.org/10.1086/519823.
115. Useem, B., & Morrison Piehl, A. (2008). *Prison State: The Challenge of Mass Incarceration* (1st edition.). Cambridge University Press. https://doi.org/10.1017/CBO9780511813573.
116. Vito, G. F., & Maahs, J. R. (2015). *Criminology*. Jones & Bartlett Publishers.
117. Webb, W. N. (2012). Ethical culture and the value-based approach to

integrity management: A case study of the department of correctional services. *Public Administration and Development, 32*(1), 96–108. https://doi.org/10.1002/pad.1602.

118. Weitekamp, E. G. M., & Parmentier, S. (2014). Restorative justice and state crime. In *Springer eBooks* (pp. 4430–4446). https://doi.org/10.1007/978-1-4614-5690-2_120.
119. Westervelt, E. (2019). *County Jails Struggle with a New Role as America's Prime Centers for Opioid Detox*. NPR. https://www.npr.org/2019/04/24/716398909/county-jails-struggle-with-a-new-role-as-americas-prime-centers-for-opioid-detox (accessed on 4th October 2024).
120. Williams, K. S. (2012). *Textbook on Criminology*. Oxford University Press.
121. Wood, W. R. (2015). Why restorative justice will not reduce incarceration. *The British Journal of Criminology, 55*(5), 883–900. https://doi.org/10.1093/bjc/azu108.
122. Worley, R. M., Worley, V. B., & Hsu, H. (2018). Can I trust my co-worker? Examining correctional officers' perceptions of staff–inmates inappropriate relationships within a southern penitentiary system. *Deviant Behavior, 39*(3), 332–346. https://doi.org/10.1080/01639625.2016.1272972.
123. Worley, R. M., Worley, V. B., & Lambert, E. G. (2021). Deepening the guard-inmate divide: An exploratory analysis of the relationship between staff-inmate boundary violations and officer attitudes regarding the mistreatment of prisoners. *Deviant Behavior, 42*(4), 503–517. https://doi.org/10.1080/01639625.2019.1695470.
124. Wortley, R. K. (2002). *Situational Prison Control: Crime Prevention in Correctional Institutions*. Cambridge University Press.
125. Xie, S., Berryessa, C. M., & Focquaert, F. (2023). The impact of neuromorality on punishment: Retribution or rehabilitation? In M. C. Altman (Ed.), *The Palgrave Handbook on the Philosophy of Punishment* (pp. 441–464). Springer International Publishing. https://doi.org/10.1007/978-3-031-11874-6_20.
126. Zamble, E., & Porporino, F. J. (2013). *Coping, Behavior, and Adaptation in Prison Inmates*. Springer Science & Business Media.
127. Zehr, H. (2015). *Changing Lenses: Restorative Justice for Our Times* (25th anniversary edition). Herald Press.
128. Zimring, F. E. (2004). *The Contradictions of American Capital Punishment*. Oxford University Press.

INDEX

D

E

Kolibri 360 GmbH
Ferdinand-Jühlke-Straße 7
99095 Erfurt, Deutschland
produktsicherheit@kolibri360.de